# FAITH & THE LIFE OF THE INTELLECT

# FAITH & THE LIFE OF THE INTELLECT

EDITED BY CURTIS L. HANCOCK &
BRENDAN SWEETMAN

*with a foreword by Richard John Neuhaus*

THE CATHOLIC UNIVERSITY OF
AMERICA PRESS

The paper used in this publication meets the minimum requirements of
American National Standards for Information Science—Permanence
of Paper for Printed Library materials, ANSI Z39.48-1984.
∞

LIBRARY OF CONGRESS CATALOGING-IN-PUBLICATION DATA

Faith and the life of the intellect / edited by Curtis L. Hancock
    and Brendan Sweetman ; with a foreword by Richard John
    Neuhaus.
        p.  cm.
    Includes index.
    ISBN 0-8132-1311-8
        1. Catholic Church and philosophy   2. Faith and reason—
    Christianity.  3. Philosophy and religion.   I. Hancock, Curtis L.,
    1950–    II. Sweetman, Brendan.
    BX1795.P47 F35 2002
    261.5′1—dc21                          2002002325

*To*

Christian Philosophers

and Scholars, past and present,

for their inspiring work and example,

and for promoting reflection on the

most interesting questions

of all

# CONTENTS

❧

*Richard John Neuhaus*

# FOREWORD

୨ବ

When did thoughtful people first begin to assume that "faith" is one thing and "the life of the intellect" quite another? Some things we "know," it is said, and that is the world of the intellect, and especially of what is called science. Other things we "believe," and that is the world of "faith," and especially of what is called religion. The great challenge, it is said, is for people who occupy both worlds to demonstrate the connections between them, showing how they are compatible and even mutually necessary.

With the authors and editors of this book, I am not at all at peace with that way of putting the question of "faith and the life of the intellect." Many thinkers trace the great bifurcation between faith and intellect, between reason and revelation, back to René Descartes (d. 1650), although I am among the minority that thinks he is usually too much blamed. Usually underestimated, I think, is the influence of the wars of religion following the sixteenth-century Reformation. Ideas that were perceived to be "religious"—in large part because they were defined as such by opposing ecclesiastical authorities—identified the parties in a conflict that almost destroyed the civil and political society of Europe. The 1648 settlement of Westphalia adopted the principle of the 1555 Peace of Augsburg that the religion of the prince would be that of his subjects *(cuius regio eius religio),* which is a formula of deliberate indifference to the question of truth—or at least of truth in connection with ideas identified as religious.

That tragedy is a primary source, if not the primary source, of the bifurcation with which we are still living. It prepared the way for the dogmas of a more militantly secular Enlightenment, decreeing that faith and religion have no legitimate place in what counts as truly *public* reason and knowledge. Many Christians have, mistakenly I believe, been happy to go along with this bifurcation. What counts as public reason, meaning mainly "science" in one form or another, deals with the "isness" of things; religion and theology with the "oughtness" of things. Reason is the prose by which we understand the real world; religion the poetry by which we try to give it a meaning that makes it psychologically and spiritually endurable. As the 1998 encyclical *Fides et Ratio* observes, ancient philosophy aimed at wisdom and opened to wonder. Most of what is called modern philosophy, following the tragic bifurcation, despairs of wisdom and shuts the door on wonder.

Postmodernism, albeit defined in maddeningly various ways, would overthrow the rule of reason entirely, dismissing it as a reductive rationalism fatally tied to the delusion of objective truth. All "truth" is poetry, all is socially constructed to meet our needs and ambitions; any number of competing "truths" can play in a contestation of power, the final resolution of which is endlessly deferred. Some Christian thinkers today welcome this postmodernist turn. It gives, they say, Christian truth claims "a place at the table" along with all the other players. And it is true that, especially in the university, the postmodernist assault on secularist rationalism has sometimes opened up space for Christian arguments and proposals. But accepting the terms of the postmodernist game, which is the price of admission, would seem to preclude arguments and proposals that claim to be the truth—public truth, intersubjective truth, truth about the way things really are, truth that, if true, is universally true.

Admittedly, the above depiction of our intellectual circumstance is painted with broad strokes. Some of the essays in this book refine those strokes, and others provide alternative ways of depicting our circumstance, and what might be done about it. But, in various ways, each author challenges the bifurcation of faith and the life of the intellect. Each is in the great tradition of Christian thought represented by Justin Martyr (d. 165) who, after searching through the many philosophies, was converted to Christianity as the most true philosophy. Much truth could be found in other ways of understanding reality, Justin said, but all truth is finally one, for God, who is the source of all that is true, is One. The "generative Word" *(logos spermatikos)* who became incarnate in Jesus Christ has sown the seed of truth very generously; no person is denied access to the truth that rescues us from the demons of falsehood and can restore us to the truth who is God.

Every Christian thinker has his or her own story to tell about how he or she came to understand the connection between faith and the intellectual life. Many years ago as a college student I was deeply impressed by a philosophy professor who declared "I am a Christian because Christianity makes more sense of more facts than any other way of thinking I know about." This is very like Justin Martyr's understanding of Christianity as the "true philosophy." Of course, being a Christian is more than philosophy, at least as the term philosophy is commonly used today. But for Christians who cannot help thinking about the truth of what they believe to be true (which would include, I suppose, all the readers of a book such as this), the philosophical task is inescapable. The authors of this book represent different "schools" of philosophy, and sometimes different approaches within these schools, but for each the life of faith and the life of the intellect is one life. Which is how it must be, if ever we are to overcome the tragic bifurcation of recent centuries and restore to public reason wisdom and wonder.

# PREFACE AND
# ACKNOWLEDGMENTS

&

There has sometimes been an uneasy relationship between religious faith and the exercise of the intellect. Religious faith has often been understood, even by some philosophers, to involve a commitment to things whose existence cannot be demonstrated, and which are finally mysterious. Reason, on the other hand, has been looked upon, depending on one's point of view, either as revealing the real problems with religious belief or as a nit-picking, materialistic, worldly endeavor not worthy of the attention of religion. This debate between reason and religion has become particularly intense in the contemporary world, a world where many see themselves as breaking away from the shackles of religious authority, and of myth and superstition, and moving toward a more "enlightened," secular era for humanity. This modern enlightened attitude is often at odds with religion; at best it relegates religion to the sidelines, at worst it is openly hostile to it and treats it with disdain. In response, religious believers are motivated by two often conflicting attitudes—a healthy suspicion of secularism on the one hand, and yet on the other hand an attempt to placate secularists, because of the cultural pressure of the secularist agenda. At the present time it is fair to say that reason and religion are mutually suspicious of each other, and it is not clear how this suspicion is going to play itself out in the future. But there can be little doubt that this tension is a special challenge in our contemporary times for the scholar who is a religious believer, and especially if that scholar is also a philosopher. This challenge, and the various ways different philosophers understand and respond to it, is the concern of this book.

Our volume is concerned with the intriguing question of the proper relationship between faith and the life of the intellect. More specifically, the essays raise and discuss, from a variety of backgrounds, perspectives, and philosophical and religious interests, the central question of how philosophers who are religious believers deal with the relationship between their religious beliefs and their research and scholarly work (and, to a lesser extent, their teaching). The essays throughout, each in their own way, ask such questions as: What is the correct relationship between one's religion and one's research aims and objectives? Does one's religious belief complement, or conflict with, one's scholarship and teaching? To what extent are Christian philosophers motivated in their work by religious faith? The contributors also consider along the way those autobiographical events or experiences which influenced their understanding of their faith, and its relation to the intellectual life. In this way, the essays often involve a fascinating detour through the personal events and experiences of the authors, events and experiences which helped shape their responses to the issues of the volume. Lurking beneath all of the essays is a more fundamental question: Can one even be at once a Christian and a professional philosopher in the contemporary world?

The questions and issues mentioned above are addressed in this volume as they apply to the Catholic philosopher, and all of the contributors would identify themselves as Catholics (and by the term "Catholic philosopher" we mean only that the contributors would identify themselves as both Catholics and philosophers).

There have been a few interesting works in recent years which have raised in a general way some of the questions mentioned, but from a Protestant perspective. This book will attempt to address the general issue of faith and the intellectual life from the Catholic perspective. We hope in this way to bring into the debate a different but equally interesting and rich perspective on vital matters concerning philosophers who are also religious believers. We also thought that it would make for a more interesting collection of essays if we did not restrict the contributors to a set formula; contributors were free to select those issues relating to the general theme which most interested them, which were most relevant to them in their own life and work. In this way each essay brings a different and fresh perspective to the issues of the volume.

The Catholic tradition has always emphasized the importance of reason in religious belief, and philosophy has always had a central place in the educational curricula of Catholic institutions. These institutions have a reputation for academic rigor, as well as for the attempt to integrate faith and reason in a liberal education. They have stressed education of the whole person, with an eye to producing well-rounded citizens, whose judgments are informed by religious and moral values grounded in God, and who have a special concern for issues of social justice. The Catholic tradition has also been a famous supporter of that approach in philosophy of religion known as natural theology—the attempt to demonstrate that it is reasonable to believe in God because of the totality of the evidence in the natural world. Faith and reason, in the Catholic tradition, are regarded as compatible and as working together in the task of faith seeking understanding.

In this way, the Catholic tradition differs from the Protestant tradition, which has often supported a more strict separation of faith and reason in religious belief and has, therefore, tended to give less of a role to philosophy in its programs of education (though this is changing). The Protestant tradition has often placed religion in one category, and reason (and sometimes science) in another, separate category, believing that each has little to say to the other. One advantage of this approach is that it protects religion from critical examination in the sense that one's core religious beliefs are not subject to rational scrutiny or to critical analysis. But this approach also comes with a disadvantage, which is that progressively over time religion becomes marginalized from the mainstream of reasoned debate, relegated to a purely private realm, where it is often not taken seriously as being "real knowledge" and is not regarded as rational. This in turn leads to all religions of every stripe, including cults, being lumped together, and being regarded by many (especially among the intelligentsia) as having no role at all to play in the public square. Religion is regarded as a second-class citizen, as unable to offer substantive ideas on the important political, legal, moral, and social debates of the day. Of course, this conclusion has important political implications, since it results in the sidelining of religion from contemporary discussion.

This problem is also compounded in the United States by the interpretation of the first amendment to the U.S. Constitution over the past few decades by the Supreme Court, ably abetted by the mainstream national media and groups such as the American Civil Liberties Union. This is the view that there should be an extreme separation between Church and State, and so religion should have no place in public life. This legal situation has affected many of our state colleges and universities, of course, and has also put pressure on private religious schools that accept federal money (which is nearly all of them). This interpretation of the Constitution fuels the belief, advanced by many today, that one simply cannot be, and should not be, a religious believer and a philosopher; in fact, this may be the prevalent view in our secularly dominated academy. This means, not that a philosopher cannot be a religious believer, but that the philosopher must always suspend his or her religious belief when doing philosophy. This claim is seldom argued for, but simply assumed (and because of this, it is often seen by religious believers as yet another attempt to denigrate religious belief). However, many thinkers, including all of the contributors to this volume, hold that this view of the relationship of religious belief to philosophy is naive and simplistic, and altogether too convenient, and they strive to articulate and defend an alternative view.

The issue of the proper relationship of philosophy to theology is obviously relevant here, and it is a theme of many of the essays. The contributors present a variety of intriguing and stimulating standpoints on this profoundly interesting question. Ancient and medieval thinkers, such as St. Augustine, St. Thomas Aquinas, and St. Bonaventure, who inspired many of the present authors, conceived of theology as the supreme discipline and of philosophy as its handmaiden. The role of philosophy was to clarify theological concepts, to defend them, and in general to complement religious faith. Certainly, in medieval times there was no clear distinction between philosophy and theology; they went hand in hand and were generally employed together in the attempt to understand, defend, and promote religious faith.

A more modern view is that theology and philosophy should be completely separate; that philosophy must be "critical" and should challenge all major claims, including, and perhaps especially, theological ones; and that, only if it remains totally independent of theology can philosophy do its job properly. In fact, one can make a good case that in the contemporary academy, not only is philosophy no longer allied with theology but it is now allied with *naturalism*. Naturalism is the atheistic view that all that exists is physical, and that everything in reality has, at least in principle, a *scientific* explanation. In this way, naturalism has become closely linked to science, and is often confused with science, and *vice versa*. This is now the default position in large parts of the academic world, and it is operationally the mainstream view at many institutions (including, it should be said, many religious institutions). It is not that naturalism has won the day in the debate among worldviews, that philosophers have argued for and established naturalism to everyone's satisfaction, or even that its merits and demerits are regularly debated in the marketplace of ideas; rather, the naturalist view is an assumption behind much modern scholarship (e.g., in the philosophy of mind); it is a "paradigm" within which many contemporary thinkers operate. It is fair to say that naturalism is to much of modern thought what theology was to much of medieval thought.

In this light, whether one is inclined to support naturalism or not, the role of the religious believer who is a philosopher has become all the more challenging. This is so because, in general, a whole slew of scholars in the profession of philosophy now hold that religious belief and philosophy, and by extension religious belief and philosophical scholarship and the teaching of philosophy, cannot go together in any coherent way. This puts an obligation on the religious philosopher to articulate and defend his or her position and approach. The naturalist, significantly, faces no corresponding obligation. There are various ways one can respond to this issue in the contemporary academy, and several of them are represented in the essays in this volume.

Another issue of great significance in the contemporary academy is the problem of relativism. Many thinkers now accept some version of either epistemological or moral relativism, or usually both. In following epistemological relativism, they subscribe to the view that there is no objective way to arrive at knowledge that is known to be true and certain; that one's "subjective point of view" in-eluctably compromises the objectivity of knowledge, and so all we have is a variety of competing and legitimate perspectives on "reali-ty." Now while we hold that this relativistic approach is false and fraught with contradictions and inconsistencies, and never defend-ed or really practiced by anyone, that is not the point we wish to make here. Our main point is that, given the dominance of this "relativistic attitude" in the modern academy, it is very disingenu-ous to claim that philosophy, if placed in any close relationship with religion, cannot be "objective." One can make *this claim* only if one is committed to the objectivity of knowledge, which many contemporary philosophers are not. Of course, if relativism domi-nates, then religious belief must have a certain legitimacy, since every worldview has a certain legitimacy. This would be a huge price to pay to get religion a legitimate place at the table of contem-porary discourse, and it is not what we mean here. We believe that the religious worldview is a rational view, and worthy of a place at the table on its merits, especially when stacked up against some of the alternatives (many of which are relativistic in nature). But the key issue here is that emphasizing these points reveals the arbitrary nature of much of the modern secular attack on religion, and such points are part of the interrogation to which theistic philosophers must subject modern thought.

Several of the contributors to this volume discuss the issue of the relationship between faith and reason, and, while they come from different perspectives and philosophical traditions, they share the view that Christian revelation and philosophical reflection are not incompatible. Some writers discuss this issue explicitly in their es-says. Others, probing the issue of the proper relationship of philos-ophy to Christian revelation, consider whether believing in revela-tion affects how one does philosophy. Several writers emphasize the value of philosophical reflection in the clarification and elaboration of theological concepts. In recent years, this objective of philosophy has gained great respect, and has led to a new branch of philosophy of religion, called "philosophical theology."

Some of the contributors to this volume are followers of St. Thomas Aquinas, and would call themselves "Thomists"; others belong to other traditions, most notably the tradition of continental philosophy; still others are somewhere in the middle, not followers of St. Thomas, yet significantly influenced by his thought nonetheless. But since Thomistic philosophy has had a close relationship with, and a significant influence on, Catholic philosophy, it is inevitable that this influence is manifest in some of the essays. Interesting questions are raised concerning Thomistic philosophy; for example, what the relationship of Thomistic philosophy is to the history of philosophy. A more urgent question is raised regarding the role of Thomistic philosophy in contemporary philosophical debate. Is the Thomistic approach out of date, or can it effectively engage modern thought? Some believe it can still engage modern thought, and further that it has an obligation to do so. But others indicate that they have learned a lot from Thomistic philosophy but have now moved beyond it to deal with more contemporary thinkers whose issues and style they see as more germane to our times.

Of course, in all of this discussion, the question of how one's religious beliefs and attitudes influence one's teaching in the classroom naturally arises. There are general concerns here which apply to all professors, not just those that are religious believers. But it is obviously important to distinguish between holding a view and being committed to that view, on the one hand, and proselytizing that view in the classroom, on the other hand. It is also necessary here to consider how both religious and secular views handle this issue.

Some people, both inside and outside the academy, after all, believe that the main role of many faculty is to make the students atheists and Marxists before they leave university! This concern indicates that proselytizing is widely practiced, and raises the question of whether this is appropriate when one is discussing religious matters. For example, could one proselytize in the classroom the view that all religions should be respected? Or the view that only one particular religion is true? And so on. These kinds of concerns are probed by some of the essayists.

In our selection of contributors we were guided by a number of considerations, chief among them the desire to get a good cross section of professors working in the Catholic tradition from a variety of perspectives. To this end, we tried to include a selection of philosophers—from the well-established to the not so well-established, younger scholars and older scholars, liberal and conservative voices, members of the religious life and lay people, men and women. It is our hope that this book will be of interest to philosophers working in the Catholic tradition, to philosophers and other professors working at Catholic or other religious institutions, and to a more general audience interested in the question of religious faith and its relationship to the intellectual life. The book may also be useful as a text for academics who teach courses on Christian philosophy and related issues, or in whose courses the topic of faith and reason is a major theme.

A number of people helped us bring this volume to completion. We would like to thank all of the contributors for their insights and wisdom, and also for their patience as the book made its way through the long process that leads to publication. We especially thank Fr. Neuhaus for taking time out of his very busy schedule to write the Foreword. We are grateful to Rockhurst University for giving us grant support, and released time, to work on portions of the book. Our thanks also to Professor Robert Knickerbocker of Rockhurst University who read the manuscript and gave us valuable advice. We also thank all those at The Catholic University of America Press for their hard work and advice. Finally, our biggest debt of gratitude goes to our families, for their always unfailing support.

*Curtis L. Hancock and Brendan Sweetman*
*Kansas City, October 2002*

# FAITH & THE LIFE OF THE INTELLECT

*Thomas R. Flynn*

# 1. ATHENS AND JERUSALEM, PARIS AND ROME

≈

Shortly after my return from Paris where I attended the last lectures that Michel Foucault delivered before his untimely death, I was invited to participate in a symposium with Rainer Schürmann and Charles Scott on the thought of Foucault. It was the first time I had delivered an invited paper to a meeting of the Eastern Division of the American Philosophical Association. I was intent on directing my talk to an APA audience in the most "professional" manner possible. In the ensuing discussion, Rainer (a former Dominican priest and colleague for a year at The Catholic University of America) challenged me to articulate the larger, metaphysical position from which I was implicitly arguing my case. Thinking that he wanted me to "fess up" to the fact that I was an active Catholic priest and (perhaps even) a closet Thomist—with all that this might entail for my audience, from easy dismissal to open ridicule—I demurred with the reply: "This is no time for an *auto-da-fé*." In fact, it was not. But the challenge and my reply continued to discomfort me for some time afterwards. A few years later, I encountered Rainer at a meeting of the Society for Phenomenology and Existential Philosophy (SPEP) and he asked me pointedly, "Are you still a priest?" When I answered in the affirmative, he countered: "Well it doesn't show in your book!" *(Sartre and Marxist Existentialism: The Test Case of Collective Responsibility).*

Now I know that many people will take this as a compliment. It indicates that a religiously committed person can take a distance on what is most profoundly his/her own in order to write with the utmost "objectivity" about a subject that at times questions or denies religious convictions. I have known several philosophers over the years who have said just that. But for someone who believes, as I do, that the religious, like the ethical, is all-pervasive, this seeming detachment may suggest either a weakened faith or a failure of nerve or perhaps even an implicit subscription to the ancient heresy of the double truth *(duplex veritas).* Let me consider each alternative.

I

*Fides debilis.* The Catholic tradition justifiably prides itself on its respect for learning and the intellectual life. The monastic scholars keeping the light of Western civilization burning throughout the "dark" ages, the cathedral schools, the great universities of the high Middle Ages—all witness to the Catholic conviction that faith and reason are colleagues, not adversaries, and that Athens has much to do with Jerusalem in the God-given task of "faith seeking understanding" *(fides quaerens intellectum).* The subdiscipline of natural theology became a hallmark of philosophy in Catholic circles. Indeed, the First Vatican Council, in a move that still strikes some as curiously circular, even defined that the existence of God could be known with certainty "by the natural light of human reason *(naturali rationis humanae lumine)*" and anathematized anyone who denied this thesis.[1]

---

1. See Heinrich Denzinger ed., *Enchiridion Symbolorum,* 28th ed. (Freiburg: Herder, 1952), §1806.

But there is another, darker side to this tradition that its critics would be quick to cite were we to forget it: the fear of learning on the part of so many, the distrust of secular society and "atheistic" philosophy (witness the infamous Index of Forbidden Books), a siege mentality leading one to view faith as a space apart rather than the leaven of a common life. The attitude of churchmen at the turn of the nineteenth century toward higher criticism in biblical studies, liberalism in politics, and psychoanalysis in psychology exemplifies a defensiveness that bespeaks a fundamental distrust of the modern age. This is one reason why the Johannine spirit of the Second Vatican Council was so exhilarating for many of us. I continue to take inspiration from the pastoral constitution "The Church in the Modern World" *(Gaudium et spes),* where the Council Fathers acknowledge that the Church must learn from the modern world as well as instruct it.[2]

Doubtless, my years of graduate study at Columbia (the academic equivalent of Harvey Cox's "Secular City") and my decades of perusing the works of two notoriously atheistic philosophers, Jean-Paul Sartre and Michel Foucault, both former Catholics, could be expected to have left their mark. As a colleague at Catholic University once put it none too obliquely, "You can always tell someone with a secular education!" Threatened by such circumstances with losing the faith "of a Breton peasant," could one hope at least to achieve what Paul Ricoeur calls a "second naïveté"? I had always subscribed to the thesis that a living faith can "mature" in the face of life's problems and that your experience of the transcendent in prayer, sacramental celebration, nature, ethical interchange, and the like can continue to ground the belief that guides and gives you

2. See "Pastoral Constitution on the Church in the Modern World" in *The Documents of Vatican II,* ed. Walter M. Abbott, S.J. (New York: Guild Press, 1966), esp. pp. 245–47.

hope. If "naïve" means "unquestioning," my belief has not been naïve since I was an adolescent. But if it means "unwavering" in the sense of never having been "suspended" by an act of will like Husserl's *epochē*, then it continues to be naïve. But rather than a "second," I would speak of a "chastened" naïveté—one that has gradually come to appreciate its circumstantial nature and to respect and admire the authentic lives of many nonbelievers. Perhaps that is what bridled my adolescent enthusiasm for an apologetics that promised to slay intellectual opponents with the *quinque viae*.

And yet the ghost of the Third Way ("Why is there anything at all and not rather nothing?) continues to haunt me. I am convinced it addresses a valid question, one that the existentialists' experience of *contingency* merely served to underscore. What the literary and philosophical experiences of contingency brought to the fore, in my mind, was something that subsequent "postmodern" discourse has merely echoed: the stakes of the choice to believe or to not-believe (rather than the cautionary choice not to believe). It comes down to the question of whether the universe resonates with our seemingly boundless drive to make sense of it or whether its existence and ours are simply brute facts to be admitted and got on with. It is a matter of life-*orientation* and of a meaning that is also a direction (*sens,* in French) based on hope rather than on either resignation or (sometimes seemingly courageous) revolt.

And the God of Abraham, Isaac, and Jacob remains present to me in the person of Jesus Christ. Again, the primacy of the lived experience *(Erlebnis).* This is why I abandoned, or rather, complemented, my Thomistic metaphysics with existential and hermeneutical phenomenology. It seemed that the concrete, situational demands of my intellectual and my faith life were not being met by a metaphysical system that appeared to discount the temporal, the personal, and the historical for the timeless, the impersonal, and the ahistorical. Yet I must admit that I have never been moved to break into prayer when reading these other philosophers as I have when reading portions of the *Summa theologiae* or the *Catena aurea*.

Still, the suspicion remains. How can anyone persist in reading and expounding such thoughts antithetical to one's Catholic faith and not be tainted in the process? A perceptive but troubled Catholic undergraduate once asked me if I had ever read Miguel de Unamuno's short story "Saint Manuel the Good, Martyr." His question was as loaded as Rainer's and I knew it. For the tale depicts a country priest who is the sole link between the world of faith and the disturbed lives of his parishioners. After decades of strengthening the belief and consoling the grief of his flock, it is discovered at his death that the pious priest had, in fact, lost his own faith years before!

*Pusillanimitas.* John Dewey introduced the expression "failure of nerve" into the philosophical literature. Like so many such expressions, it trades on a fundamental ambiguity. One person's "nerve" is another's foolhardiness. Nietzsche, for example, is praised by some for his "heroic atheism" and castigated by others, e.g., Karl Jaspers, for being a personal and philosophical "shipwreck." The expression denotes one's unwillingness to follow one's principles/arguments to their logical conclusions. (Parenthetically, I have always thought this was the weakness of philosophers who oppose all forms of infinite regress save one.) In my case, "failure of nerve" would take the form of sympathetically explaining Sartre's ontology of brute, factical existence without succumbing to its allure. Why, I ask myself, is this not an object lesson in Sartrean bad faith? And Michel Foucault's critique of rationality? Though it might open the door to a fideistic "leap," its implicit relativism makes one disinclined to claim that anything is nonnegotiable, including religious commitment. In sum, how does one avoid either Sartrean bad faith or Foucauldian skepticism when traveling in such company? The "logic" of their respective positions would seem to demand the suspension of religious belief, at least in any recognizably Catholic sense.

There are at least two ways of answering this objection. The first is to propose an "existentialist" appeal to concrete thinking (something of the sort that Gabriel Marcel practiced) and to attack the excessively rationalist demand, implicit in the objection, that one reason in a vacuum. No one ever does, as Foucault has clearly shown us. When it is a matter of life choices (what Sartre called fundamental choices), one is coming down on the side of a line of reasoning that speaks to the heart (in Pascal's sense) and that values the good (in the Thomistic sense that belief requires an awareness that it is good to believe—a theme taken up by William James in a pragmatist context). The "faith" of Sartrean "bad faith" is based on what he calls "insufficient" evidence. But that, in turn, presupposes a concept of "sufficient" evidence that is rationalist and acontextual. If bad faith simply means believing when one knows one could do better epistemically speaking, then it should be eschewed in accordance with a kind of ethics of belief. But when that is not the case, then good faith may well counsel that one give the assent in a commitment that is firm and loyal ( for example, when its object is another Person, which is how I conceive Christian faith). It then becomes a matter of "working out" one's faith by the life-choices one subsequently makes. As Sartre pointed out, we can do an existential psychoanalysis of a person's deeds and products to discover the authenticity/inauthenticity of their lives. Faith, in other words, is not a proposition or even an attitude of mind ("Not those who cry 'Lord, Lord' will enter into the Kingdom of heaven . . ."), but a doing, a praxis, an orientation. If Sartre didn't teach me this in the first place, his work confirmed it in many respects.

Like most skepticisms, the Foucauldian variety is more a proposal than a thesis (lest it get mired in self-referential inconsistency). I read Foucauldian discourse analysis as a warning more than a command: be cautious in your commitments; do not leap blindly; be aware of the unworthy motives behind your most innocent gestures; think against yourself; consider that you might be mistaken. This last is the most difficult one; the one that seems to undermine interpersonal commitment; the one I find incompatible with faith or with true love, for that matter. Yet I take heart at discovering it suspended in Foucault's own personal commitments and in his remarks on the "constancy" of friendship *(philia)* as distinct from the instability of the love relation in ancient Athens.[3]

*Duplex veritas.* Condemned by ecclesiastical authority in the Middle Ages (correctly or not, it was associated with Averroës, the brilliant Islamic philosopher), the theory of "double truth" held that one and the same proposition could be true in faith (theology) and false in reason (philosophy) or *vice versa.* Versions of this doctrine are implicit in the arguments of those philosophers in modern times who seek to avoid confrontation between faith and "science" at all costs. As one of my graduate professors, the late John Herman Randall Jr., argued, there can be no contradiction between the claims of these two domains if they remain within the confines of their respective disciplines because their fields of discourse are completely heterogenous. Wittgenstein's appeal to alternative language-games and *Lebensformen* can be read as a version of this position. It is an especially attractive stand among postmodernists because it turns on the postmodern thesis of the plurality of rationalities or "games of truth." In this latter sense, I too have found it tempting. But I have always been troubled by the domain/form of life/lan-

---

3. See Michel Foucault, *The Uses of Pleasure* (New York: Pantheon Books, 1985), p. 201. See his remarks on friendship as "a way of life" in *Foucault Live* (New York: Semiotext(e), 1989), pp. 206–7.

guage-game in which the problematic "one and the same" proposition was articulated in the first place.

So again, the ghosts of Aristotle and Aquinas return to challenge me: Assuming in such a pluralist context that one can even speak of the same "proposition" rather than "inscription" or "expression," can the same proposition be both true and false in the same respect and at the same time? Does not the very meaning of this statement presume that it cannot? Has not history recounted genuine conflicts between religious and scientific truth in the past? Who can forget (even a rehabilitated) Galileo? Does not some of the fruitfulness of theological reflection stem precisely from the need to answer objections from the natural or the social sciences? The double truth and even the Kantian "two viewpoints" (nature and freedom) hypotheses strike me as too slippery an exit from the impasse that often generates religious discomfort in many believers. Existential *Angst* may not be the key to religious authenticity, but Pascal, Kierkegaard, and many others have made me realize that it is an extremely effective way to gain our religious attention! On the other hand, there is something spiritually soporific about the ease of the double truth theory; it resembles a sensory deprivation tank!

The pluralists have an answer. It is robustly pragmatic, when articulated philosophically, and otherwise simply asserted as a matter of fact: We do live with a great deal of inconsistency (what the psychologists call "cognitive dissonance") and it does us little or no harm. In fact, it may be healthier for our peace of mind than the torments inflicted by the logical principles of excluded middle or noncontradiction. "Life is larger than logic and laughs at it," says the romantic. A foolish consistency, Emerson once remarked, is the hobgoblin of little minds! Perhaps so. But intellectual honesty seems to argue that one not gloss over the apparent contradictions when they arise. And the pluralist solution, like that of the double truth, strikes me as a little too slippery.

But, the dialectic continues, would you be willing to commit intellectual suicide in order to protect your beliefs? Is your loyalty as blind (and as dangerous) as that of "My country, right or wrong"? Is this not the impoverished line of the skeptic who, rather than risk being mistaken, resists the chance to know the truth? "Nothing ventured, nothing lost"—that's my idea of failure of nerve; it's the motto of *les petites natures*.

## I I

This excursion into the possibilities of failing to reconcile religious and professional commitments may be getting us nowhere. But it has at least raised several issues that stalk the believer who is in continuous dialogue with those who question the validity of that belief. Let us return to the general theme of faith and the intellectual life.

On the assumption that intellectual schizophrenia is unhealthy, I wish to sustain the thesis that a *living* faith and an *active* intellectual life are indeed mutually compatible, without relegating one to the closet for festive occasions or assigning the other to the security of the study. But, as with any living relationship, they undergo a change in the course of their development. This should come as no surprise to Catholics who have lived through the sea changes of pre- and post-conciliar theology and religious practice. In fact, I have thought that my pre-conciliar commitments and convictions (along with a rather sanguine disposition)[4] have enabled me to maintain a

4. Not long after I had received my Ph.D., Paul Weiss confronted me with "Young man, you will never be a philosopher!" "Why not?" I countered, rather pained at his prognostic. "Because you smile too much!" was his reply.

certain equilibrium amidst the "purification" process of the intervening years when so many serious Catholics felt betrayed by changes in worship and church discipline. Likewise, my early interest in existentialism enabled me to accommodate myself to the challenges of contemporary French thought with a certain openness and tolerance that made me the kind of interpreter whose fairness or at least lack of bias Rainer Schürmann remarked over a decade ago.

What I have come to appreciate in my own "solution" to the problem of reconciling religious faith and the intellectual life is that philosophy both in its study and in its communication is *not* apologetics. I do believe there is an apologia to be given for the faith that one holds but that this "statement" is made primarily by the authenticity of one's life—for the Christian, in the daily living of Gospel values—rather than in the "proofs" and "arguments" that one musters. Decades of working with college-age students have taught me to respect their idealism and their almost Nietzschean nose for hypocrisy as well as the power of Christian example to move hearts. Once I was freed from the need to "defend" the faith in the classroom, I could get on with what was for me the matter at hand, namely, an informed, competent, and enthusiastic examination of the topic of the day, whether Aristotle on friendship, Sartre on bad faith, or Foucault on power-knowledge. Of course, many students are keen to ask Rainer Schürmann's question. And those who do so get a direct but tailor-made response in the privacy of my office or over a pizza in a local parlor. Such contexts are more conducive to dialogue than the "bully pulpit" of the classroom and they enable me to share with a student what matters to me most in an atmosphere that is respectful of his or her reason for raising the question in the first place. (I should add that for the last twenty years I have been teaching in a private college with an official tie to the Methodist Church but with a student body as heavily Jewish and Catholic as Protestant. As in most such elite schools, the atmosphere is rather secular.)

Once a graduate student in a seminar I was conducting on Foucault's *The Archaeology of Knowledge* brought me up short with the interjection: "Professor Flynn, we would be disturbed if we thought you really believed all of this!" Variations on the Schürmann theme, though I suspect Rainer hoped I did so believe. I recall reading somewhere Etienne Gilson's prefatory warning that he would probably shock his auditors because the philosophical position he was about to present was one he actually believed![5] From exposition to espousal to advocacy: have I somehow short-circuited the natural progression? Or am I, as one colleague suggested, like an anthropologist who has stumbled upon an exotic tribe whose curious customs and beliefs I duly note without in any way subscribing to their content? There is perhaps nothing wrong with such a practice except for the constant threat of "going native," not to mention the (Foucauldian) question of one's right to be there at all! But when the subject matter is philosophy, when it touches on the very conditions of sense-making in a society, is such detachment desirable or even possible? Has not one already made a commitment to abide by the rules by deciding to "play the game" in the first place? And when those very rules are in question, when one is in the midst of a *crisis of criteria,* as in the case of our postmodern condition, how does one maintain a critical stance? Again, my solution is to shift from the "apologetic" mode—in this case, from the need to mount an apology for "Platonism" or for any of what Whitehead called its footnotes—to a fair and sympathetic account of the position at

5. I thought this occurred in his William James Lectures at Harvard (Etienne Gilson, *The Unity of Philosophical Experience* [New York: Scribner's, 1937]), but I have not been able to locate it.

hand. Part of that exposition must include the paradoxes that this new position engenders as well as the consequences it entails for received philosophical wisdom. But that is the risk of any properly philosophical experience. That risk is heightened when the very legitimacy of philosophy as an autonomous discipline is at issue.

### III

As a student in Bernard Lonergan's classes at the Gregorian University in Rome, I was struck both by the subtlety of his argument and by the honesty of his dialogue with contemporary thinkers. Despite several previous years of textbook Thomism, this was probably the first truly philosophical experience of my life. His thought has served as a beacon through the years and his life as an example of the productive wedding of faith and the intellectual life. The author of *Insight* taught me that one can pursue a hypothesis to the utmost as long as one keeps one foot grounded in experience. It was the distinction between faith and understanding in Anselm's *fides quaerens intellectum* that has kept me open to and interested in the most "atheistic" of thinkers, without thereby feeling the depth of my religious commitment in jeopardy. But no more than Lonergan thought he could fathom the mystery of the Trinity via the "intelligible emanations" around which his speculative theology revolved, do I believe that Sartre or Foucault (or Aquinas or Augustine, for that matter) has the last word on a reality that exceeds our grasp both in its depth and in its extent. Of that much my faith continues to assure me. I can now see how philosophers with a mystical bent (or mystics with a philosophical bent) like Nicholas of Cusa could play havoc with the principle of noncontradiction and feel at home with the metaphorical mode. Like some early Renaissance deconstructionists *avant la lettre,* they communicated a feeling of extreme freedom flavored with a degree of skepticism that never weakened the faith commitment that grounded (and issued from) an experience that sometimes overwhelmed them.

Parodying a famous description of Robert M. Hutchins's University of Chicago, a priest friend once described me as "a Catholic priest in a Methodist university teaching atheistic philosophy to Jews!" What moved me toward recent French philosophy? Why did I choose to devote the major part of my scholarly research to the works of Sartre and Foucault in particular? I would offer distinct reasons for the choice of each.

Aside from the intrinsic interest that characterizes both thinkers for me, in the case of Sartre the reasons are biographical and ethical. As an undergraduate in Carroll College (Montana) in the mid fifties, I became interested in existentialism, writing an honors thesis on the concept of choice in Kierkegaard. The topic was still current and it enabled me to enrich my Aristotelian-Thomistic background with personalist and historical considerations that I thought were foreign to these philosophers. I recall the excitement of reading Maritain's newly translated book on the philosophy of history in my senior year. It made me realize that one could deal with such issues even in a Thomistic context.[6] My four years at the Gregorian opened my eyes to speculative theology and, in particular, to so-called "transcendental Thomism." But as if to confirm the suspicions of its more traditional Thomistic critics, this Maréchalian approach also introduced me to the thought of the German idealists and Martin Heidegger. Upon completion of my Licentiate in Theology, circumstances intervened to require that I return to Montana

6. I type these words with a certain mixture of nostalgia and piety as I look out my window at the Institute for Advanced Study toward the Princeton campus, which was Maritain's home for so many years. I paid my respects, as it were, in an essay, "Time Redeemed: Maritain's Christian Philosophy of History," in *Understanding Maritain,* ed. Deal W. Hudson and Matthew J. Mancini (Macon, Ga.: Mercer University Press, 1988), pp. 306–24.

to teach philosophy and, to my surprise, French. The latter would have a definite effect on my decision to move in the direction of French rather than German philosophy. In fact, I began the study of Sartre's then untranslated *Critique of Dialectical Reason* my first semester at Columbia and have continued to reflect on it ever since. Like a good intellectual mentor, Sartre introduced me to areas of philosophical concern as vast and variegated as his own catholic interests: phenomenology and dialectics, psychoanalysis and hermeneutics, social and political philosophy, ontology, history and biography, plastic and literary art, and, of course, moral responsibility. This last ran through his thought from start to finish like the *cantus firmus* of some elaborate contrapuntal creation. I chose to write my dissertation on collective responsibility as the *experimentum crucis* for a Marxist existentialism and as a particularly apt locus for bringing my religious and my philosophical convictions into tandem if not into full synthesis. I found that Sartrean social ontology and Catholic social thought have much in common. And while Sartre makes many claims (as does Aristotle) that are not valid matter for baptism, his prophetic identification with the oppressed and the exploited in our society is quite in line with authentic Christian teaching—and is equally discomforting to merely cultural Christians. It was the strength of his moral courage that kept my interest long after the hyperbolic remarks of his occasional writings had faded away. Moreover, Sartre never coveted disciples. So I have never felt I was betraying him by pursuing his thought in my own way. He did it to others and expected it to be done to him.

My reason for choosing Foucault is somewhat different. As I worked through the extensive Sartrean corpus, I encountered responses to the many critics he had occasioned along the way. Frankly, I found the brightest and most original of these to be Michel Foucault. And, like Nietzsche, he wrote so well! It seemed that he not only met Sartre issue-for-issue but that he did so from a position that was truly revolutionary: spatialized thinking countered dialectical temporalization; system challenged a shopworn humanism; the call of discursive practice disturbed an anthropological slumber, and so forth. And while he was every bit as much the polymath as Sartre (even more so because of his command of the history of science), he was even more difficult to categorize. Was he philosopher or historian? Literary critic or political theorist? Structuralist or post-structuralist? Perhaps an anti-theorist and even a "good" cynic? Curiously, none of these alternatives is implausible; each has had its defenders. One thing was clear, as his friend Paul Veyne remarked: Foucault was a "kaleidoscopic" thinker. He challenged us to turn the cylinder of our received opinions ever so slightly and watch the pieces fall into new and surprising configurations. He referred to his works as "fictions" that nonetheless had something to do with truth and characterized his thought as a tool chest from which we were free to borrow whatever we found useful. In sum, the kaleidoscopic metaphor captured the project of "thinking otherwise than before *(se déprendre de soi-même),*" which he described on several occasions as the ethic of an intellectual in our day. I call this turning of the cylinder the "Foucault experience," the name I gave a three-week seminar for college professors that I conducted at the National Humanities Center in North Carolina. I continue to find it intellectually stimulating.

But is it true? Does the Foucault experience appeal to our desire for wisdom or merely to our curiosity, to borrow a distinction from Saint Thomas? To the extent that "wisdom" denotes the ordering of things under a single principle, Foucauldian diagnostic is the antithesis of wisdom. In fact, it is as profoundly anti-Platonic in character as is the thought of Nietzsche, which Foucault admired so much. But the various forms that Foucault's thinking assumed in the course of his career, namely, archaeology, genealogy and "problematization," challenge us to reconsider the received wisdom and takens-for-granted that form the commonplace of our intellectual existence. And this, if not the "end all," may well be the "begin all" in our search for wisdom. It can be seen as radicalizing the Socratic ideal of the examined life in an admittedly unPlatonic (but more properly Socratic?) manner. In any case, Foucault never thought he had offered the last word on any topic. Indeed, his life was a series of reassessments of what went before, including his own previous opinions. Perhaps its chief contribution to our search for wisdom is to liberate us from . . . the search? Some will make that claim. But I see it as an emancipation from the self-satisfaction accompanying the belief that the end is at hand, that we have, if not all the answers, at least all the important ones, and that we have had them in hand since the thirteenth century or the end of the eighteenth or whenever. Like the "good Cynics" on whom he was lecturing at the time of his death, Foucault seeks to disturb the complacencies that keep us from realizing the possibilities that accrue from thinking otherwise.

The matter of truth is more complex. Though he was concerned with truth in its various forms and often spoke of "games of truth" in his later lectures and interviews, Foucault's chief concern was with the *effects* of truth, with the difference that truth claims make in the resultant power of the one authorized to speak the truth, to settle arguments, to resolve difficulties, to reform the deviant and normalize the aberrant. These are aspects of the exercise of truth that were commonly overlooked or ignored by mainstream philosophers in their focus on the epistemic and their love of truth in the abstract. This brief survey of Foucault's approach to the problem of truth indicates why his thought has been more influential with social scientists than with philosophers in the traditional sense.

Despite its implicit critique of the status quo in nearly every field of inquiry, Foucault's "histories" do not seem to lead to social involvement and reform as readily as the works of Sartre. Of course, Sartre is one of the prime targets of Foucault's criticism of the "universal" intellectual who seems to be in possession of the big picture and anxious to impose his solutions on other peoples' problems. But if this skeptical reluctance kept Foucault from making the big mistakes of which Sartre was often accused, it did not leave him in a state of ethical quietism. His archaeology of mental illness contributed to the anti-psychiatric movement and his genealogy of the penal system to a movement of penal reform. In fact, he and Sartre worked together in support of the Vietnamese "boat people" and other social causes. Still, I think it safe to say that Sartre was closer to the spirit of Catholic social teaching than was Foucault, chiefly because of the "prophetic" and even "apocalyptic" character of Sartre's later thought.[7]

## IV

And so I return to Rainer Schürmann's question one last time. John Herman Randall once asked whether my interest in Sartre's Marxism was not "a little too ecumenical." Clearly, he was perplexed by a priest devoting his time to so apparently antithetical a thinker. Unresolved Oedipal problems, as one person queried? I dismiss such suggestions for their basic logical error: the genetic fallacy. I prefer to close with the thought that my devotion might be the exercise of a boundless desire to know, steadied by the hope that it does all make sense in the long run and encouraged by the conviction that there are many ways to pursue a Truth that is One as

7. See his last interviews with Benny Lévy, "Hope . . . , Now," *Dissent* 27 (Fall 1980), pp. 397–422.

well as truths that are multiple. Perhaps it is never precisely "the same" proposition that is at issue in statements of faith and philosophy. This at least is a "postmodern" hypothesis worth investigating. In any case, when I have completed my present task,[8] I intend to undertake a project in which my religious and intellectual interests clearly converge, a book tentatively entitled "(Postmodern) Faith and (Enlightenment) Reason." When one turns the kaleidoscope in a certain direction, an awesome configuration emerges, one that cannot be kept at a distance but that seems to reflect into and out of one's very soul. Could that be an image of the gift of faith?

8. Volume two of my study *Sartre, Foucault and Historical Reason,* subtitled *A Post-Structuralist Mapping of History.* Vol. 1 is subtitled *An Existentialist Theory of History* (Chicago: The University of Chicago Press, 1997).

*Brendan Sweetman*

# 2. A RATIONAL APPROACH TO
# RELIGIOUS BELIEF

❧

## I

I grew up in the Republic of Ireland, in a small village in County Dublin called Lusk (population then about 1,000), which is about twelve miles north of Dublin City. It is five miles north of Swords, where Dublin Airport is located. Ireland in those days (the 1960s and 70s) was very much a Catholic country, with around 95 percent of the population belonging to the Catholic Church, and about 90 percent practicing. People went to religious services regularly, including weekly mass, mass for holy days of obligation, funerals, weddings, baptisms, and so on. Religion formed part of the fabric of social life, and anything else was more or less unthinkable. As the Irish writer Brendan Behan reputedly said when he visited America and was asked whether he was a Catholic, "What else is there?"!

Of course, there were also Protestants in Ireland, most coming from English families during colonial times, stretching back over several hundred years. Most towns in the south of Ireland had not only a Catholic church, but also a Protestant one, and each town had several prominent and well-respected Protestant families. However, the Protestant church had little influence in Irish life, had little input into government, law, education, the media, etc. I also never knew of anybody who converted from Protestantism to Catholicism or *vice versa,* although I am sure it did happen. But one did not usually meet converts in Ireland; one stayed with the religion into which one was born.

The Catholic Church had complete control over education in the sense that religious orders ran most of the country's schools, orders such as the Christian Brothers, the Sisters of Mercy, and the Loretto Nuns. And those schools that were not run by orders were still run by Catholic lay boards. They were all Catholic schools in the sense that most (usually 100 per cent) of the pupils and teachers were Catholic. The Catholic religion was taught in those schools, many had daily prayer, and each school observed all Catholic feast days, etc. Another interesting point about them too is that, unlike American schools, they were all funded by the state, including the teachers' salaries. Most schools in Ireland, including all of those I attended, provided a free education.

The elementary and other primary schools were usually run by the local parish priest and a local committee. In primary school, we were taught our catechism in the old question-and-answer method (Q: What is prayer? Answer: Prayer is a lifting up of the heart and mind to God); we were also prepared in the schools for our first communion and our confirmation. In secondary schools, religion was taught as a subject, although there was no national examination in it, as there was in every other subject. The secondary school which I attended, Swords Christian Brothers (*Colaiste Choilm* is its name in Irish), was the best school in my area at the time; unlike most schools, it required passage of an entrance examination to gain admission. Religious instruction was not emphasized very much in my school. The principal, Brother Devine, was a very tough Christian Brother, and whatever else one might say about him, he did keep discipline! But most of the teachers were lay people; our religion class was usually taught by a lay person, who was often reluctant to push religion on the class. In fact, these classes were often used more broadly to discuss issues such as capital punishment, various moral problems, the dangers of drugs, and world religions.

Growing up in Ireland, I never experienced the oppressive Catholic Ireland that Irish writers like James Joyce and Brian Moore described in their novels and that many Irish journalists continue to rant about in their columns. I seldom heard, for example, a fire and brimstone Sunday sermon, and I never heard a priest publicly (or even privately) morally condemn anyone for their actions. I never even met a priest who could be described as intolerant or lacking in understanding or compassion. All of the priests, brothers, and nuns whom I knew—they were many—were good people, who did their best in their positions. When Irish writers speak of a priest-ridden Ireland, I do not recognize what they mean. After about 1970, this Ireland had more or less ceased to exist. Of course, I know that at least one of the things they mean is that they do not like the influence of a Catholic worldview on the Irish people, and they would prefer the Irish people to follow their secular, liberal view—for which they proselytize in the papers every day—but that is another story for another time!

However, in all of this climate, religion was a subject of profound interest to me, though in these early days the really interesting questions were just beginning to stir within me. But I was a practicing Catholic, believing in God and in the doctrines of the Church, and saying my prayers regularly. It was not until I went to University College, Dublin (UCD), on the far side of Dublin City from where I lived, that I began to study philosophy, and to engage seriously with influential thinkers and writers on the major issues. This was when I began to subject my religious faith to critical scrutiny, as one might imagine. I went to university originally interested in studying for a B.A. degree in English literature because I was interested in becoming either a secondary teacher or a sports journalist (I was and still am an avid soccer fan, and to those in the U.S. who can't appreciate the majesty of this game, all I can say is that you have my profound sympathy!).

In our first year at university we had to study three subjects; then in subsequent years we dropped one and took our degree in the other two. In Irish universities, as in British ones, we do not take a variety of "core" courses, and then "major" later on in a particular subject. Rather, we specialize from the beginning in our chosen subjects, and after the first year, we then study exclusively those subjects we are taking for the degree. In my first year, I took Economics, English, and Philosophy. Philosophy was regarded as a good "third subject," one you would study for a year because it was interesting, and then drop to concentrate on your degree subjects. Everybody I had asked about studying Philosophy before I went to university told me it was very interesting and that I, in particular, would enjoy it. (They were certainly right about that!) In any case, I intended to drop it after the first year, and to study English and Economics for my degree, which would have been a good combination for the two careers I had in mind. But in that first year I found Philosophy so fascinating, and Economics so boring, that I decided to take my degree in English and Philosophy. This turned out to be a fantastic combination, as many people I had asked for advice at the time predicted it would be. At this time, I had no thoughts of a third-level academic career.

One of the questions which fascinated me concerned the rationality of religious belief, and the rationality of Christianity when compared to other worldviews. I studied with Patrick Masterson, Desmond Connell, Gerald Hanratty, and Richard Kearney, the better known people in the Department. Masterson went on to become President of UCD, and later President of the European Institute in Florence. Connell is the current Cardinal Archbishop of Dublin. Kearney built up an international reputation in continental philosophy. I studied English and Philosophy side by side, and it proved to be a fascinating combination for an enquiring mind. There was considerable overlap between the two subjects: in philosophy we pursued the debate about the existence of God, realism vs. anti-realism, language and its relation to reality, the nature of the self, in such thinkers as Plato, Aristotle, Augustine, Aquinas, Descartes, Locke, Hume, as well as Russell, Moore and Ayer, the existentialists, and later continental philosophers. In Literature, we read Old English, Middle English, Shakespeare (in my first year we read ten of Shakespeare's plays), Donne, Milton, the Romantics, and lots of modern literature, such as T. S. Eliot, Faulkner, Whitman, and, of course, almost all of Anglo-Irish literature, including Yeats, Joyce, Beckett, Shaw, and Heaney. You name it, we read it.

In all of this fascinating journey through some of the great minds in history, two questions stood out for me: the ultimate origin of reality and the nature of the self. I was particularly gripped by the idea that one could provide an argument to show that religious belief is rational. We went through the whole debate about whether or not one could prove the existence of God—which was a popular issue in philosophy of religion at that time—but I sided with those who held that it was not necessary to actually prove that God existed, but was sufficient to show that religious belief was a rational view of the world, as rational as atheism, secular humanism, and so on. We read and discussed Bertrand Russell, A. J. Ayer, and Anthony Flew attacking religious belief, and we all raised doubts and difficulties ourselves in class and in our conversations outside of class. But the more I came to think about this matter, the more it seemed to me that religious belief was more rational than the various atheistic and secular alternatives, especially if one pursued them to their logical conclusions. It seemed to me then, as it does now, that the cosmological and design arguments for the existence of God are very good arguments. More than that, when these arguments are added to the other arguments—the moral argument, the argument from the nature of mind, the argument from religious experience, etc.—one has a strong cumulative case that some non-physical being of roughly the theistic variety exists beyond the physical world. I was less interested in the question whether we could know the nature of God in order to adjudicate among the world's religions, but it seemed to me that, once the existence of God is presented in a rational way, then atheism and secular humanism are challenged. This is so, not just because these views do not stack up against religion in terms of rationality, coherence and explanatory power, but because they are then no longer the default position in modern thinking. In the light of a rational analysis of religious belief, I found the atheism and secular humanism of a James Joyce or a Samuel Beckett or a Jean-Paul Sartre very shallow, and not at all convincing. Modern atheism seemed to me to be an assumption, rather than a carefully worked out position, and my friends and I debated this question frequently in the college restaurant.

I believe that, by appeal to the arguments of natural theology, a very good case can be made for the claim that it is reasonable to believe in God. I have argued this elsewhere and I have space here only to sketch two of these arguments, but I urge readers to check out this material for themselves, especially contemporary presentations of these arguments.[1] The cosmological argument revolves

---

1. For arguments for the existence of God, see St. Thomas Aquinas, *Summa Theologiae,* Part I, q. 2, a. 3, in *Introduction to St. Thomas Aquinas,* ed. Anton C. Pegis (New York: Random House, 1945); Frederick Copleston, *Aquinas* (Harmondsworth:

around the fundamental question of the ultimate cause of the universe. Where did this vast and fascinating universe, with its one hundred billion galaxies (including our Milky Way), come from? The possible answers are: (i) the universe is eternal, and so, the argument goes, does not need a cause; or (ii) it "popped into existence out of nothing"; or (iii) it was caused by something other than itself, something outside the physical order. I am very convinced by the arguments which maintain that the first two possible answers are unreasonable. William Lane Craig has argued, on both philosophical and scientific grounds, reviving an old argument of St Bonaventure's, that an actual infinite series of physical events is impossible in the real world. In any case, I think St. Thomas showed that even if the universe is eternal, it still needs a cause, because a contingent series of events cannot cause itself, *no matter how many members are in the series.*

The cosmological argument leaves us with a supernatural cause for the universe, a cause which is *outside* of or beyond the physical order. It is also reasonable to conclude that this cause is personal and powerful; for the other alternatives, that the cause might be an impersonal force or an unknown quantity, are unnecessarily vague. And it is important to bear in mind that one popular objection to this argument from contemporary naturalists is illegitimate. This objection, expressed in different ways and with varying rhetoric,

Penguin, 1955); William Lane Craig, *The Kalam Cosmological Argument* (New York: Harper & Row, 1979); Richard Swinburne, *The Existence of God* (Oxford: Oxford University Press, 1991 2d ed.); R. Douglas Geivett and Brendan Sweetman, eds., *Contemporary Perspectives on Religious Epistemology* (Oxford: Oxford University Press, 1992); Curtis L. Hancock and Brendan Sweetman, *Truth and Religious Belief* (New York: M. E. Sharpe, 1998). For criticisms of natural theology, see David Hume, *Dialogues Concerning Natural Religion* (Indianapolis: Hackett, 1980 ed.); John Mackie, *The Miracle of Theism* (Oxford: Oxford University Press, 1982); Bertrand Russell, *Why I am not a Christian* (London: Allen & Unwin, 1957); Richard Dawkins, *The Blind Watchmaker* (New York: Norton, 1986).

holds that the cause can't be a supernatural being because a non-physical entity simply can't exist. But this objection is obviously question-begging. For we are not entitled to conclude that nothing non-physical exists if the existence of God is yet to be decided.[2] In short, since the debate about the existence of God is a debate about whether something non-physical exists or not, a prejudice in the debate toward physical explanations begs the question.

The modern version of the argument from design is based on the notion that we live in a universe that shows clear evidence of design or order, and that this order suggests an orderer or a designer behind it. The order referred to here is not the overt order in nature that the eighteenth-century natural theologian William Paley referred to, but the underlying order in the whole universe, i.e., the laws of physics. The argument from design is based on the notion that we live in a lawful universe, not a lawless or chatoic one, such as one might expect to find if the universe really were a product of chance. The analogy of spilling a can of alphabet soup is useful here as a metaphor for how modern atheism thinks our universe came about. If the can is toppled by accident, what are the chances that the letters would spell out "Rockhurst University is number one" or "Arsenal Football Club"?! Not very high, I suggest. Yet of all the possible universes we could have ended up with, if it truly was an accidental occurrence, we ended up with a lawlike one, an ordered one, one which follows laws consistently, laws which make life possible, one which, in short, plausibly spells "God exists." It is common for skeptics to appeal to Humean objections to this argument, and while such objections are interesting, they are not nearly as effective as modern atheists claim. In fact, I believe that Richard

2. See Dallas Willard, "The Three-State Argument for the Existence of God" in Geivett and Sweetman, *Contemporary Perspectives on Religious Epistemology,* pp. 212ff.

Swinburne has replied effectively to these kinds of objections in his work.[3]

One might also briefly mention here another version of the argument from design that has gotten attention in the last few years—the argument from the fine-tuning of the universe.[4] The idea here is that scientists have discovered in the last few decades that the existence of intelligent life on earth depends on a very complex and delicate balance of initial conditions given in the big bang itself. The upshot of this discovery is that the emergence of life depends on a fine-tuning that is difficult to comprehend and the probability of which is so low that it is almost incalculable. Again the conclusion of the fine-tuning argument is very reasonable: that our universe very likely did not happen by chance, and is the product of a designer. This is the only conclusion the evidence supports.

The appeal by naturalists like Richard Dawkins to the theory of evolution to explain the order and design in the universe does not succeed because the theory of evolution obviously cannot explain the origin of the universe, or the laws of physics. It cannot explain the origin of matter, since the theory must *presuppose* matter and an environment in order for evolution to take place, and it *presupposes* the laws of physics, just as all scientific theories do.[5]

## II

In 1987, my wife and I came to the United States, where I enrolled in the Ph.D. program in philosophy at the University of

3. See Richard Swinburne, "The Argument from Design" in Geivett & Sweetman, *Contemporary Perspectives on Religious Epistemology*, pp. 201–11.

4. See William Lane Craig, "Why I believe God exists" in *Why I am a Christian*, ed. Norman L. Geisler and Paul K. Hoffman (Grand Rapids, Mich.: Baker, 2001), pp. 62–80, for one of the best statements of this argument. My brief account of the argument here relies on Craig's.

5. See Richard Dawkins, *The Blind Watchmaker* (New York: Norton, 1986).

Southern California in Los Angeles. I came into a department under the control of analytic philosophy, and while the department was not hostile to philosophy of religion, it was indifferent to it, did not offer courses in it or encourage its study. I was, however, also very interested in continental philosophy, especially the work of Husserl, Gabriel Marcel, and Martin Buber, and the critique of postmodernism. I began to study with Dallas Willard, who is a Husserl scholar of international stature. In recent years, he has become very widely known through several best-selling and influential books on religion. Dallas is unique among philosophers in that, while he is a phenomenological realist, and thoroughly steeped in the continental tradition, he also works in analytic philosophy and has profound knowledge of the history of philosophy. There are not many working in philosophy departments today who can match this breadth, and his students down through the years have greatly benefitted from his overall, deep knowledge of philosophical issues. He is a wonderful teacher and thinker, and a man of great moral character and compassion, and I count myself very fortunate to have studied with him, and to count him amongst my friends. His honest, logical, and common sense approach to philosophy, and his modeling of the life of the philosopher, have had a deep influence on me. In his courses, I came to really appreciate the value of intellectual honesty, the necessity of having detailed knowledge of one's area in philosophy, and the need to be careful, rigorous, and fair in stating one's positions and arguments.

If one is interested in the philosophy of religion, America is a very interesting country to live in. Here, the debates about religion and politics, religion and science, and religion and morality differ quite a bit from comparable debates in Ireland. The contrast between the two societies (and perhaps between Europe and the United States generally) has served to crystallize the issues for me and to sharpen focus of my interests in philosophy of religion. Given my general position that religious belief is rational and has nothing to fear from atheism, American society has proved a catalyst in further working out my position, especially on the issue of the role of religion in public life, and on the relationship between religion and morality.

One interesting cultural fact about the United States is that it has a long tradition, under the influence of Protestantism, of holding that faith and reason are in two separate and usually mutually exclusive categories, and therefore that religion has nothing to fear from reason, or from science. One can even see the influence of this view on the religious philosophy of Alvin Plantinga, who has argued in an interesting and provocative way that belief in God is a basic belief, not inferred from other propositions, and yet is still a justified belief. Although I admire Plantinga greatly, and would be among the many who would say that he has inspired me, I believe his approach is a risky way to defend religious belief, and that natural theology is a more effective approach.

The advantage of Plantinga's approach is that placing religion in a separate category of faith tends to protect religion from critical discussion. In the life of a believer, the practical effect of this is that one does not have to raise critical questions about one's view, or have to defend one's view against contrary evidence, or have to worry about one's religion being rational and coherent and capable of meeting secular challenges. This is an advantage of sorts, because it enables religion to avoid critical debate. However, the disadvantage of this approach is that, eventually, religion is seen as belonging purely to a private realm with no place in public life. Also, over time religious belief tends to be regarded, especially by the intelligentsia, as a worldview which cannot be taken seriously because it seems that its main beliefs are not subject to rational examination.

Eventually, this conception of religious belief becomes marginalized in society; and we get the schizophrenic situation where one finds oneself practicing and defending one view privately, but following another view publicly (e.g., on abortion). Some religious believers are greatly troubled by this conflict and don't fully understand it, but some embrace it and are quite content to restrict their religion to the private realm. This describes well, I think, the current situation with regard to much of religious belief in American society.

Religion in America has been adversely affected by the public vs. private distinction currently invoked in religious, social, political, and legal debates in our society. This distinction was recently employed with significant effect in the 1997 debate in Oregon concerning euthanasia, where the pro-euthanasia side insisted that the arguments against euthanasia were religious arguments. It was argued that, since religion is a totally private affair, religious arguments are not appropriate when the subject is a public issue, affecting all citizens. This view influenced a lot of people, and the churches were unable to deal with it rhetorically, and so the pro-euthanasia side carried the day. The private/public distinction was used here to put religion on the defensive. In this way, this distinction suits atheists and secular humanists because it enables them to diminish the influence of religion on modern political and social policy. I believe this interpretation of the American founding documents concerning religion is erroneous, but I cannot argue that here. My main point here is that as long as this is the dominant view it affects religion adversely.

One of the strengths of Catholicism is that it has always been a great defender of reason in religious belief, of the attempt to show that belief in God is a rational belief, and that religious belief is more rational than any atheistic alternative. In his recent encyclical *Fides et ratio* ("Faith and Reason"), Pope John Paul II made a very interesting point when he noted the irony that it is now the Church who is among the foremost defenders of reason and truth, of the objectivity of knowledge, of common sense, whereas many times throughout history those who claimed to defend reason and truth ridiculed the Church for being on the side of superstition and myth. The Catholic Church, in particular, has always insisted on a significant role for reason in religious belief and in theology. It has always defended the view that faith and reason are compatible—that the truths of faith are not incompatible with reason, and, more significantly, that religious faith is a rational response to the ultimate mystery of the universe and of human life. The Catholic Church has great resources to defend its worldview and its philosophy of the human person against secular opposition and criticism. This is one of the reasons the Catholic Church is much disliked by many intellectuals—because it represents a serious and rational alternative to their worldview, and hence is a threat to their worldview.

In developing and discussing these matters, I have been very influenced by a number of thinkers, especially the key philosophers of the Western tradition, Plato, Aristotle, St. Augustine, and St. Thomas Aquinas. But I have been most especially influenced by the thought of the French philosopher Gabriel Marcel,[6] a theistic existentialist, because of his attempt to engage the modern world with a Christian vision of the human person, all in an existentialist sense rather than in a theoretical sense.

Marcel is one of the lesser known of the existentialists; he is often eclipsed by his more illustrious atheistic counterpart and contemporary, Jean-Paul Sartre. Nevertheless, Marcel is one of the most significant philosophers of the twentieth century. I was drawn to Marcel for several reasons, which dovetailed with some of my

6. See Gabriel Marcel, *The Mystery of Being,* 2 vols. (Chicago: Regnery, 1951).

own ideas and experiences. What first drew me was his critique of Cartesianism, where he argued that the epistemological dualism of subject and object which Descartes began with and which eventually plunged him and modern philosophy into either skepticism (the view that we cannot have any real knowledge of anything) or anti-realism (the view that the mind modifies the objects of consciousness in the act of knowing and so we never know things as they are in themselves) was very much mistaken. Marcel argued that the skepticism, anti-realism, and relativism which has been the unwitting legacy of Descartes to modern philosophy was based on a false epistemology. After studying Marcel in detail (in my Ph.D. dissertation) and other thinkers who were close to him such as Buber, Heidegger, and Husserl, I came to believe that he was basically right in his critique of Descartes, although his position needed both clarification and elaboration, something I have since tried to do in my own work on Marcel.

A second theme which appealed to me in Marcel was his defense of a Christian philosophy of the human person. What I found interesting about his view was the fact that he did not simply assume Christianity and go on from there to explain and defend the Christian view of the human person; rather, he developed his philosophy of the human person independently of religious tradition or of particular religious thinkers, and supported it by appeal to reason and human experience. What intrigued me was that he still came out very close to the Christian view, and, in ethics, to the natural law tradition, even though he was not influenced by these positions, and did not espouse them at that time. Over a period of years, he came to realize that his position was very close to Catholicism (even if arrived at independently), and eventually he went from agnosticism in his own life, to conversion to Catholicism in 1929 at the age of forty.

A third theme in Marcel, and in existentialism generally, which I found interesting was the critique of contemporary culture. In Marcel, this flowed directly from his epistemology. Marcel's phenomenological analysis of the human person is based on his critique of the "spirit of abstraction" at work in modern culture, a critique which leads to his famous distinction between problem and mystery. Marcel argues that the realm of conceptual knowledge (or what he calls "primary reflection") is concerned with *problems* of various kinds. Problems require conceptual generalizations, abstractions, and an appeal to what is verifiable in human experience. However, the realm of the problematic cannot do justice to what Marcel's calls the *being-in-a-situation* of the human person, the person's *fundamental involvement* in the world at the level of personal experience. This involvement takes place, according to Marcel, in the realm of *mystery*, a realm where the distinction between subject and object breaks down. Many of our most valued and profound experiences occur at this level. These experiences are all mysterious because they intimately involve the questioner in such a way that the meaning of the experience cannot be fully conveyed by means of an abstract conceptual analysis. This realm of mystery includes the "concrete approaches" of love, hope, fidelity, and faith, experiences which are being lost in the modern world, a loss which is ushering in new forms of alienation. This alienation is characterized by a withdrawal from the intersubjective nature of human relations and the behavior appropriate to these relations; one focuses instead on one's self as the center of meaning and value. To adopt this kind of attitude is to exhibit an "unavailability" *(indisponibilité)* to the other, whereas what we urgently need is a kind of "spiritual availability" *(disponibilité)* toward our fellow human beings. In my study of Marcel, many of my interests came together—the question of the rationality of religious belief, the phenomenological analysis of the nature of the human person, ethical issues, and epistemological questions relating to modernism and postmodernism. This confluence has had a major influence on my current interests and research in philosophy.

### III

I would like to spend the last part of my paper discussing more directly how, in the light of my description of my religious beliefs and interests in philosophy, these ideas relate to my work in philosophy, and to my role as a teacher and thinker. One interesting question to consider is whether my religious beliefs influence me when I engage in philosophical research; in particular, do they influence the results of my research? And if they do, should they? How would my approach differ say from the approach of a scientist to his or her research? A scientist presumably would not allow religious beliefs to interfere with his or her research. This is an interesting question and a discussion of it will serve to further clarify some of the issues.

It is when we get into this question that the rationality of one's beliefs becomes critical, I believe. As I have pointed out above, it is never a good idea to believe simply on faith and give little or no thought to whether one's beliefs are rational, or could be true, or whether they make sense. This is true of all worldviews, not just religious worldviews. I use the example of the Abominable Snowman Worship Society to make this point. If you came across such a society, would you be inclined to join it if the members of the group emphasized to you that their religion would lead you to meaning in life, spiritual fulfillment, happiness, and so on?[7] But they stressed that they did not get into distracting, silly questions about whether the abominable snowman actually existed or not, or was worthy of worship!

7. This issue is discussed further in Hancock and Sweetman, *Truth and Religious Belief,* Chapter 1.

My position, as I have described it above, is that religious belief in general is quite rational and can form the basis for a perfectly respectable worldview. Philosophy, therefore, should not be considered as apologetics for one's religious view. That is to say, the role of philosophy is not to provide a defense of one's religious beliefs, *after* one has committed to these beliefs in advance. In my view, one arrives at one's religious beliefs, as a philosopher, by using philosophy to justify one's fundamental beliefs (e.g., in the existence of God), and to defend them. Of course, not all religious believers approach the issue this way, but we are talking specifically about the approach of the philosopher here. Religious believers commit to their religious beliefs for all sorts of reasons, and whatever these reasons are, it is possible for the beliefs to be rational even if a specific believer cannot explain why he or she holds various beliefs, and cannot defend them philosophically. It would be very unrealistic to expect *every* religious believer to be capable of philosophically defending what he or she believes (just as it would be unrealistic to expect this of every marxist). But the goal of philosophy is to explore questions in a rational, logical and historically informed way, and then to arrive at a coherent set of beliefs which can be defended. In this way, I disagree with those medieval thinkers (such as St. Bonaventure) who believed that theology was prior to philosophy, and that the primary job of philosophy was to clarify and defend the insights of theology.

Of course, some mysteries of the faith cannot be proved in a strict philosophical sense, because they are ultimate mysteries forever inaccessible to reason. Nevertheless, I believe it is rational to accept the general reliablity of revelation, given the general rationality of religious belief. One can come to believe that the general truths of revelation are true based on the overall evidence for religious belief, on an independent phenomenological analysis of the nature of the human person, and after an examination of the evidence for each particular revelation claim. This, at least, is how I suggest addressing the question of whether in general it is reasonable to believe in the miracles of the Bible. Philosophical theology can help us to clarify and better understand religious doctrines, as well as to illustrate their compatibility (if not their accessibility) to human reason. But the most important point to make is that the truths of faith are not incompatible with reason; and the doctrines presented in revelation cannot be ruled out because of an *a priori* commitment to some form of naturalism.

Let us turn to the question of whether a philosopher who is a religious believer should proselytize his or her religious beliefs in the classroom. I do not think proselytizing is appropriate for two reasons. By proselytize, I mean attempt to convert the students in one's classes to one's point of view on a particular issue, or even worldview—I am not referring to merely informing one's students what one's view is on a particular topic. First, philosophy should involve a fair and balanced presentation of a question, or subject, or issue, and, in my view, if one does this, certain positions such as realism, the rationality of religious belief, and the objectivity of value will stand out as rational (whether or not one comes to adopt them). Second (and closely related), in philosophy one must consider honestly all points that are pertinent to the discussion of an issue if one is to do the job properly (and one should do so in the light of the best scholarship, both past and present). In this way students will be properly informed and can make up their own minds. This, in fact, is supposed to be how an individual philosopher arrives at his or her own beliefs: by rationally analyzing the subject fully and honestly, and coming to a conclusion. If one presents an issue honestly and thoroughly, from all sides, then the danger of misleading students or prejudicing them in one direction rather than another is avoided, I believe. For example, if one is discussing the question of the evidence for the existence of God, one should discuss the problem of evil as a possible challenge to religious belief. Or if one is discussing John Rawls' political theory, one should bring up the question of whether he contradicts himself by covertly appealing to his own view of the good when he says one should not do this (I once took a course devoted wholly to Rawls in which this question was never raised). Or, finally, if one is discussing postmodernism, one should honestly discuss the problems of relativism and self-contradiction which that position invites.

One can state one's views and arguments in the classroom and then present the alternative arguments; the alternative arguments should also, ideally, be reflected in the class reading assignments. This is fair, and standard practice, I believe. In fact, it is probably the best way to teach philosophy (particularly in graduate courses). It is better than always being neutral in one's presentations, because an approach characterized by permanent neutrality runs the risk of sending the message that philosophical arguments are unimportant, and that philosophy ends up, for all practical purposes, in relativism. Defending one's view cannot be regarded as proselytizing, for the students are always free to dissent. It is essential that in grading exams, for example, a student must not lose points for disagreeing with the professor. If the student presents very well the strongest possible argument against a professor's view, he or she may very well be worthy of a top grade, even though the professor does not agree with the conclusion (and so does not think the overall argument is convincing). This approach insures fairness.

It can be instructive to compare religious belief to other worldviews on this matter, and to ask if it is legitimate for a professor to proselytize his or her beliefs in the classroom, as long as those beliefs are not religious. Of course, an affirmative answer to this question would require some very good reasons for why religion should be singled out for this kind of discrimination. While I cannot discuss this interesting issue fully here, a number of observations may be made in the limited space we have left. First, in fact professors from the full range of disciplines do proselytize in the classroom. One only has to think of the proselytizing of radical feminist thinkers, or of those who teach various courses in multicultural studies. But these are only the most obvious cases. Professors across the board proselytize, and not just in the humanities, but in the sciences, law, business, etc. That is to say, many professors try to convince their students that their worldview is the right one, and they try to get the students to subscribe to that worldview (at least in part). And this is not just because a certain amount of proselytizing is inevitable in the classroom, it is because the professors are intentionally proselytizing. The fact that a good many of them, if challenged on this point, would deny it, or would not want to consistently allow this opportunity to all disciplines, is beside the point.

A second observation relates to the fact that if proselytizing in these other areas is okay, why is it not acceptable if the view being proselytized is religious? If one can proselytize radical feminist philosophy, why can't one proselytize religious beliefs? Now I have already given my own answer to this question. My view is that one should not proselytize *any* subject, but should try to present it in a fair and balanced way. However, it is important to point out that those who proselytize their own views today, but who want to deny religious belief this opportunity, are on shaky ground. This is because one of the main arguments they use to exclude religious belief is that it is a private view, which is not subject to rational examination, and so should have no role in public life, especially in education.

I have indicated above that I do not accept the view that religious belief is a private view, and not real knowledge, especially if one is going to claim that other views, such as marxism, secular humanism, etc., are not subject to the same constraints. This is simply an argument that will not hold up against religion. Religion is no more a private view than marxism is. The other important point is that those who hold this view are usually themselves operating from a background of relativism, especially if they come from the feminist, postmodernist, or multicultural camp, and so are not in a position to exclude a view because they believe it cannot be objectively demonstrated. For one of the main beliefs of many opponents of religion today is the belief that knowledge is relative to either the culture (cultural relativism) or the individual (extreme relativism). This approach is rampant in the academy. But this general view of knowledge as relative is inconsistent with precluding religious views based on the metaphysical status of its knowledge claims. All this simply serves to show that much of the criticism against religion in many areas of our educational establishments is arbitrary and cannot be justified. And this is a crucial insight for anyone concerned with the issue of the relationship of the intellectual life to religious belief.

# 3. FAITH, REASON, AND THE
# PERENNIAL PHILOSOPHY

ॐ

It has been an object of wonder to me that I aspired to the study of philosophy. My family background was not disposed to education. They were pioneer stock, having migrated to Oklahoma with the original settlers in the late nineteenth century. Only a small percentage of Oklahomans, no doubt, received a college degree until after World War II. I was the first person to earn a college degree in my family, including the vast extended family of both my parents. My mother had eleven siblings; my father, five. But from my earliest years, especially on occasions when I was feted to Sooner football games, my father would remind me that I was expected to go to college some day—to the University of Oklahoma. Where else? At age eighteen, I dutifully complied.

I attended the university on a track and cross-country scholarship. At the time, I would have told you that athletics was my sole motive for attending college. But I would have been disingenuous, of course. While I was not a star pupil during my twelve years of public school education, I was naturally curious and read voraciously, especially history, science, science fiction, sports literature, and adventure tales. For some reasons, which I have never really analyzed, I was disposed to philosophical reflection. I believe that this was partly encouraged by the wonder evoked by living and playing among the prairies and hills of Oklahoma, a place palpably tinctured by Native American mysticism, if one is attuned to it. I enjoyed the friendship of many Indians during my childhood, especially members of the Cherokee, Kiowa, and Osage tribes, and their heritage suggested a respect for contemplation that may have influenced me.

This influence was curiously mixed with my childhood Protestant training, since I attended a Southern Baptist church with many Native American members. I remained a member of that church until my university years. One of my compelling memories from childhood was the experience of attending Sunday School and realizing quite strongly that something significant was being valued and discussed. That experience and my early faith formation generally were more important than I was at first willing to admit years later during my agnostic phase, which, not unpredictably, coincided with my undergraduate university years. Nonetheless, my earlier Protestant formation had equipped me with a certain biblical literacy and a modest conversance with evangelical theology, both of which would serve me well when, in my mid-twenties, I openly explored the Christian faith again, a re-examination that within a few years led to a conversion to Catholicism.

This background, along with the brazen declaration of philosophy as my major before I even matriculated at the University of Oklahoma, convinced me, retrospectively, that philosophy was for me a vocation. And yet, my early encounters in philosophy were uncongenial to my religious sensibilities, since I was mainly tutored by positivists, who thought that it would actually dignify religious utterances to declare them false. Rather, religious beliefs were to be condemned to the flames of nonsense. The only balance to the positivists in the department were a couple of "death of God" theologians and a few philosophers of religion, whose mission was to proselytize Rudolph Bultmann to the Oklahoma plains. I was sitting in classes with other undergraduates whose beliefs were routinely catalogued for de-mythologizing.

As it often happens in such a milieu, the student comes to believe that philosophy, indeed the intellectual life in general, must be at loggerheads with religion. I embraced that anti-religious creed for two or three years. What else could I do? Was there anything besides positivism or de-mythologized religion? I sought advice but found it wanting. Yet, I knew I was not content. My heart sought rest and another direction for my philosophical studies.

I am thankful that Providence smiled. During my senior year I enrolled in a class taught by a Thomistic philosopher, Francis Kovach, whose commitment to the work of St. Thomas Aquinas was rivaled only by his fierce allegiance to his Hungarian homeland. That there was a professor committed to and vocal about the Catholic intellectual tradition was itself a marvel in Oklahoma, given that, positivists and deconstructionists notwithstanding, Oklahoma is the Bible Belt, where matters Catholic are seldom visible or publicly discussed, at least not favorably. Beyond Ayer and Bultmann, there is always looming Oral Roberts. But to complicate that state of affairs, a wealthy Austrian benefactress, apparently distressed that students could not encounter Catholic wisdom on the Oklahoma grasslands, endowed a Chair for the study of medieval philosophy. Francis Kovach, who had been teaching at Villanova, was awarded that Chair, and I had the good fortune to hear his lectures for several years. True, his Thomism was more "paleo-" than "neo-" (which was, and is, all right by me), and in its rigid, mechanical presentation it lacked grace. Nonetheless, his lectures were sometimes powerful and persuasive. As an antidote for what ailed me at the time, his tutelage was a reviving elixir.

Francis showed me that there was another tradition in the history of philosophy, one which had the resources sufficient to reconnect faith and reason, according to the light of the unity of truth. This tradition Jacques Maritain and others have called the *perennial philosophy,* which, at cost of oversimplification, refers to the way the Western tradition, culturally animated by the Catholic Church, absorbed and developed the Greek conviction that the human mind can know both physical and, to a modest degree, metaphysical things and that the human person, on account of the mystery of mind and morality, is more than just flesh and bone. As Pope John Paul II has recently explained in his encyclical *Fides et ratio,* these convictions are implicit in all cultures when sound philosophy develops. For that reason the perennial philosophy speaks to all philosophical generations and is open to truth regardless of cultural, historical, or geographical source.[1]

1. Pope John Paul II, *Fides et Ratio,* September 14, 1998, 4–5. The following quotations express the Pope's appreciation of inclusivism implicit in the perennial philosophy:

> Although times change and knowledge increases, it is possible to discern a core of philosophical insight within the history of thought as a whole. Consider, for example, the principles of non-contradiction, finality, and causality, as well as the concept of the person as a free and intelligent subject with the capacity to know God, truth and goodness. Consider as well certain fundamental moral norms which are shared by all. These are among the indications that beyond different schools of thought there exists a body of knowledge which may be judged a kind of spiritual heritage of humanity. It is as if we had come upon an implicit philosophy, as a result of which all feel that they possess these principles, albeit in a general and unreflective way. Precisely because it is shared in some measure by all, this knowledge should serve as a kind of reference point for the different philosophical schools. . . . On her part, the Church cannot but set great value upon reason's drive to attain goals which

Needless to say, my lessons with Professor Kovach were liberating, since they revealed that so many of my former professors had omitted arguments in the history of philosophy that called into question their own narrow and arbitrary view of the nature and limits of knowledge. At that time, I also enjoyed the friendship of Joseph Pappin, who happened, like earlier friends, to have both a Native American and a Protestant background. He also had been wandering in the intellectual deserts before stumbling upon Francis Kovach. Together in our conversations we saw the perennial philosophy opening up alternative philosophical explanations and pathways which we had presumed were closed. My readings of St. Thomas and his predecessors, especially the ancient Greek philosophers Plato, Aristotle, and Plotinus, convinced me that sound philosophy rests on classical realism, the judgment that the content-determining cause of our knowledge is ultimately things outside the mind, and that the classical Greek view of knowledge and of the human person, open to and revitalized by the contributions of other philosophical cultures, can reinforce and advance the Christian faith.

So it was that my early philosophical experience conformed to Francis Bacon's observation "that a little or superficial knowledge of philosophy may incline the mind of man to atheism, but a further proceeding therein doth bring the mind of man back again."[2] I have seen this pattern repeat itself in the philosophical pilgrimage

---

render people's lives ever more worthy. She sees in philosophy the way to come to know fundamental truths about human life. At the same time, the Church considers philosophy an indispensable help for a deeper understanding of faith and for communicating the truth of the Gospel to those who do not yet know it.

2. Francis Bacon, *The Advancement of Learning,* in *Great Books of the Western World,* vol. 30, ed. Robert Maynard Hutchins (Chicago: Encyclopedia Britannica, 1952), p. 4.

of friends and colleagues, such as Joseph Pappin, and I have come to regard it as natural for those sincere in cultivating breadth and depth of philosophical understanding. In the thought of St. Thomas I discovered a way to make sense of the relation of faith to reason. This development is possible when reason is an ally of faith. From acquaintance with St. Thomas' modern commentators, such as Etienne Gilson and Jacques Maritain, I came to realize that reason is not an enemy of faith but that it preserves and protects it, either from a confused fideism or from the encroachments of atheism.

I became convinced that the Christian philosophy of St. Thomas was my surest guide. But I was not content to study St. Thomas as though he existed disconnected from earlier influences. To understand St. Thomas, I spent several years reading in medieval thinkers. But eventually I developed an interest in ancient philosophy, especially Hellenistic thinkers, in my efforts to find distant influences on St. Thomas. I was struck by the fact that, while St. Thomas is often described simply as an Aristotelian, his citations of Neoplatonists, such as Pseudo-Dionysius and the author of the *Liber de Causis,* are most frequent in his texts. So it happened that my exploration of influences on St. Thomas led to an interest in Neoplatonism, an interest that perhaps had some resonance with my vague sense of Native American mysticism in the ambience of my childhood. I met Leo Sweeney, S.J., and spent several years in Chicago at Loyola University researching the thought of Plotinus. With Father Sweeney's direction, I wrote a dissertation entitled *Act and Potency in the Enneads of Plotinus.* This research rewarded me in ways that I never anticipated. I was able to acquire at last a comprehensive perspective on ancient philosophy, since act and potency are foundational principles for Plotinus, opening up his entire metaphysics, and since these principles radiate out of the earlier work of Plato and Aristotle. Thus, in order to understand Plotinus, I had to become conversant with earlier classical Greek metaphysics. In the end, the dissertation had the subtitle, *A Reaction to Plato and Aristotle.* This work helped me to appreciate how influential Neoplatonism has been on Western philosophy. In fact, it is not an exaggeration to call Plotinus' *Enneads* a kind of *Summa Theologiae* of ancient philosophy. It synthesizes Plato, Aristotle, and the Stoics according to Plotinus' own monistic and mystical vision of the universe. All subsequent medieval philosophy is under Plotinus' influence. Reading Aquinas is never the same after reading Plotinus and the Neoplatonists, even if it is true that in the end Aquinas' grasp of the real distinction between Creator and created enables him to escape the monism or pantheism which Neoplatonism, at least as Plotinus envisioned it, entails.

While my graduate study explored the history of philosophy, I was always on guard against the dangers of a historical dilettantism, a fate to which some Thomists succumb. Good friends such as Joseph Pappin, Alan Lacer, Randy Feezell, and George Cornecelli kept me from suffering that fate. They would commend the historical erudition whenever I appealed to an ancient or medieval argument, but would always follow up with important questions: Is it really a good argument? Does it persuade us today? Does it cohere with what we know about modern science? Et Cetera. This forced me to be a philosopher, not just a historian of philosophy. They saw earlier and more clearly than I that the history of philosophy can provide an escape from the demands of engaging the philosophical debate in our own culture. Historical knowledge is important but it does not absolve one from the call to restore sound philosophical thinking in our own time. I am distressed by the number of fine thinkers who have an impressive grounding and training in St. Thomas, but who have retreated from the cultural debate into their own arcane studies. I understand the temptation, but classically trained philosophers ought not to avoid "dirtying their hands," given the intellectual and moral confusions endemic in today's culture.

These remarks indicate that my debt to the perennial philosophy is not just academic but personal. And I have done my very small part as a teacher and as a professional to keep the lamp of the perennial philosophy lit during these times. This is not an easy job, given the postmodernist malaise we are living in. In fact, some skeptics go so far as to say that the perennial philosophy is dead, which would be an ironic state of affairs for a philosophy that professes to be "perennial." Yet, I do not despair. I am convinced, as others have said before me, that the perennial philosophy will survive to bury its undertakers.

To demonstrate that survivability, philosophers who labor in the vineyard of St. Thomas—whom I take to be the best representative of the perennial philosophy—need to engage in a countercultural criticism of two presumptions prevalent in today's culture, especially among the intelligentsia. These presumptions Alvin Plantinga has called "Perennial Naturalism" and "Creative Anti-Realism."[3] The first holds that matter alone exists, and that matter is sufficient to explain all reality, including human nature and behavior. The latter holds that the human mind knows only its own contents, manufactured by language, culture, or perhaps its own psychological structures and states. Such a viewpoint rests on a wholesale skepticism and must be dismissive of any tradition advancing realism. This is neo-Protagoreanism: the mind is free to make its own reality and value. It is anti-realism, but of a "creative" kind.

If the Christian philosopher is able and willing to assess both

3. Alvin Plantinga, "On Christian Scholarship," in *The Challenge and Promise of a Catholic University,* ed. Theodore M. Hesburgh (Notre Dame: University of Notre Dame Press, 1994), p. 228.

creative anti-realism and perennial naturalism in the classroom, he or she is bound to have a rewarding pedagogical experience. As a teacher, I have discovered that a number of students have been influenced by these worldviews. Their awareness of this influence is more inchoate than refined; nonetheless, when first encountering philosophical discourse and argument, many students will take epistemological and moral skepticism as axiomatic, reflecting the influence of anti-realism. Their response is partly emotive: objective truth and value sounds suspiciously authoritarian to them. In a culture where freedom of "choice" is highly valued, they are reluctant to endorse a position that sounds as though one is "imposing one's views on others." The rhetoric of relativism panders to this sensibility, and it persuades them unless they are shown that relativism, whether of the moral or the epistemological kind, has serious difficulties.

Additionally, they will prejudge discussions about God or the human soul as pointless, since science, which they often confuse with naturalism, has no need of these "hypotheses." Of course, that there is science at all does not cohere well with their anti-realism, but they have not yet had to bother with such a fine point. At any rate, the students' prior allegiance to these worldviews provides a unique opportunity for the Christian educator to show that anti-realism and naturalism are highly troubled philosophies and that a philosopher borrowing from the Christian and Greek realist philosophical traditions can explain more convincingly human knowledge and reality. Educators who do not address the weaknesses of anti-realism and naturalism in today's classroom are, in my opinion, doing their students a considerable disservice. Much of the confusion under which they and their culture labor is due to an uncritical acceptance of modern skepticism and dogmatic materialism.

It is especially beneficial to inoculate students against the pretensions of skepticism. To engage skepticism in a frank debate will expose that it is a bizarre and counterintuitive way to approach philosophy, and this will give the students some resistance to the extremes of modernist and postmodernist culture. Once they can discern that skepticism underpins many of these extremes, they are less likely to take them seriously and are prepared to warn the wider culture against them. In today's philosophical classroom professors usually present the problem of skepticism as *the* uncontroversial and obligatory starting point for philosophical inquiry. But, of course, this is not true. A more balanced perspective is Etienne Gilson's in his book *Methodical Realism,* where he explains that the philosopher has the right to begin philosophizing any way he or she chooses.[4] Nonetheless, he adds, that right does not change the fact that skepticism is unnecessary and arbitrary as a philosophical beginning, in spite of the protests of generations of philosophers who *a priori* rule out philosophizing from any other starting point. That vigorous criticism of skepticism seldom occurs is a sign, Gilson believes, that we live in a stale intellectual age, in which thinkers have become inured to skepticism and have ceased to regard it as bizarre.

If students are shown that there are philosophers like Gilson who have boldly criticized skepticism, regarding it as no more than another idol of the modern intellectual tribe, they will let their own common sense judgment spring forward and they will criticize skepticism themselves. They will identify its incoherencies and will offer alternative, more plausible ways of looking at problems of knowledge. That many students today never engage in a critical discussion of skepticism is because their professors often present the problem of skepticism (which presumes that the human is appar-

---

4. Etienne Gilson, *Methodical Realism,* trans. Philip Trower (Front Royal, Va.: Christendom Press, 1990).

ently constrained to know only its own states and cannot know extramental things) as something supposedly beyond criticism. Unfortunately, this conveys the impression that genuine philosophy, and all liberal education for that matter, is built on (or fractured by) the rock of skepticism. However, once the students are shown that skepticism has been subjected to criticism by great minds over the centuries (recall St. Augustine's *Contra Academicos*), they are encouraged to exercise their own common-sense belief that genuine knowledge of the external world is possible and they are afterward wary of professors and peers who maintain that skepticism is axiomatic for the life of the mind.

With a little Socratic coaching, the students often come to see that the problem of skepticism is unconvincing. When discussing Descartes, students will sometimes point out that skepticism is self-refuting. They will see that the skeptic presupposes realism when setting up the very problem of doubt in the first place. To doubt whether the mind can know the external world results from a concern for error. But whence arises error? One learns error from ordinary experience, in which there sometimes occur mistakes in judgment about objects. Descartes himself, the celebrated modern skeptic, admits this. We recognize error, he observes, when we see that in water the stick appears bent only to realize later that it was really straight. Once the student puzzles over this example for a few moments, he or she will usually locate the skeptic's incoherency. After all, the skeptic's implicit admission—that ordinary experience itself supplies the distinction between truth and error—is to surrender skepticism. For if the veracity of ordinary experience is presupposed to set up the problem of skepticism—the worry about error—then a knowledge of the external world is admitted. Since the standard for skepticism—truth versus error—emerges out of ordinary experience, the skeptic knows what he or she doubts.

Ask the students to finalize their response to skepticism and they will often do so by analogy or illustration, modes of explanation which so often clearly vindicate common-sense judgment over counterintuitive types of belief. They observe that one can be taught to believe anything, but that does not mean it is really credible. It is as though it has become acceptable to believe that the sun will not come up tomorrow because we can, by a hyperbolic effort of our imagination, consider the possibility. Of course, it is far and away more reasonable to believe that it will come up. But if absolute certainty is the standard for knowledge, even hyperbolic doubt becomes decisive against what is plausible. If one were to obligate everyone to make this doubt authoritative over all their beliefs and behavior, then one would have an analogy illustrative of what modern philosophy has done to us. Modern philosophy's presumption that skepticism is obligatory for philosophical discourse is like the demand that we change our whole behavior because we cannot be *absolutely certain* that the sun will come up tomorrow. There is no reason to change our attitude about life because there is a remote chance a comet will wipe out the solar system. Life should be based on what is reasonable, on what is plausible. In light of such an analogy, students will discern that skepticism is neither plausible nor persuasive, even if, as Gilson concedes, one has a "right" to accept it.

Students have reinforced my conviction that modern skepticism is counterintuitive and that the mind has to be trained to accept it as reasonable. To turn the counterintuitive into an idol of the intellectual tribe is no mean trick. Struggling to account for so odd an historical fact, Eric Vogelin has remarked that modernism is a kind of gnosticism, since it is unnatural to think this way about the external world. One must be trained by an elite culture to accept something so uncongenial to the way ordinary people know the world. Jacques Maritain observed that modern philosophy is not really philosophy at all, but "ideosophy," according to which the human mind has only its own states as objects of knowledge.[5] Philosophy is wisdom, and wisdom must know, at least in part, what is real. After cultural training, nowadays entrusted to departments of philosophy, that which is not philosophy, indeed that which is anti-philosophical because it denies the possibility of knowing the real, becomes by an Orwellian twist the conventional use of the word "philosophy."

Our common awareness of things is the place where philosophy begins, not ends, according to the classical realist tradition. This name describes the philosophical attitude of the ancient Greeks who coined the word "philosophy" and founded the discipline. Classical realism is as defensible today as it was during their time. A return to realism will correct much of the philosophical disorder of our own time, even if that disorder is now of a postmodern, not a modern kind. But, of course, this is a distinction without a difference. There is, in fact, no real difference between the age of Hume and the age of Nietzsche. These are just two episodes of the same culture. I am amused when I observe critics of postmodernism invoke Enlightenment philosophy as its sure remedy. This solution would only aggravate the symptoms, not cure them. I believe the times are so turbulent, not because a new philosophical age may be appearing, but because we are experiencing the death agony of modernism. Postmodernism is modernism as it struggles to write its own epitaph. Perhaps classical realism can take root in our cultural soil again. Thereby, modern culture will escape the radical irrationalism that seems to fascinate it.

5. Jacques Maritain, *The Dream of Descartes,* trans. Mabelle L. Andison (New York: Philosophical Library, 1944).

Of course, some postmodernists will protest by saying that their intellectual outlook is really different in kind from modernist skepticism. Heideggerians, for example, deny that they are committed to the problem of skepticism, since they overcome, or ignore, the subject-object distinction skepticism implies. But their protests strike me as just another covert way of taking for granted the modernist project: to expand the neo-Protagoreanism to its farthest possible limit. Postmodernists do this by a bold stroke of poetic imagination in which they identify the world and the self. Spirit and the world become one. What is this but an extreme consequence of the modernist belief that consciousness manufactures knowledge? The human mind—its culture, language, psychology—is the measure of all things.

Creative anti-realism has had significant impact on intellectual attitudes about religion. This is not surprising. If one believes that knowledge is just a personal or social construction, then such an attitude is bound to apply to religion. The result has been that many intellectuals look at religion either as a sociological phenomenon or as a matter of private belief. In the first case, there arises the common belief that it is pointless to defend the religious claims of one society over the claims of another. How could one social construction about religion be really more true or false than another? Anti-realism reduces religion to a kind of cultural relativism. Accordingly, there is a widespread willingness to *describe* religions in cultural terms and to compare them. It is becoming less and less common, however, to find Christian thinkers engaged in a defense of Christian belief, if that defense entails the conclusion that Christianity is the fullness of truth about reality, the human condition, right conduct, and the human relationship to God. The relativist sensibilities of modernist anti-realism will not accept such a defense. This is why a contemporary Christian philosopher who wants to defend

Christian wisdom in the public square must be prepared to tangle with the cultural relativism implicit in creative anti-realism.

Additionally, the Christian thinker should also appreciate that anti-realism is often behind the popular tendency to dismiss religion as a purely private belief system. If truth is a personal construction, then religious "truth" for you may not be religious "truth" for me. For you to debate your view with me and to maintain that it is more truthful than mine is a subterfuge for imposing your religion on me and others—a device for substituting your "truth" for the "truth" of others. Hence, religion must be consigned to the sphere of private experience and belief and not permitted to occupy a position in the public square. Of course, the same result seems to apply to all kinds of knowledge, if knowledge is merely a construction. The same reasons that compel us to hold that religion is a purely private matter compel us to make the same judgment about every other way of knowing, even of science! These are implications about knowledge that make some contemporary philosophers nervous. In practice, the Christian thinker can discern an inconsistency here. Creative anti-realists let some ways of knowing into the public square—e.g., scientific claims and often liberal politics—but arbitrarily preclude other ways of discourse. The standard for "legitimate discourse," then, very often becomes political coercion. Certain views are permitted by the postmodernist intelligentsia, some are not. It devolves to a matter of power. That is the scary side of our postmodernist malaise. The Christian philosopher should not be naïve about that.

Nor should she or he be naïve about the second presumption I mentioned above—the belief Alvin Plantinga calls "Perennial Naturalism." While Plantinga has pointed out that it is a common belief among the intelligentsia, it is worth noting that it has also percolated down to the popular culture, partly through the work of naturalist proselytizers, such as Carl Sagan, Steven Hawking, Richard Dawkins, and Stephen Jay Gould. It behooves the Christian philosopher to address naturalism as much as to address anti-realism. Naturalism has been imbibed uncritically by many of our students and by many persons in the wider culture. This has spawned several confusions that the Christian philosopher can constructively address, including distortions about the precise relationship between science and naturalism and about the relationship between faith and reason.

Naturalism is commonly accepted because many educators (those who have generally escaped anti-realism) suggest that science is the only way of knowing. This suggestion serves naturalism by dismissing *a priori* ways of knowing that might consider non-physical objects, such as God and the human soul. Such objects are dismissed as matters of purely private religious feeling. They are not issues that can be part of rational human inquiry or the genuine pursuit of knowledge. In this way, naturalism is often smuggled into scientific discourse. Of course, that statement itself—that "science, along with mathematics, is the only genuine way of knowing"—is not a scientific statement. As a matter of fact, it is a self-refuting utterance, for it is neither through experimental method nor through mathematical demonstration that such a statement is justified. As it happens, the statement is a philosophical, indeed an epistemological, judgment, and hence is self-refuting.

In spite of this, many naturalists have convinced others that whenever naturalism is spoken somehow science is spoken too. I often ask my students whether the following statement is a philosophical statement: "The Cosmos, the totality of the distribution of matter and radiation in space-time, is all that is or was or ever will be." Some students will immediately reply that it must be a scientific statement, not a philosophical one. Why? The reason seems to be that it is uttered by Carl Sagan at the beginning of his popular science program, *Cosmos.* If a prominent scientist says something in a science program, it must be science, right? Secondly, hasn't science somehow proven that only matter exists? Once asked to think about this remark, students quickly detect the fallacy: science could not prove any such thing without begging the question. Science of its very nature is constrained to examine only physical things. Obviously, just because science is limited to the study of physical things, it does not follow that only physical things exist. Nor does it follow that one should deny the possibility of other ways of knowing the universe—such as metaphysical or theological knowledge. With this realization, they see clearly that Sagan's remark is a dogmatic assertion of naturalism, and as such is a philosophical, not a scientific, claim.

Such confusion affects people's ability to think clearly about the relationship of faith and reason. The naturalist's conviction that only science counts as genuine knowledge is one source of the common belief that science and religion must occupy totally different spheres of inquiry. They cannot contradict each other because science (reason) concerns knowledge, while religion (faith) involves only symbolism, poetry, pure imagination, and feeling. Sometimes this separation of faith and reason into hermetically sealed spheres is advanced as a comfort to religious persons. "Religion need not fear scientific claims, because religion and science occupy different realms of inquiry. Science concerns facts; religion tells stories, whose legitimacy is based on edifying feelings and symbols, not on facts. The two need not conflict because they are simply different." Many religious persons enthusiastically accept this separation of religion and science, believing that it empowers them to embrace both the truths of science and of religion. But, of course, they might not notice that the naturalist is using the word "truth" equivocally. For the naturalist, scientific "truth" is factual. Any judgment that contradicts such truth is false. Religious "truth," however, is poetic—truth that only conforms to feeling, not to fact. A feeling that contradicts poetic truth, which is merely another feeling, need not be false. By these assumptions, the naturalist is able to marginalize religion from the public square, prejudging that religion cannot criticize scientific findings because religion has different objects and language. To presume that religion could speak to science would confuse apples with oranges. As I said, many religious persons themselves accept this description of religious knowledge, even if they employ it inconsistently. Let a scientist like Darwin or Shockley advance racism, say, and these same religious persons who agree that religion cannot criticize science are the first to queue up (and quite justly, by the way!) to condemn such scientists. But they do this at the expense of their earlier position that science and religion occupy altogether separate realms of inquiry, between which there is no linguistic or conceptual intercourse about truth.

This separation is objectionable when one considers that religion can be rational, even if ultimately it deals with objects that are mysterious. But while religion may embrace the non-rational, it need not accept the irrational. By calling it "rational," I mean that religion can use philosophy (reason) to express and support its beliefs as *factual.* Such a view of religion prevents reducing it to mere poetry or perhaps even to the irrational or the superstitious. Escaping this caricature of religion, the Christian philosopher, as St. Thomas explained, can regard religious truth *analogously,* not equivocally. It is certainly different from science in many respects, but ultimately it is like science in that religion seeks to know and express what is real—to know and express genuine truths about the world. It is not merely poetry. Beyond its poetic elements, there is a propositional content to religion; that is to say, some religious expressions profess conformity with reality. In other words, credal propositions in religion can be *logically* true, not just *poetically* true. As such, they can be really contradicted. When this takes place, the opposing proposition is false, if the religious proposition is indeed true. Of course, it is possible that the religious belief is mistaken and its contradictory opposite is true. If religion professes to make truth claims of a logical, not just a poetic kind, it must be open to the possibility of error and falsification. To escape that risk, some theologians have surrendered to the idea that religious utterances are mere poetry, but that is to make a bargain, it seems to me, that seriously compromises the credal objectivity and integrity of religion, and is to advance a revisionist view of the Christian religion that would not be recognizable to the Apostles, the Martyrs, or the Saints.

If one grants that religion sometimes makes *assertions,* statements that are true or false, then another possibility can obtain: when religion and science disagree on an issue, they may both be mistaken, in which case their opposite judgments are contraries, not contradictories. Contradictories cannot both be false (e.g., if atheism is false, then God must exist) but contraries can both be false (e.g., if monotheism is false, it may also be the case that polytheism is false, for it might be that atheism is true). Without belaboring the point further, logical discourse entitles science to judge whether religious statements are false, but likewise that same discourse entitles religion to judge science.

Of course, science and religion can also agree. When science and religion express their respective truths, they complement each other. To say they occupy separate spheres and to say that religious beliefs are irrelevant to science, and to the life of reason generally, is to suffer a fragmentary view of truth that disorders the human intellect. Truth is a unity and thus religion and science can complement and speak to each other in the language of their respective attainment of facts, logical truths.[6]

6. Needless to say, my discussion of logical versus poetic truth and of the credal,

Addressing naturalism in the classroom affords one the opportunity, of putting Christianity and the perennial philosophy next to Sagan's naturalist worldview and to test each for cogency. When one does this, the students are quite struck by the fact that it is Sagan's naturalism, not Christian wisdom, that founders. Perennial naturalism can be shown to be highly troubled when one asks about (1) the origin of the universe, (2) its order (physical laws), (3) the emergence of life, and (4) the existence of consciousness. The naturalist encounters grave difficulties in trying to explain any one of these facts of the universe. By addressing these difficulties, the Christian educator can give his or her students an experience that they are not likely to have again. For they have seldom heard naturalist assumptions criticized, and they are not likely to hear them again in the academy or in the wider culture. Students who have come to believe that science tells the only story worth reading are often edified and surprised to find that modern science appears to vindicate theism rather than atheism. An assessment of naturalism will invite them to revise their uncritical acceptance of it, especially when they brood on observations such as the following:

1. "That matter exists" is no answer to the question "Why is there something rather than nothing?" for it is the existence of matter in the first place that the question addresses. There are several philosophical and scientific problems with the assumption that matter is just an eternal stuff that has existed forever and thus requires no explanation. The idea that the universe could have an infinite past is replete with internal difficulties (as St. Bonaventure argued in the thirteenth century), and it is now called into doubt by Big Bang Cosmology and the Second Law of Thermodynamics.

---

propositional nature of religious language relies heavily on Mortimer Adler's excellent book *Truth in Religion* (New York: Macmillan, 1990), pp. 10–39.

2. That the behavior of the physical universe is regulated by laws is another fact that naturalism cannot plausibly explain, as Richard Swinburne has outlined clearly in his writings on theism.[7] That highly regulative physical laws describe the behavior of matter in the universe seems to defy naturalistic explanation. Some naturalists, such as Richard Dawkins, try to overcome this difficulty by arguing that evolution itself, expanded beyond biology and applied to the cosmos, can account for the laws of nature. But this is a sleight of hand, of course. Evolution, whether biological or cosmic, presupposes two things: (a) that certain entities exist and (b) that they develop because of specified potential behaviors. In order for something to remain an entity as it evolves, there must be an order governing how the evolution takes place. Accordingly, there can be no evolution of any kind without there being entities governed by laws furnishing an ordered environment in which the entities can develop. One can no more explain physical laws by processes of evolution than one can argue, as Leibniz pointed out, that the laws of mechanics are instituted by the laws of mechanics. As Dallas Willard has put it, there is a "logically insurpassable limit" to any attempt to apply evolution to the questions of origins and order in the universe. Evolution *presupposes* origins and order. It cannot explain them.[8]

3. Darwinian naturalists have argued that life is just a certain arrangement of physical compounds; that the organic is reducible to the inorganic. There is little evidence for this beyond the much-

---

7. Richard Swinburne, *The Existence of God* (Oxford: Clarendon Press, 1991 rev. ed.) Also see his essay "The Argument from Design: A Defense," *Religious Studies* 8 (1972), pp. 193–205.

8. Dallas Willard, "The Three Stage Argument for the Existence of God," in R. Douglas Geivett and Brendan Sweetman, eds., *Contemporary Perspectives on Religious Epistemology* (Oxford: Oxford University Press, 1992), pp. 217–18.

discussed Urey-Miller experiment in the 1950s, the success of which has been greatly exaggerated.[9] Life is far more than amino acids and urea. In a recent book, George Sim Johnston cautions the naturalist not to make rash claims.

> Nor are we any closer than the Victorians to explaining the origin of life. Life only seems to come from life. But even if some day the origin of life were proven to be a mechanistic phenomenon (which is not very likely), I would be unperturbed, because such a mechanism would not be incompatible with the Catholic doctrine of creation. Creation from nothing is beyond scientific explanation. The greatest scientific genius will never be able to produce being, or even to discuss it with his scientific vocabulary. Ditto for human consciousness.[10]

4. Mind seems especially resistant to physical explanation. Naturalists often talk as though the discovery of physical correlates with consciousness—e.g., when one has a toothache, potassium chloride is secreted in the amygdala—is evidence that mind is reducible to matter, consciousness to brain. But none of these correlates, even if they are causes, are ontologically the same as awarenesses. Hence, it is difficult to see how any exhaustive description of the physics of neurology can demonstrate that consciousness is neurology.

Naturalists also suffer a difficulty when dealing with moral understanding. This is particularly embarrassing for many naturalists, who have often argued that naturalism assumes the high moral

---

9. Stanley Miller and William Urey provoked excitement in the naturalist community when they produced amino acids after passing electricity through a closed flask containing hydrogen, methane, and water.

10. George Sim Johnston, *Did Darwin Get It Right? Catholics and the Theory of Evolution* (Huntington, Ind.: Our Sunday Visitor, 1998), pp. 124–25. Earlier, Johnston remarks that "even if someday a scientist were able to accomplish the seemingly impossible task of creating from inert chemicals a biologically functioning protein, it would still not prove a materialist scenario for the origin of life, because it would be human intelligence that produced it" (p. 77).

ground. "Would that the world were peopled by naturalists," they often proclaim, "it would be progressive and peaceful, not wicked and violent as is the world fashioned by the Judeo-Christian ethics." And at this point, the litany of woes supposedly perpetrated by Christian civilization—from the Spanish Inquisition to the Galileo episode—are paraded before beleaguered Christians. The one hundred million plus people killed as the direct result of the machinations of twentieth-century politicians who explicitly abjured Christianity, such as Stalin (a naturalist) and Hitler (a neo-pagan), are usually conveniently omitted from such discussions. But upon a moment's reflection one sees that to claim the high moral ground is an embarrassment to the naturalist, because naturalism cannot sustain a belief in free will. If all behaviors are the result of purposeless matter in motion governed by physical laws, it is determinate cause and effect that explains human thought and action, not liberty. If there is no liberty, there is no moral responsibility, and if there is no responsibility there is no morality. Naturalism is determinism and determinism cannot assume the moral ground, whether high or low.

As I indicated above, the presumption of many naturalists that matter alone is sufficient to explain any one of these facts (origins, laws, life, and mind) commonly circulates in the educated culture. At times naturalism appears to be a prerequisite for admission to that culture. But if the Christian thinker is aware of the limits of the naturalist worldview, he or she will be able to show that naturalism as a philosophy is far weaker than it may at first appear, and that the Christian worldview *can explain better* the above facts while naturalism founders.

Perennial naturalism and creative anti-realism, by advancing oversimplifications, if nothing else, have fostered many distortions about religion and about the nature of knowledge generally. Postmodern society suffers the intellectual and practical consequences of these distortions. One effect is the malaise in which people suffer a loss of meaning. This is another reason why the Christian philosopher should challenge these worldviews, so as to help people understand that "the way we look at ourselves has changed from seeing people as noble, special, and created with a purpose, to seeing people as meaningless, hopeless, and caught in a silent universe."[11] But I am optimistic. These worldviews are at last being seriously challenged. In the century ahead I believe they will be increasingly discredited. They are collapsing of their own weight. The Christian philosophy of St. Thomas is indeed perennial. His defenders, such as Gilson and Maritain, were right: the perennial philosophy yet survives to bury its undertakers.

11. John Whitehead, *Grasping for the Wind: Humanity's Search for Meaning* (New York: Insight Media Videos, 1999).

*John D. Caputo*

# 4. CONFESSIONS OF A POSTMODERN
# CATHOLIC: FROM SAINT THOMAS
# TO DERRIDA

৵

In a very lovely sentence, a mere aside in *From the Sacred to the Holy,* Emmanuel Levinas says that while the Talmud is not philosophy, "its tractates are an eminent source of those experiences from which philosophers derive their nourishment," and then a bit later, in another aside, he says, "[p]hilosophy, for me, derives from religion."[1] Without religion, without the nourishment that philosophy draws from religion, I, too, like Levinas, would have had little to do as a philosopher (beyond marking blue books). For me, philosophy has always been nourished by religion, has always drawn its stock of problems from religious experience, and finally takes the form of putting its perplexities and intimations into a language in which we can all debate. But that means that for those of us who, like Levinas, draw upon religious experience, the language in which philosophers conduct their business is continually being interrupted by

1. Emmanuel Levinas, *Nine Talmudic Readings,* trans. Annette Aronowicz (Bloomington: Indiana University Press, 1990), pp. 4, 182. My thanks to Tirdad Derakhshani for drawing my attention to these texts.

the oddity of religion's voice, its Hebraic, Aramaic, and biblical voice, which is the voice of an alterity upon which philosophy cannot quite get a fix. The result is that philosophy is never completely at ease with itself, never assured that it is not missing something important, and that uneasiness is deeply and profoundly productive, keeping philosophy on its toes, on the watch for something different, *tout autre,* Levinas likes to say, "wholly other."

I hope to establish, or at least to illustrate, this point—about the continual nourishment and disturbance that religion effects in philosophy—by way of the following little narrative, my own little story.

## I. POSTMODERNITY AND POSTSECULARISM

A few years ago, after I had given a paper which had taken a typically postmodern twist, a very distinguished phenomenologist, a sober man and an insightful student of phenomenological seeing in the Husserlian style, said to me that my paper had helped him better understand what he really did not like about the postmodern turn things had taken in the last two decades. That, of course, was a nice way to say that one of the things he liked about my paper was that it helped him understand more clearly why he did *not* like my paper. What made him so uneasy, he explained, was that this critique of modernist reason was leaving the door wide open to religious faith, and that was going to undo all the good done in the Enlightenment, instead of bringing the Enlightenment to a happy conclusion in phenomenology. That, I responded, was for me the main idea. I did not know whether to declare myself exposed or simply understood. As an astute phenomenological seer he was more at home with the light of Enlightenment reason, which puts what we do not see on the shelf, than with this critique of Enlightenment, of what the Enlightenment called reason, which produced for him what phenomenology could only regard as a certain blindness.

I, on the other hand, much as I love phenomenology, as often as I have had recourse to the protection of its methodological rigor, have my doubts about pure seeing. I tend to see seeing as a fragile thing. For just as we are not immune from believing what we want to believe, so we are not immune from seeing what we want to see and from not seeing what is staring us in the face. That is because, as I believe, seeing is very much structured by certain presuppositions, by a certain *faith* which is, if you will, a *certain* blindness. For example, the more someone pounds on the table and repeats "don't you see?" as if the assertion gained in luminosity by the pounding and the repetition, the more one succeeds only in making one's own *presuppositions* conspicuous.[2] That is why I have always favored "hermeneutical" phenomenology, which says that seeing is always seeing *as,* that seeing always has a certain slant, and that is why I do not take my phenomenology straight up.

I do not think that the divide between reason and faith makes for a clean cut. There is too much faith in reason when reason is properly understood and too much know-how in what we call faith for this distinction to hold up. *Credo ut intelligam.* Faith is for me the driving force of thinking, not an obstacle but an impetus, an impulse, a wellspring, a source of nourishment, as Levinas says, a beginning of thinking. The distinction between faith and reason was certainly not invented by the Enlightenment, but that is when it became an invidious opposition and was given teeth sharp enough to cut. In the Middle Ages this distinction was much cherished, but always as a way to mark off stages along the way in a ris-

2. Martin Heidegger, *Being and Time,* trans. John Macquarrie and Edward Robinson (New York: Harper & Row, 1962), p. 192.

ing ascent, like markers along a path as one climbs a mountain road, or like the stages of a lovely growth, and reason was often conceived as a way to explain a faith in which reason finds itself already situated. The distinction was not intended to erect a barrier, or hold anyone down, or keep anyone out, or point a finger at those who have gone too far and fallen into madness and the abyss. Faith was not the outside or the "other" of reason, but a something that precedes, follows, and punctuates the laborious steps of reason. But in its typically *modern* form this distinction became a divide or an abyss, and that is what I resist. That is also an important part of the reason I am interested in what is today called *post*modernism, although this word has been almost ground senseless by overuse and itself suggests too sharp a divide and periodization of intellectual and cultural history. Postmodern thinkers distrust clean binary oppositions, and they try consistently to show just how much unrest there is beneath the surface of the serene divides and clean cuts— like philosophy and religion, reason and faith, subject and object, fact and value (or modern and postmodern!)—around which modernity and a lot of what likes to call itself "meta-physics" is organized.

Take Kant, who is for me the archetypal modernist, the philosopher par excellence of reason, autonomy, and liberalism, and a philosopher who even was, God help him, a university professor. Now, I love Kant very much, and I have always loved the way he loved those simple people of common decency who served as the exemplars of what he called "pure practical reason," a term they would hardly have understood, which signified that it was not necessary to understand the categorical imperative in order to abide by it. But Kant seems to me like a transcendental surveyor, a man out in the field looking through his glass, waving some fellow with a stake first to the right, then to the left, first closer, then farther, causality here, freedom there, spontaneity here, receptivity there, until the whole field is staked off and everyone knows where and where not to step and how to stay within the lines. The field of thought is thoroughly mapped out by Kant, and patrolled by the police of "Critique," by a border patrol whose job is keep everyone within limits, above all to make sure that no one walks off the edge of pure reason and falls into the abyss of unbridled enthusiasm. That is too tidy to be right.

We Catholics tried mightily, and rightly, to be modern. We eagerly assured our fellow Americans that John F. Kennedy was not going to turn the White House over to the Vatican, that we no longer subscribed to geocentrism, and that we thought Galileo was a fine fellow. But the truth is that we have never been quite at home with modernism and perhaps with modernity itself. While we have no wish to return either to the divine right of kings or to geocentrism, we were never able to settle easily into the Cartesianism and rationalism of modernity, its affection for pure critique and the transcendental subject, its secularism and its division of labor among the various human faculties, like science, ethics, art, and religion, which seems to put things into boxes, inserting religion in particular into a box of privacy and even of irrationality. So when a movement comes along calling itself *post*modern, that at least should attract our attention, for here at least is a tendency of thought that, like Catholicism, also wants to put some space between itself and modernism. Postmodernism offers Catholicism an opportunity to counter a great deal of what it dislikes about modernity without undertaking a full-scale retreat into *pre*modernity or *anti*modernity. It provides an opportunity to return to our premodern sources in a way that preserves the progress modernity has made, effecting a return which moves forward, not in reverse. Postmodernity relieves us of the need to measure up to the requirements of modernity which have come under fire from other quarters, which is why I am all ears for what these postmodernists are saying. For if modernity means secularism, how can postmodernism fail to be postsecular?

That is why Heidegger's *Being and Time* played an important role in my thinking, why it played so well among many Catholics of my generation. (Catholic universities are still by and large the place in the United States to study continental thought.) For this classic of twentieth century thought is in no small measure a smashing critique of the Cartesian subject, a dismantling of a bloodless thinking thing disengaged from its concrete setting in the world, a subject which brushed against the grain of our Aristotelico-Thomistic sensibilities, our sense of an embodied, acting being in the world. When I first read what Heidegger said about "being-in-the-world" and how the question of whether there is a world makes no sense for beings whose Being is being-in-the-world, that struck a chord that resonated deeply with the "realism" of my Catholic philosophical upbringing. We were all realists, afraid it seemed that someone was going to steal the world out from under us if we so much as took our eye off it, and if the world, then why not God or, God forbid, this would surely be the final straw, the pope. The neoscholastic obsessiveness with "realism," with the epistemic defense of realism, is linked very closely to the Vatican defense of infallibility; they are both distinctly nineteenth-century events that reflect a lot of Cartesian, and very modern, anxiety. But St. Thomas himself seems to have lost no sleep worrying about whether the world would be there when the monastic bell awoke him the next morning. Then Heidegger came along and said that the project of *proving* or *establishing* the existence of the world, or realism, or certainty, the need for a proof to back up whatever knowledge we have managed to acquire, was already too late. For *as soon as Dasein comes to be* it is already in the world and in the truth, and the very being of Dasein has already laid skepticism to rest: the very fact that the skeptic is in the world and discloses it has already put down in advance any possible skepticism.[3] So much for Cartesian, Kantian, modernist anxieties. That was for many of us our first *aggiornamento,* a way of getting *past* Cartesianism by getting *back* to the situated self of the Greeks and medievals (and the Scriptures).

In graduate school, I felt I had to prove to my professors that I knew the modernist map, that I could fill a blackboard reproducing its boundary lines, and that I could take apart and reassemble all the parts of the mechanisms in Kant's transcendental surveyor's kit.[4] But my most abiding desire, my most hidden, simmering instinct was to twist free of all that, to escape across the borders in the dark of the night while the unsuspecting border patrol nodded off. To transgress the boundaries of modernity, to violate the limits imposed by what modernity calls pure reason, especially when this transgressiveness took the form of helping faith slip furtively across the borders, is to a great extent, as I look back, what I have always done and am still doing. So now I can conceive this and announce it publicly to have been my life-plan, pretending that I knew this all along, this announcement having the advantage, coming late enough in life as it has, to have excellent predictive power. The proper subject of philosophical reflection for me is the living subject—ethical as well

---

3. *Being and Time,* pp. 249, 271.

4. It is a matter of some amusement to certain readers of my *Against Ethics* and *The Prayers and Tears of Jacques Derrida* that one of my first articles was an analysis of Kant's critique of the ontological argument that deployed a certain amount of symbolic logic. See John D. Caputo, "Kant's Refutation of the Ontological Argument," *Journal of the American Academy of Religion* 42 (1974), pp. 686–91.

as theoretical, believing and reasoning, thinking and bleeding, feeling and hoping, situated deeply in social, political, economic, religious, historical, and gendered networks that stretch out farther than eye can see. One begins where one is, in the midst of contexts we can never saturate, structured in advance by multiple faiths whose measure we cannot take and whose very existence we do not as yet suspect. Without faith, from the sheerest, merest perceptual faith all the way up to the dark and probing movements of religious faith, I would have had nothing to analyze and nothing to do. I would have been unproductive, unpublished, and alas unemployed (read: untenured!).

The idea is not to ridicule reason, God forbid, but to make reason *porous,* a little "im-pure," or better, to defend the porousness of reason against those who would make it a solid impenetrable well-rounded sphere. I have always sought to show that the sharp lines that Kant drew were blurred, and I have tried to establish and maintain lines of *communication* among the various parts of ourselves, like philosophy and faith, feeling and duty, masculine and feminine, straight and unorthodox. The rigorousness of Enlightenment reason seems to me like so much *rigor mortis.* What tends to be called reason, to call *itself* reason, to congratulate itself on being rational, turns out to be a kind of "blackmail," as Foucault calls it, practiced by the Enlightenment. They want to consign those who disagree with their position into irrationalism and to blacken their name, rather the way a government tries to portray the people who disagree with its policies as disloyal to the country.

My loyalties to faith, to the multiple forms of faith by which we are structured, does not render me disloyal to reason. It simply puts me at odds with the policies of the Enlightenment establishment on reason, policies which I think have been discredited by a wide range of thinkers on both sides of the English Channel. As I have argued at length in *Radical Hermeneutics*,[5] reason is a much more flexible and supple thing than the Enlightenment thinkers let on, and it is at its best when it lacks just the sort of rules that modernists lean upon, the methodological guidelines with which modernists love to identify reason. Reason operates in intimate cooperation with deeply held and inchoate beliefs and practices that we perhaps do not even know we hold (because they hold us), and it is dependent upon clues and instincts and insights that operate far below the radar of rules. What too many philosophers today call reason is what reason got to be called in the seventeenth and eighteenth centuries; it is historically constituted. It could be constituted otherwise, and in the Middle Ages, where it moved in intimate cooperation with faith, it was in fact constituted otherwise, and in these days of late capitalist, free market, high-tech, advanced communications, what is called reason is open to still further discussion and complications. But I absolutely resist the idea that reason is what Kant and the Enlightenment said it is, which makes everything look programmable and makes folks with religious faith look a little tipsy. On the contrary, as I am arguing in this little tale, faith is what drives reason and gives philosophers something to do with themselves (even after they are awarded tenure).

## II. SAINT THOMAS, THE LATER HEIDEGGER, AND MYSTICAL RELIGION

The first question to engage me philosophically was how to think about reason and what lies outside or beyond reason. That is what eventually led me years ago to Heidegger, and in particular, to

---

5. John D. Caputo, *Radical Hermeneutics* (Bloomington: Indiana University Press, 1987), pp. 209–35. See also *The Very Idea of Radical Hermeneutics,* ed. Roy Martinez (Atlantic Highlands, N.J.: Humanities Press, 1997).

my still favorite book by Heidegger, which was the focus of my doctoral dissertation, *Der Satz vom Grund,* translated as *The Principle of Reason.*[6] It will perhaps scandalize some of my more conservative friends, if I still have any, that Martin Heidegger came to occupy a place in my young intellectual life that was once occupied by Jacques Maritain, and that *Der Satz vom Grund* eventually became for me a better way of doing the work that once was done for me by *Les Degrés du Savoir.* When my passion for philosophy was first fired, I found that I had conceived what any self-respecting Protestant must consider a most unnatural offspring, namely, a dual love of Søren Kierkegaard (who, more than anyone, has influenced my intellectual style, my "how" and my habitus) and Saint Thomas. Not long ago, again after a lecture I had given, someone said that she always said "Aquinas" and she wanted to know why I said "Saint Thomas." The answer of course is deeper than I can say, archi-primordial, deeply embedded in being "Catholic." It has to do with the fact that when first I opened my intellectual eyes there was Saint Thomas, his angelic hand (if that is not an oxymoron) outstretched to lead the way, and I have always, always been unable to repudiate that beginning, even after I had strayed off to different and stranger sites and very heterodox opinions. Two conflicting loves, the great philosophical reconciler of nature and grace, faith and reason, the author of several nimble and much anthologized proofs of God's existence, along with the great champion of the leap of faith who made merciless mockery of every such proof.

That is why, as a tormented youngster, I turned to French Thomists for help, for in Paris Thomism had a heart. Maritain, a French Thomist who managed to combine a love of the theory of

---

6. Martin Heidegger, *Der Satz vom Grund* (Pfullingen: Neske, 1957); *The Principle of Reason,* trans. Reginald Lilly (Bloomington: Indiana University Press, 1991).

intentionality of John of Saint Thomas with a passion for art and mysticism (a feat which paled in comparison with his managing to combine marriage with celibacy), was clearly a man even more conflicted and tormented than I. Maritain laid out in a synchronic way how the various strata of reason, faith, and mystical union are layered, how the gears mesh, how all things work unto one in a culminating, fulminating vision of God. It was for a similar reason that I had recourse to the work of another passionate French Thomist, Pierre Rousselot, someone on the Jesuit side this time, a bit of a precursor of transcendental Thomism, whereas Maritain was on the Dominican side. Rousselot's *The Intellectualism of Saint Thomas*[7] was a beautiful, soaring account of how the very dynamism of what Thomas called intellectus pressed by its own momentum beyond the limits of *ratio,* the latter, as Rousselot pointed out, having been described by Thomas as a *debilitas intellectus,* a feebleness or weakness of human reason, of the particular model of reason with which human beings came equipped, which should not be confused with the very structure of intellect as such. The intellects of the angels, in which I was greatly interested at the time, had higher, upgraded versions of *intellectus.* Angelic intellection moved with the swiftness of intellectual intuition—my phenomenologist friends would have greatly admired angelic *Wesensanschauung*—not with the poky clunkiness of human ratiocination, the piecemeal discursivity of rational argumentation, which slowly patches together a quilt of major terms and minor terms and middle terms. Angels, our students would point out to us today, had much faster chips.

What interested me, what tormented me, what kept me up at

---

7. Pierre Rousselot, *The Intellectualism of St. Thomas,* trans. James O'Mahoney (New York: Sheed & Ward, 1935). For an account of Rousselot and what I made of him, see my *Heidegger and Aquinas: An Essay on Overcoming Metaphysics* (New York: Fordham University Press, 1982), pp. 265–71.

nights, was this conflict. On the one hand, the *necessity* we are under to pull our trousers on one leg at a time, to reason and argue, to
do the best we can piecing together the fragments of the world
around us, to make ourselves clear and entertain objections. On the
other hand, the *limits* of this sort of thing, the way it tends to falsify
what it is trying to reassemble, to get in its own way and trip over
its own feet, to throw up obstacles in its own course, to have a lame,
wooden, hard-headed, obstinate way of thinking about things, to
allow its hands to be tied by its own methodologies, which were
supposed to be ways of helping it along the way. Everybody knows
that we know more than we can prove, as any frustrated prosecutor
bound by the rules of evidence can tell you (which is also why defense lawyers can afford such nice houses). Maritain and Rousselot
tended to portray this crossing of the borders from reason to its beyond as a movement into a deeper, higher, truer, simpler region, an
ascent to a more intuitive union or unitative vision, to a kind of hy-
per-presential contact with God. My young heart skipped a beat.

Heidegger supplied this question of reason and its other or beyond with a history and a genealogy. In giving things this historical
twist, Heidegger was the first place in which I ran into a convergence of the premodern and the postmodern, of the before and the
after of the Enlightenment. Heidegger produced a profound meditation upon the limits of reason, upon the delimitation of what
calls itself reason, which he contrasted with "thinking," or what
"calls" us into thinking, *was heißt Denken?* But unlike the French
Thomist friends of my youth, Heidegger cast all this in terms of a
*history* of reason and "ground," and he proposed that "reason" was
an historical construction whose birth date can be more or less
traced to the seventeenth century. Heidegger's history of reason
stretched from his rather fanciful rendering of *logos* in Heraclitus
(although I believed it at the time), through the Aristotelian notion

of the rational animal, through the medieval rendering (or sundering, even distortion, Heidegger would have said) of this as the *animal rationale,* up to Leibniz's *principium rationis,* the principle of sufficient reason, "nothing is without reason" *(nihil est sine ratione, nichts ist ohne Grund).* When I discovered that Heidegger's history led up to a brilliant contrast between Leibniz's principle and Angelus Silesius's mystical verse "The Rose Is Without Why," and when I learned that Silesius was to a great extent versifying Meister Eckhart of Hochheim, and when I then found that Eckhart was a Dominican who pushed to a mystical extreme what he learned from "brother Thomas" (Saint Thomas), that *deus est suum esse,* well, then, *eureka,* my heart was afire and skipped another beat.[8]

This story has a point. Far from blocking or cutting off, preventing or otherwise presenting an obstacle to philosophical thinking, you can see that the religious tradition, my religious tradition (not in the sense that it belongs to me but that I belong to it), and the communication of philosophical thinking with this religious tradition, is what *fires* my work, what "nourishes" it, what gives it passion, interest, and urgency. That is what keeps me up at night, transforming what I do from some merely technical problem into a passion of life, a passion for life, a salvific work. The essential thing in philosophy, the only thing that makes it worth putting up with the middling pay and the torment of departmental meetings, is that philosophy be a matter of passion and personal survival, a matter of prayers and tears, the way we get through our days. Although it certainly requires technical abilities, philosophy must not regress into a simple technical craft, a way of solving problems and cracking riddles, which is, alas, what happens all too often in "analytic" philoso-

---

8. I develop these matters in some detail in *The Mystical Element in Heidegger's Thought* (New York: Fordham University Press, 1986, rev. ed.).

phy. I do not deny that there are other ways to summon this passion—art, e.g., or even science—but the way I have found, the way
that worked for me, the way that worked its way with me, whether
I liked it not, was to allow religious questions to boil up and over-
flow into philosophical ones. Without religion, how could I philosophize? What would there be to do? Philosophy for me has always
been religion becoming philosophical, getting philosophical about
itself, and so, thus far, a gift of religious life. But let it not be forgotten, one must keep this whole process *porous,* for even as philosophy ought not forget the religious springs by which it is fed, religion must not be turned into a shadow of itself, a philosopher's
invention which replaces the Holy Spirit with hyperventilating
philosophical speculative long-windedness, telling religion what it
is supposed to be. The language of philosophy ought to be beset by
a deep unease about its own inability to get at what really interests
it, and this unease is productive. When philosophy lacks this uneasiness, when there is nothing to disturb philosophy's comfort,
nothing to stop it, it is insufferable.

Heidegger himself thought that philosophy and faith were ene-
mies and Christian philosophy a square circle, because he thought
Christian faith does not need philosophy and philosophy cannot
tolerate faith, which puts questioning to sleep. This was but another of the many points that I was beginning to discover about which
Heidegger, much as I owed him, had blundered; it was a very modernist way of thinking which built up boundaries between things
instead of seeing their porousness. Furthermore, it was a highly
ironic and ungrateful thing for Heidegger himself to say, given the
extent to which his own thought from the very start is fed by theological springs, given how much theology has been bootlegged into
his work, given how much secularization of theology lies beneath or
within what we call today "Heidegger." I would say, against Hei-

degger, that the name of God is what makes everything questionable, and is the most questionable and question-worthy name we have. For the name of God is the name of what we love, and we always want to know what we love. "What do I love when I love Thee?" Augustine ask in that very wonderful book which told the beautiful story of his prayers and tears (*Confessions,* X, 6). That for me is the first, last, and constant question. When Augustine found God, he simultaneously found himself saying *quaestio mihi factus sum,* that is, he found he had become a question for himself, a sentiment that Heidegger did not hesitate to put to work in *Being and Time* and which played a central role in the genesis of *Being and Time.*[9] The awakening of religion is the awakening of questioning, and the loss of one will always be at the cost of the other, for the name of God is the unnameable name whose sense and reference, meaning and urgency, point and impact, we are always, endlessly seeking to probe.

As a career matter, when I discovered Heidegger's *Der Satz vom Grund* I had discovered the topic of my doctoral dissertation and the web of problems around which I would weave my first two books. Eckhart waved the wand of mysticism over the metaphysics of St. Thomas, which later took the form of the mystical poetry of Angelus Silesius, who became a touchstone for Heidegger's task of "overcoming metaphysics," of the delimitation of "onto-theologic." The later Heidegger wrote a historical, genealogical delimitation of metaphysical reason that culminated in the autonomy of modernity's "transcendental" subject, which he opposed to a more

---

9. See *Being and Time* and *Phänomenologie des religiösen Lebens,* 1 *"Einführung in die Phänomenologie der Religion"* (Wintersemester 1920/21), ed. Matthias Jung and Thomas Regehly; 2. *"Augustinus und der Neuplatonismus"* (Sommersemester 1921); 3. "Ausaurbeitung und Entwürfe," ed. Claudius Strube, *Gesamtausgabe,* B. 60 (Frankfurt/Main: Klostermann, 1995).

self-effacing *Denken,* a notion that is modeled after mystical *Gelassenheit* in Meister Eckhart, where instead of imposing transcendental conditions of possibility upon the world Eckhart says that we must give up our attachment to the ego and live "without why." Eckhart was a Dominican who had radicalized the idea of *intellectus* so deeply as to declare its primacy over *esse* itself, which became his own version of speaking of God as "without being" or "beyond being," and his appropriation of "brother Thomas" was very much guided by his love of Christian Neoplatonism. For Eckhart, *Gelassenheit* meant the radical uprooting of the ego, of the "faculties" of knowing and willing, in order to "let God be God" in us, to let God give birth to God's Son in the soul. This deeply mystical idea from a medieval master drawing upon Saint Thomas and Christian Neoplatonism became the "model" for what the later Heidegger called "thinking," by means of which Heidegger meant to delimit the deep constraints imposed upon us by modernity. The metaphysics of modernity—for modernity is an epoch, a cut or slice, of metaphysics—is for Heidegger a metaphysics of the subject, of representational knowing and willing, whose deepest limit is its failure to let Being be, to let Being be Being in us. Heidegger's "postmodernity," if such it be, always had recourse to the premodern, and invoked not the newest of the new but the oldest of the old. Accordingly, although he did not put it this way, Heidegger had delimited the secularism of modernity by way of a medieval mystic, thereby setting the terms for what we today call "postmodernism" in a way which is, like it or nor (the Nietzscheans *hate* it), also a highly porous "postsecularism."

### III. ETHICS AND A-DIEU (TO HEIDEGGER)

So far I have not said a thing about ethics, about which, I have to confess—*confiteri tibi in litteris*—I had forgotten. Fortunately, it was not too late. *Sero te amavi.* The great religious tradition which nourishes and sparks my work had tended to mean for me up to this point mystical and apophatic religion, the relation of the speculative elegance of the metaphysics of St. Thomas to the great mystical tradition on the one hand and to the later Heidegger's overcoming of metaphysics on the other hand. In *Radical Hermeneutics* all that changed. The more I worked with "hermeneutics" in the early 1980s, and with Gadamer in particular, the more I came around to the view that what we call reason ought to be seen on the model of practical reason, of what Aristotle called *phronesis,* another pre- and post-Enlightenment point drawing this time upon another and hitherto neglected side of my Aristotelico-Thomistic youth. This favoring of *phronesis* also very much informed the Heidegger of the 1920s (despite his often professed beginning in Aristotle's *Metaphysics*), and this shows up in *Being and Time* in the central notion of *Verstehen* (§§31–32). "Understanding" *(Verstehen, phronesis)* means a certain know how, an ability to make one's way around the world, to cope with shifting circumstances, to dodge the bullets of daily troubles, to make it through the day, guided only by more or less general "schemata" which provide at best a loose fit for the singularities of concrete circumstance. The principal difference, I thought, between the current hermeneutical situation, in our late modern or postmodern day, and the one that Aristotle faced, is that for Aristotle there was at least a certain agreement about the schemata, and the problem was to learn how to apply them.

Our postmodern situation, I mused, greatly differed from this very hierarchical, top-down, leisure-class, aristocratic Aristotelian *polis* on just this point, that we have as many schemata as we—especially "we" highly pluralized, late-twentieth-century Americans, who can hardly say "we"—have ethnic groups, genders, sexual orientations, races, religions, nations, languages, social classes, and perhaps even neighborhoods (if we still have any). So what *we* needed, I argued, was a kind of radical or meta-*phronesis* for a more radical hermeneutical situation in which the very schemata which we require were not agreed upon and settled.[10] Whence the two pressing questions that bit into the hide of this line of argumentation: (1) the question of the *other*, of the one who falls outside the reigning schemata, whose "alterity" rattles the security of the frameworks within which we generally move about; (2) the question of *singularity*, of the shifting circumstances in which judgments are made, practical reason being, as Aristotle said, the ability to judge things that change, whereas speculative reason deals with things that have the courtesy to remain the same. That these problems sound a little like the "problemata" in *Fear and Trembling*, should come as no surprise. For the "categories" of the "other"—the "widow, the orphan, and the stranger" of the Jewish Scriptures thematized by Levinas—and of "singularity"—what lies in the heart of each one, whose tears, indeed, the very hairs on whose head God has counted—are deeply biblical categories that leave Aristotelianism behind. Once again, the attempt to get beyond modernist reason lands us back on ancient and biblical terrain.

In writing *Radical Hermeneutics* I had become increasingly uneasy about Heidegger, increasingly disturbed by his "mythologizing" tendencies, his penchant for turning what is on many levels a penetrating historical-genealogical critique of reason into a tall tale, a "meta-narrative," as Lyotard said, about the Great Greek Beginning, the Shining Spot that once was Greco-Camelot, of which the Germans were the Appointed Heirs (self-appointed, of course). I had gotten fairly weary of that line and, I insist on this, had published a critique of it on strictly philosophical grounds before *it*

10. See *Radical Hermeneutics,* pp. 257–264.

*happened.* It happened first, in 1987, when Farias published his notorious *Heidegger and the Nazis.* Farias troubled me but I did not
quite believe him, because the whole thing was a patent frame job,
and whatever facts were to be found there were buried under an
undisguised attempt to blacken Heidegger's name. Then Hugo
Ott's book appeared and it was all clear enough, so clear that to this
day only the most fanatical Heideggerians of the Strict Observance
still deny it. On a purely personal level, Heidegger was up to his
ears in National Socialism, and not only in 1933–34; he held right-
wing extremist and nationalist views before and after that time, and
remained a loyal supporter of the war throughout. He had dropped
out of Party life, more or less at the Nazi's invitation, on the
grounds of his political ineptness and incompetence, not because of
a change of heart. He had become disillusioned by the fact that the
Nazis were not going to make him the intellectual and academic
Führer of the movement, even though he was the only one who understood the place of the National Socialist revolution in the history of Being, something whose point seems to have been lost on the
Party apparatchiks. That is why he withdraw from Nazi politics,
not because he saw the light. He was transmuted into a hyper-
essential, *Seinsgeschichtlich,* mountain-top Nazi by whom the party
leaders were utterly mystified and dumbfounded, although they
were glad enough to have the support of a famous professor, whatever it was that he was talking about.

Then he said it. After the war, he broke his silence and pro-
nounced the dictum of *Denken* upon the Holocaust, the best that
*Denken* could do. He said that the *essence* of the Holocaust and the
*essence* of modern agriculture are the same, they are *im Wesen das-
selbe,* because in both there is the same technologization of the
earth, the same extinguishing of Being's shining beauty, the same si-
lencing of the resonating harmony of *Sein, Schein,* and *Schönheit.*

That was the most he could come up with, and it was at best an insensitive embarrassment, at worst a nightmare. I remember first reading that passage and I remember being dumbfounded, and I have not recovered from it. I had criticized Heidegger for "mythologizing" the history of metaphysics. Now I saw that this mythologizing clearly took the form of an "essentializing" in which the fabric of what in the 1920s he had called "factical life" vaporized into some event in the history of Being, and I saw that this was clearly dangerous. What becomes of the stuff of life, above all of suffering men and women and children, when everything is thought through to its "essential Being"? The answer is: it suffers the worst thoughtlessness. This *Wesen,* by the way—whether it be the essential being of poetry, history, language, architecture, agriculture, or the Holocaust—always turned out to be the same, namely, the rising up of things into the glow of day, lingering and shimmering there for a moment, only to fall back into the dark blue *Schwarzwald* blackness of *lethe,* in the sacred groves of *a-letheia,* at the sound of which every Heideggerian head shall bow. *A-letheia, a-men!*[11]

The whole thing would have been humorous were it not so dangerous. The momentum of Heidegger's mountain path of thought had carried him to an absurdly sublime height, a point which allowed him to neutralize the distinction between murder and agriculture, a point where it was possible to bracket murder in favor of the *Wesen* of Being. A point I would say of scandalous *ethical* insensitivity, where a certain "phainaesthetics," an aesthetics of Being's beauty, produces an anesthetics, an insensitivity to murder, misery, and suffering. This too had a religious significance for me. (Each move I have made along the way has had a religious coefficient.) I

---

11. The argument is made in detail in John D. Caputo, *Demythologizing Heidegger* (Bloomington: Indiana University Press, 1993), esp. ch. 7.

had finally seen that the "later" Heidegger's thought, whose religious charge had held me captive for fifteen years or more, was, on the one hand a *meditative* or *mystical* religion—I was in love with its deep affinity with Meister Eckhart, and with Buddhism, for that matter—but it was, on the other hand, and this was the down side, a quite *pagan* religion with a dubious ethico-political pedigree. The later Heidegger had very much parted company with his *biblical* roots, and I think with unhappy results. He renounced them in no uncertain terms during the National Socialist years when he celebrated the Greco-German Event of Being, the gracious *Ereignis* that granted us Greeks, Germans, and National Socialists, gifts which are, I submit, as good an example of *Ver-gift-ung* as one is likely to come upon.

Levinas's criticisms of Heidegger, which I had always taken with a grain of salt, were now ringing in my ear. Although I would not have wanted Levinas to be in charge of the Environmental Protection Agency, or to head up a committee on animal rights, and although I would not have entrusted Levinas with the fate of the Palestinians, for all his talk about openness to the other, he was nonetheless right about Heidegger. The later Heidegger's thought is a neopagan celebration of earth gods in which the fate of human flesh, of suffering humanity, really played no significant role. If "mortals" wielding handmade swords battled each other upon the "earth" and under the "heavens" and murdered each other mercilessly in the name of their local "divinities," then what could Being do but smile benignly upon the antics of its children who played the play of the Foursome in sprightly, pre-technological splendor? Heidegger had lost his way, and he had lost his way for just the reason that Levinas had given, which is also why Celan left his visit to the *Hütte* shaking his head. Heidegger had done theology and religious reflection an enormous service by means of his powerful delimitation of "onto-theo-logic," a project that is very close to the theological project of de-Hellenization, but he had lost his way. This neopagan mythology which hearkens to the call of Being had lost its ear for the laments of "the widow, the orphan, and the stranger" around which a biblical ethics is woven. (One possible biblical ethics, we should add, for there is no denying that there is a fair amount of merciless monotheistic slaughtering in the Bible, as Regina Schwartz has recently shown so courageously.)[12] In *Demythologizing Heidegger* and *Against Ethics* I let off a good deal of ethical steam about Heidegger and I have, since then, tried to ward off being appropriated by the *Ereignis* and I have kept a safe distance from Heideggerianism of the Strict Observance.

## IV. LEVINAS, DERRIDA AND PROPHETIC RELIGION

I would say that my work, never far removed from the ambiance of the Scriptures, has since then taken on a more and more *biblical* twist, thanks in no small part to Levinas. Levinas, when you think about it, did something extraordinary. He succeeded in gaining a hearing in the heady, highly secularized world of Parisian philosophy for the biblical notion of the "widow, the orphan, and the stranger" and for the idea of God as the "wholly other." Not many people could have done that. He had been around almost forever, like the Ancient of Days himself, and had even first introduced Husserl and phenomenology into France, if one can even imagine French philosophy *before* phenomenology. But the point of Levinas's work seemed to descend upon the contemporary philosophical scene in the 1980s—especially in the United States—with a par-

---

12. Regina Schwartz, *The Curse of Cain: The Violent Legacy of Monotheism* (Chicago: University of Chicago Press, 1997).

ticular force, like an aging prophet whose day had come, like a visitation upon postmodernism by a new Abraham, a kind of Abraham of Paris.

Levinas's work provide a very good exemplar of how biblical experience relates to philosophical reflection. I have been claiming throughout this little intellectual autobiography that, far from impeding philosophizing, religious experience is a driving force of my philosophical thinking, that just as Levinas says, it supplies philosophy with inexhaustible materials for reflection even as it disturbs philosophy's love of "immanence," of cutting things down to philosophical size, cutting them to fit the requirements of philosophical conceptuality. Religious experience is one of those deep sources of "factical" life, as Heidegger used to call it in the 1920s, upon which philosophy nourishes itself. I am happy to think of myself as a kind of midwife who assists in the birth of religious ideas into philosophical parlance, helping to infiltrate philosophy with religious offspring and implantations. I especially cherish the way that religious experience shocks philosophy, which is a Greek word and a Greek idea (almost—a highly conceptual philosophical tradition is also found in classical Indian thought), and forces philosophy to rend its garments. I love the way that religion, like a scraggly, half-naked Jewish prophet shouting in our ear, visits upon aristocratic Greek philosophy events and categories that jolt philosophy out of its Greco-ontological routine and raise its Hellenistic eyebrows. That is what both Levinas and Kierkegaard have done for the contemporary philosophical scene. Kierkegaard said that if we can't come up with categories other than "universality" and "ethics," then Abraham is lost! Greeks and moderns would like nothing better than to lose Abraham, to shake loose of him. Religious experience provokes wonderful disturbances in philosophy, like the story of Abraham, confronting philosophy with its "other," with one of them at least.

The "other" is something to which philosophers today pay a lot of lip service, but nothing is more likely to clear a room of philosophers if it is mentioned that this "other" is religion, that is, other than what the philosophers of alterity expected, an other for which they were not prepared (too *tout autre*). But while I have always held such a view about philosophy and religion, the difference now is that by religion I do not so much mean a *meditative* or *mystical* religion that puts discursive reason out of play but rather a *prophetic* religion, the religion of the prophets. The call that rouses philosophers from a sound sleep is not the call of Being but of justice, the call *for* justice, to let justice flow like water over the land. Or even *messianic* religion, the call of a justice "to come."

That prophetic dimension is why I would claim, today, to the scandal of both the faithful and "deconstructionists" alike, that Jacques Derrida is the single most interesting case of the interaction of philosophy and religion in last quarter of the twentieth century.[13] Levinas is the most obvious case, but Derrida is the most interesting case, because Derrida is an atheist, at least he says of himself, "I quite rightly pass for an atheist."[14] If I may be allowed to put this somewhat paradoxically, his atheism allows Derrida to pursue the religious element in philosophy in a purer form, since he has no theological line to tow, no rabbis or bishops to please, no financial supporters to placate. What is so very delicious to me about this is that Derrida is the *enfant terrible* of the lovers of the Good and the True, the proponent it seems of a shameless neo-Nietzschean nihilism, which dances on God's grave. Derrida seems to those he

13. I have made a detailed argument for such a reading of Derrida in John D. Caputo, *The Prayers and Tears of Jacques Derrida: Religion without Religion* (Bloomington: Indiana University Press, 1997).

14. Jacques Derrida, "Circumfession," in Geoffrey Bennington and Jacques Derrida's *Jacques Derrida* (Chicago: University of Chicago, Press, 1991), p. 155.

frightens the most to revel in the utter breakdown of meaning, sense, reference, truth, and above all of God. God above all, for the very idea of God is the idea of a stable center which arrests the play in which Derrida and his fellow Parisian nihilists love to frolic. Such was and is the take on Derrida, from the liberal pages of the *New York Review of Books* to conservative religious circles, Catholic, Protestant, or Jewish. But Derrida has turned out to be, more and more since 1980 or so, a religious thinker, a thinker of a certain religion, of what he calls a "religion without religion,"[15] without the institutional base of organized religions, and without religious dogma, who is passionately interested in deeply religious structures like the messianic, the gift, hospitality, confession, prayer, witnessing, forgiveness, and the name of God.

The notorious "free play of signifiers," the equally notorious critique of "presence," the impudent declaration that there is nothing outside the text, all of that turned out to be a critique of the idols of "presence," so that Derrida is more like Moses letting Aaron have it for the golden calf than like some kind of neo-Nietzschean nihilist. The deconstruction of presence has turned out to be part of the resistance offered by deconstruction to the idea that what we long for and desire could ever take definitive form. The "deconstruction" of institutions, literature, metaphysics, or the work of art arises not from an irrational impulse to level everything in sight but from a desire to keep things open to the coming of a Messiah who is always to come, structurally to come, the coming of something *undeconstructible,* so that whatever does arrive in the present is liable to deconstruction. Deconstruction turns on an undeconstructible Messiah, whose coming we cannot see or foresee, in whose coming

15. Jacques Derrida, *The Gift of Death,* trans. David Wills (Chicago: University of Chicago Press, 1995), p. 49.

we can only have *faith,* for whose coming we can only *pray and weep.* The critique of presence turns out to be not a form of nihilism but of the kenotics of faith. *Il faut croire,* Derrida says at the beginning and the end of *Memoirs of the Blind.*[16] One of his favorite figures for deconstruction in recent years has been blindness, not the blindness of a tragic hero like Oedipus, or the blindness that is exchanged for higher sight, like the blindness of the Greek seer, which is, on the whole, a good deal, but the blindness of blinding tears, of the woman weeping at the foot of the cross depicted in an exquisite drawing in the Louvre by Daniele da Volterra, reproduced at the end of *Memoirs.* Deconstruction turns on faith in the incoming *(invention)* of the *tout autre,* Derrida says, of the "wholly other," who will upset our present schemata like the tables of the money changers in the temple.

The messianic figure is, for Derrida, the figure of justice and hence a deeply ethical and political figure. The holy one who is coming, for whom we pray and weep, the one in whom we place all our faith and hope, all our love and desire, is the justice to come, the justice that will run like water over the land. By justice Derrida means not some Greek rank-ordering that keeps everybody in their fated and appointed place, but a very biblical justice for the neighbor and the stranger, justice for the other, lifting up the least among us, healing the lame and even raising the dead, hospitality to the immigrants and foreigners who show up at our door, a justice which finds a place for those who lack one, who have no place to lay their head. The work of Derrida, who rightly passes for an atheist, is very close to Levinas, who draws directly upon biblical and rabbinic sources, and perhaps, I might say, on this point at least, it

16. Jacques Derrida, *Memoirs of the Blind: The Self-Portrait and Other Ruins,* trans. Pascale-Anne Brault and Michael Naas (Chicago: University of Chicago Press, 1993), pp. 1, 129.

draws close to St. Paul, who said that God has chosen *ta me onta,* the nothings and the nobodies of this world, the least among us, to manifest his strength. Indeed, one of the oppositions for which Derrida's work makes trouble, I would venture to say (at the risk of giving still more scandal), is the binary opposition of theism and atheism. He throws the love of God and the love of the neighbor into a holy undecidability. There is a sense in which it is not at all clear that Derrida does *rightly* pass for an atheist.

## V. CONCLUSION

The case of Derrida illustrates as pointedly as possible the point I would make. Philosophy is a gift of faith, the gift of what faith gives us to think and put in words. The idea is not to make the faith pass into knowledge, which is what Hegel had in mind, but the opposite. The idea is to come to see the extent to which what we think we know is structured by faith, by a certain unseeing, a certain uncertainty, which remains structurally open to what we do not, cannot see, our condition being one of a certain blindness. Our beliefs and practices are beset by a certain lack of clarity, by a constitutive fallibility, even as the demands of life press in upon us and demand action, not excuses. So we move ahead by faith, like a blind man tapping the way ahead with his stick, Derrida says, through a glass darkly, St. Paul would say, where we take our lead from neither circumcision nor uncircumcision, neither Greek nor Jew, male nor female, but from the love of God which is in us, where it does not cease to be necessary to ask, with St. Augustine, what do I love when I love Thee, my God?

I regard philosophy as caught up in a kind of structural lag behind the facticity and situatedness and concreteness of experience, in a game which it can never win. Philosophy always arrives on the scene just as factical life passes by, just as existence has moved on.

Philosophy has the impossible job of trying to report back to its readers what life is like *before* philosophy arrived on the scene. Philosophy never catches up with life and never catches more than life's back as it leaves the scene. For the moment that the philosopher issues his report, formulates or conceptualizes life, he has turned life into a philosopher's creation, "mummified" it, as Nietzsche quipped. Philosophy moves back and forth in a kind of losing game between the tumultuous inconceivability of the rush of life and the comforting stability of its own concepts, allowing its concepts to be nourished by life and giving life transient conceptual form, even as these concepts come undone by life's ebb and flow. That is why philosophy is at its best when it is being continually disturbed from within, continually provoked and made ill at ease with itself, continually exposed to its other. That is why religion is so important to philosophy, such an important resource and source of nourishment for philosophy, providing it with an *elemental form of life* which—like artistic experience, or perceptual experience, or ethical conflict—nourishes philosophical reflection by supplying it with experiences for which philosophy can barely find words. I treat religion as an irreducible form of passion, of our love and our desire, for which philosophy gropes for words. The question philosophy should ask is not, "does God exist," or "do I or should I love and desire God?" but rather, "what do I love and desire when I desire and love God?"

The *particular religions,* the *determinate* faiths, offer *determinate answers* to that question, whereas a paler, more pallid, more generalizing philosophical reflection resists that degree of determination. For me, philosophy and religion differ, not as reason and faith, but as an indeterminate faith differs from a more determinate one. Philosophy tends to say in a more indeterminate and abstract way what is deeply embedded in the concrete symbols, specific stories, particular traditions, and identifiable beliefs of the particular religions. It is not a higher form of which the concrete religions are particular cases, but a more abstract, desert-like image or trace of a form of life that antedates it both historically and genealogically.

Religion is an elemental passion of life, driven by an irreducible faith, a passion for the *tout autre,* for something that takes us by surprise, that overtakes us, a passion for the impossible, for with God all things are possible, including *the* impossible. Religion is a passion for the inconceivable, for God is *id quo majus cogitari nequit;* religion is impelled by a faith in *the* impossible, in which we hope, of which we dream, for which we pray and weep. Religion is a prayer and a tear for justice, that justice may flow like water over the land. Philosophy is the child of those prayers and tears, *filia istarum lacrymarum,* the son and the daughter of these tears, like the women weeping at the foot of the cross.

My current area of research centers on this question, or constellation of questions, very serious indeed, which takes us back to the heart of the *Confessions,* with which I leave you, which I give to you as a gift: Praying and weeping—is that the stuff of men or of women, of children or adults, of insight or blindness, of faith or reason, of religion or of philosophy?

*Peter A. Redpath*

# 5. PHILOSOPHIZING WITHIN FAITH

❧

In *Recent Philosophy: Hegel to Present,* Etienne Gilson says that the object of Pope Leo XIII's encyclical *Aeterni Patris* was to indicate that the Church has continuously "put natural reason at the service of Christian faith" to defend the faith or elucidate its meaning.[1] According to Gilson, Pope Leo maintained that to combine the exercise of philosophical reason with religious obedience to faith, as did early Christian apologists, Church Fathers, and the major Medieval scholastics, especially St. Thomas, is "the best way of philosophizing."[2]

Commenting on Pope Leo's encyclical several years ago, Armand A. Maurer said: "The reader of the encyclical can hardly fail to notice its repeated reference at the beginning to the mode, method, and right use of philosophy. Its right use leads the way to the true faith; it aids one to understand it better and to defend it against errors. This is said in no way to destroy the independence and integrity of philosophy for it enjoys its own method, principles and arguments."[3]

1. Etienne Gilson, Thomas Langan, Armand A. Maurer, *Recent Philosophy: Hegel to Present* (New York: Random House, 1962), p. 339.

2. Ibid.

3. Armand A. Maurer, "Gilson and *Aeterni Patris,*" in *Thomistic Papers VI,* ed. John F. X. Knasas (Houston: Center for Thomistic Studies, 1994), p. 95.

Maurer maintains that Gilson considered Christian philosophy to be "a way of philosophizing," and "not a philosophical system," or a hybrid third wisdom distinct from the two formally distinct wisdoms of philosophy and theology. Gilson considered philosophy and theology to be essentially distinct, definable through their principles and methods. Christian philosophy, on the other hand, is "the way of philosophizing used by the Church Fathers and Medieval schoolmen and productive of the brilliant philosophies of Augustine, Bonaventure, and Thomas Aquinas": a mode or method of doing philosophy, not a formally distinct order of wisdom.[4]

Gilson thought that a professional theologian like Aquinas placed his philosophy in the service of theology. At the same time, according to Maurer, Gilson contended that, because philosophy has its own distinct principles and methods, we can remain open to the influence of Christian revelation and the guidance of theology without formally being Christian theologians. In support of his interpretation of Gilson, Maurer cites Anton Pegis's authority and refers to several of Gilson's works in which, Maurer says, "Gilson philosophizes within faith but uses the method and order of philosophy, not those of theology."[5] Maurer singles out especially *The Unity of Philosophical Experience* and *Being and Some Philosophers* as instances of Gilson's "quite novel method of philosophizing on the data of the history of philosophy," and maintains:

These are often taken to be works in the history of philosophy, but in fact they are philosophical, using experience in the history of philosophy as a basis for philosophical reflection. From a sort of "experimentation" with that history Gilson draws intelligible ideas and laws that, in his estimation, transcend history and belong to philosophy itself. Here too we find him writing as a Christian philosopher and not as a theologian.[6]

4. Ibid., p. 97. See also, Etienne Gilson, *The Philosopher and Theology*, trans. Cécile Gilson (New York: Random House, 1962), pp. 175–99.

5. Maurer, "Gilson and Aeterni Patris," p. 104 and n. 48.

6. Ibid., p. 105.

I make reference to Gilson's novel way of philosophizing because my main purpose in writing this paper is to make intelligible to readers my way of doing philosophy within faith and the benefits that have accrued to me from this practice. While I never took a class from any of them, Maurer and Gilson, in addition to Jacques Maritain, have had a tremendous influence on my philosophical practice in relation to faith. To make my way of philosophizing as intelligible as possible, and to explain how it relates to my faith, the easiest way to proceed is through reference to the work of these three thinkers.

In *The Unity of Philosophical Experience,* Gilson makes the sage observation that philosophers should beware of their disciples because what masters hold as conclusions disciples often hold as premises, "with the consequence that their own conclusions can never be their master's conclusions."[7] While I am no disciple of Maritain, Maurer, or Gilson, I consider myself their student. And I think that the observation Gilson makes about disciples often applies to students. Apparently, Gilson took as a conclusion about Christian philosophy something I take as a flawed premise.

If it is true that, as Pope Leo maintained and Gilson apparently believed, to combine the exercise of philosophical reason with religious obedience to faith, after the model of the Christian apologists, Church Fathers, and the major Medieval Scholastics, especially St. Thomas, is "the best way of philosophizing," then why would any Christian philosopher, including Gilson, seek to philosophize in any other way? In *The Unity of Philosophical Experience* and *Being and Some Philosophers,* and some of his other works, did Gilson only try to give us his second best? I doubt it. And I think that to comprehend Gilson, Maritain, and a host of other Christian philosophers,

7. Etienne Gilson, *Unity of Philosophical Experience* (New York: Charles Scribner's Sons, 1937), p. 240.

we do well to recall Maritain's distinction between philosophers of fact and philosophers of intention, and Gilson's quip that we philosophize the way we can, not the way we wish.[8] Is it possible, in short, for Christian philosophers to remain open to Christian revelation's influence and theology's guidance without doing philosophy theologically? I think not. I do not think Gilson's own principles support this possibility. And I do not think I practice philosophizing in this way.

Maurer maintains that Gilson thought Christian philosophy is no system or body of knowledge. This is true of the later Gilson, but Gilson's earlier way of describing Christian philosophy appears to suggest just the opposite. And Maurer's statement does not apply to Maritain's early understanding of Christian philosophy. In *The Spirit of Medieval Philosophy,* based upon his 1931–1932 Gifford Lectures, Gilson specifically articulates his view of Christian philosophy historically and in terms of a "system." He says, for example:

> Consider any given philosophic system. Now ask if it is "Christian," and if so by what characteristics you can recognize it as such? From the observer's standpoint it is a philosophy, therefore a work of reason. The author is a Christian and yet his Christianity, however telling its influence on his philosophy has been, remains essentially distinct from it. The only means at our disposal for detecting this inner action is to compare this data which we can outwardly observe: The philosophy without revelation and the philosophy with revelation. This is what I have attempted to do. And since history is alone capable of performing this task, I have stated that history alone can give meaning to the concept of Christian philosophy. . . . I may say, then, that Christian philosophy is an objectively observable reality in history alone, but that once its existence has been thus established, its notion may be analyzed in itself. This ought to be done as Mr. J. Maritain has done it; I am in fact in complete agreement with him.[9]

8. Jacques Maritain, *Bergsonian Philosophy and Thomism,* trans. Mabelle L. Andison and J. Gordon Andison (New York: Philosophical Library, 1955), pp. 1–28, and Gilson, *Unity of Philosophical Experience,* p. 302.

9. Cited in Jacques Maritain, *An Essay on Christian Philosophy,* x, n. 1.

In *The Philosopher at Large,* Mortimer J. Adler attributes his own view of philosophy as "a body of knowledge, not a set of opinions," to Maritain, especially to Maritain's lectures and works of the 1930s, such as *The Degrees of Knowledge* and *An Introduction to Philosophy.*[10] In *An Essay on Christian Philosophy* and *Science and Wisdom,* Maritain, in turn, attempts to explain Christian philosophy systematically, as did Gilson, but in terms of a distinction between the nature of "pure" philosophy abstractly considered in its absolute nature, and its historical state as it exists in the human subject.[11]

In *From Unity to Pluralism: The Internal Evolution of Thomism,* Gerald A. McCool is one of the few contemporary thinkers to realize that a serious flaw exists in the contemporary Thomistic attempts to reconcile philosophical activity with Pope Leo XIII's desire to revive the practice of philosophizing within faith. I disagree with McCool's analysis of *Aeterni Patris,* the history of modern Thomism, and the role Gilson played in the Neo-Thomistic movement.[12] Still, in the above work, I think McCool hit on something crucial about modern Thomism and Gilson's role in its revival: that a gradual change occurred in Gilson's articulation of his views of Scholasticism, Thomism, and Christian philosophy from his earlier to later works.

Early in his research, Gilson, like Maritain, articulated his understanding of Christian philosophy in terms of a system, or body

10. Mortimer J. Adler, *Philosopher at Large* (New York: Macmillan, Collier Books, 1977), p. 298.

11. For a more detailed critique of Gilson and Maritain's views of Christian philosophy, see my "Romance of Wisdom: The Friendship between Jacques Maritain and St. Thomas Aquinas," in *Understanding Maritain: Philosopher and Friend,* ed. Deal W. Hudson and Matthew J. Mancini (Macon, Ga.: Mercer University Press, 1987), pp. 91–113. See, also, F. Copleston's apparent approval of my critique of Maritain in his review of *Understanding Maritain,* in *Heythrop Journal* 32 (1991), p. 444.

12. See my critique of McCool, "Unity of Thomistic Experience—A Gilsonian Rejoinder to Gerald McCool, S.J.," in *Thomistic Papers VI,* pp. 69–90.

of knowledge. As Gilson noted in the above block quote, in framing the notion of Christian philosophy as a system, he took an observer's, a historian's, not a practitioner's, a Christian philosopher's, standpoint. In so doing, he maintained that this historical standpoint is the only means we have to detect this inner action as an objectively observable reality, by comparing this data that we can outwardly observe: the philosophy with and without revelation. Once we have historically established the existence of Christian philosophy, Gilson maintained that we could analyze the notion in itself. He added that we ought to do this the way Maritain had done it, and that he was in complete agreement with Maritain.

Later on, in framing this same notion in works like *Introduction à la philosophie chrétienne* (1960) and *The Philosopher and Theology* (1962), Gilson appears to have taken more of a practitioner's than an observer's standpoint, and to have stressed more Christian philosophy as "a way of philosophizing," or as Maurer has called it, "a style," and not a system.[13]

Gilson's early articulation of his view of Christian philosophy is unfortunate for at least four reasons:

1. As I have argued elsewhere, Maritain's understanding of Christian philosophy is seriously flawed and, in my opinion, essentialistic. It appears to me to be based upon a misunderstanding of St. Thomas's teaching about the actual composition of existence *(esse)* and essence in finite beings.[14] If, during the 1930s, Gilson was in

13. Armand A. Maurer, "Translator's Introduction," in Etienne Gilson, *Christian Philosophy: An Introduction,* trans. Armand A. Maurer (Toronto: Pontifical Institute of Mediaeval Studies, The Etienne Gilson Series 17, 1993), p. XIV. See, also, Etienne Gilson, *Introduction à la philosophie chrétienne* (Paris: J. Vrin, 1960) and *The Philosopher and Theology,* pp. 100–101.

14. "Romance of Wisdom: The Friendship between Jacques Maritain and St. Thomas Aquinas," pp. 99–113.

complete agreement with Maritain about the notion of Christian philosophy, during this time Gilson's notion of Christian philosophy was essentialistic.

2. Gilson appears to me to be wrong to maintain that the historical standpoint is the only way we have objectively to observe Christian philosophy. According to Gilson, "Christian philosophy" is a phrase he used to express a "theological notion of a reality observable in history."[15] If such be the case, the Christian theological-historical standpoint, not the historical standpoint as such, would be the only way to observe this reality in history. The ordinary historian would lack the requisite skill to recognize this reality. Furthermore, why must the historical observer be the only person capable of detecting the inner action of Christian philosophy as an objectively observable reality? Cannot the practitioner, the Christian philosopher, objectively observe this reality in the present? Is history the only way we can objectively establish the existence of philosophical realities? or Christian philosophical realities? Can we not objectively establish them by exercising philosophical acts in relation to philosophical habits, by relating formal objects to our own faculties in the exercise of our own acts?

3. In this early description of Christian philosophy, Gilson made the unfortunate mistake of talking about it as a "system." And, even in as late a work as *The Philosopher and Theology,* he said that, in using the phrase "Christian philosophy," he

felt somewhat embarrassed to have to characterize the philosophy of the middle ages by a formula of which the history of that philosophy provided practically no example. Indeed, a master of theology teaching in the thirteenth century would never have considered himself as having a philosophy, even a Christian one.[16]

15. Etienne Gilson, *The Christian Philosophy of St. Thomas Aquinas,* trans. L. K. Shook (New York: Random House, 1956), p. 441, n. 20.

16. Gilson, *The Philosopher and Theology,* p. 178.

And he added:

[W]hat other name could one find for this body of doctrines so deeply marked with the seal of the Christian religion? Since, indeed, such a large portion of it was so truly rational that modern philosophy has appropriated it, one could rightly call it a philosophy, and since this philosophy was quickened by a genuinely Christian spirit, there was no escape from calling it a "Christian philosophy."[17]

When we couple the above two statements to Gilson's early description of Christian philosophy as a system, Gilson appears to be telling us that, during the early 1930s, he understood Christian philosophy to characterize a philosophical system, body of knowledge, doctrine, or common philosophy of the Middle Ages. Yet in a letter to me dated 1 December 1999, Maurer wrote:

Regarding Christian philosophy, I think you are right in not seeing it as a system. Too often that has muddled the controversy over that subject. Gilson may have used the term "system," but he never meant it in a Kantian sense. The French "système" has a wider meaning.[18]

In a subsequent letter dated 11 September 2000, Maurer added:

You are right to emphasize that Christian philosophy is a way of philosophizing. Gilson did not waver in this description, from his early debates on the subject in the 1930's to the end. There is no early and later Gilson in this regard. He never regarded Christian philosophy as a doctrine or a system. As a way of philosophizing, it can produce various Christian philosophies, like Augustine's, Bonaventure's, and Thomas's. But it itself is no one doctrine.[19]

4. Gilson's own early and infelicitous way of expressing his views about Christian philosophy can obscure, instead of clarify, Thomas's unique way of "philosophizing within faith." It easily lends itself to

---

17. Ibid., p. 179.
18. Letter from Armand A. Maurer to Peter A. Redpath dated 1 December 1999.
19. Letter from Armand A. Maurer to Peter A. Redpath dated 11 September 2000.

the conclusion that, while Christian philosophy might not be a single philosophical system common to the Middle Ages, as a way of philosophizing, it still consists of being a system or of system building.

What, then, are we to make of Christian philosophy? Of philosophizing within faith? McCool rightly realizes that Gilson's discussion of Christian philosophy creates trouble for people who mistakenly consider Thomism to be a philosophical system, and that it eventually created problems for Gilson to make his views intelligible to fellow Thomists, not to mention others. Whether, as Maurer says, the French notion of "system" has a wider meaning than the Kantian sense does not appear to me to be a main cause of the problem. I concur that this term has a wider meaning for the Frenchman Gilson. I doubt that the same is true in the case of the Frenchman Descartes.[20] Gilson's meaning of system is wider than Kant's primarily because it is realist and derives from the thought of St. Thomas, not because it is French.[21] Whatever the case, talking about Christian philosophy as a system created some problems for Gilson, and creates problems for other Thomists, because, in its primary sense, as Maurer has well documented, Thomas does not consider philosophy to be a system.[22]

20. For a more complete presentation of the notion of system in the thought of Descartes and Kant, see my *Cartesian Nightmare: An Introduction to Transcendental Sophistry* (Amsterdam and Atlanta: Editions Rodopi B.V., 1997) and *Masquerade of the Dream Walkers: Prophetic Theology from the Cartesians to Hegel* (Amsterdam and Atlanta: Editions Rodopi B.V., 1998).

21. Armand A. Maurer, "The Unity of a Science: St. Thomas and the Nominalists," in *St. Thomas Aquinas 1274–1974 Commemorative Studies,* Vol. 2, editor-in-chief Armand A. Maurer (Toronto: Pontifical Institute of Mediaeval Studies), pp. 269–92.

22. For Maurer's analysis of the origin of the notion of philosophy as a system and St. Thomas's understanding of philosophy, see Maurer, "The Unity of a Science: St. Thomas and the Nominalists," pp. 269–92.

My understanding of Christian philosophy is philosophizing within faith. And my understanding of philosophizing within faith starts from a twofold realization:

1. From Gilson and Maurer I have learned that philosophy is not a system or body of knowledge.[23] Today, I think most "philosophers," including many self-professed Thomists, mistakenly consider philosophy to be a logically coherent system of ideas. I believe they are mistaken. Such a notion is a poetical, even sophistical deconstruction of philosophy, not philosophy.[24] As Werner W. Jaeger tells us: "The innovation of the Ionians lay in the fact that they did not begin with uncontrolled traditions and fictions, as did the mythical thinkers of earlier times. . . ."[25] Nor did the Ionians start their reasoning with controlled fictions or impossible dreams, as did Descartes and his progeny.[26] Instead, as Jaeger says, the first philosophers "took as their point of departure the things they found in experience, which they tried to explain in terms of itself alone."[27]

2. From Gilson, Maurer, Maritain, and St. Thomas, I have learned that all philosophy is essentially realist in character. Gilson forcefully drives home this point in several works, especially *Methodical Realism* and *Thomist Realism and the Critique of Knowl-*

23. Ibid. See also Etienne Gilson, *Methodical Realism,* trans. Philip Trower (Front Royal, Va: Christendom Press, 1990), and *Thomist Realism and the Critique of Knowledge,* trans. Mark A. Wauck (San Francisco: Ignatius Press, 1986).

24. For a more detailed critique of this mistaken notion of philosophy, see my "From Sophistic Animism to Philosophy," in *Contemporary Philosophy* 20, nos. 3 & 4 (1998), pp. 36–43; *Cartesian Nightmare, Masquerade of the Dream Walkers,* and *Wisdom's Odyssey from Philosophy to Transcendental Sophistry* (Amsterdam and Atlanta: Editions Rodopi, B.V. 1997).

25. Werner W. Jaeger, *The Theology of the Early Greek Philosophers* (Westport, Conn.: Greenwood Press, 1960), p. 102.

26. For a detailed critique of this mode of reasoning as unphilosophical, see my *Cartesian Nightmare* and *Masquerade of the Dream Walkers.*

27. Jaeger, *The Theology of the Early Greek Philosophers,* p. 102.

*edge.*[28] And in his classic *Being and Some Philosophers* he goes so far as to say:

The magnificent "systems" of those idealists who bear the title of "great thinkers," and wholly deserve it, belong to the realm of art more than in that of philosophy. . . . No more than science, philosophy cannot be a system, because all systematic thinking rests on an assumption, whereas, as knowledge, philosophy must rest on being.[29]

Maritain makes a similar point in *The Peasant of the Garonne,* but in much stronger language. There he refers to the practice of modern subjective idealists as "secularized theology," says that "a Christian can not be an idealist," and states that modern subjectivist idealists

impugn from the very outset the very fact on which thought gets its firmness and consistency, and without which it is a mere dream—I mean the reality to be known and understood, which *is here* seen, touched, seized by the senses, and with which an intellect which belongs to a man, not to an angel, has directly to deal: the reality *about which and starting with which* a philosopher is born to question himself: if he misses the start he is nothing. They impugn the absolutely basic foundation of philosophic research. They are not philosophers.[30]

As Jaeger rightly understood, philosophy started among the ancient Greeks with the realist problem of the one and the many. As I have said elsewhere:

What first distinguished early Greek philosophers from other people who wondered about the world, in particular from the theological poets, was that the philosophers began to look, by uninspired reason alone, into the nature

28. See note 22 above.
29. Etienne Gilson, *Being and Some Philosophers* (Toronto: Pontifical Institute of Mediaeval Studies, 1961), pp. 212–13.
30. Jacques Maritain, *The Peasant of the Garonne: An Old Layman Questions Himself about the Present Time* (New York: Holt, 1968), pp. 100–102.

of things. They looked to their knowledge of physical things, instead of to their own imaginations and revelation by the gods, as the source of their reasoning principles."[31]

St. Thomas understands the first philosophers in much the same way. "In the consideration of the nature of things," he says, "the Ancients proceeded according to the order of human cognition."[32] By this Gilson understands Thomas to mean, "our knowledge begins with sensible things, and from them it progressively rises to the intelligible by a series of ever-deepening abstractions."[33] As Gilson says, "Wisdom begins with notions that are certainly abstract but endowed with a content extracted from the real world by a mind whose light discovers in forms the light itself of which our mind is an image."[34]

Philosophy begins in wonder, not in doubt or impossible dreams of pure reason. Wonder is a sensory, emotional activity related to our human condition of sensing the being of physical things. St. Thomas identifies wonder, with which philosophy starts, as a species of fear.[35] The initial cause of this wonder is something within physical being, and ourselves: principles of knowing that escape the immediate grasp of our senses. We first grasp these principles as objects of sense experience, not as principles of demonstration. This means, as Gilson clearly understood, that the being of sensible things and our sensory and abstractive faculties are principles of apprehending being that are prior to and regulative of the principles

---

31. Redpath, *Wisdom's Odyssey,* p. 5.

32. St. Thomas Aquinas, *Quaestiones disputatae: De potentia,* ed. Paul M. Pession, 9th ed. (Turin: Marietti, 1953), q. 3, a. 5.

33. Gilson, *Christian Philosophy: An Introduction,* p. 17.

34. Ibid., p. 72.

35. See St. Thomas Aquinas, *Summa theologiae,* I–II, q. 41, a. 4, especially his reply to objection 5.

of demonstration. Hence they are the regulative first principles of philosophy for the ancient Greeks and for everyone for all time.

This helps to explain why, as Gilson notes, philosophy's "first stage corresponds to the sensible perception of the qualities of bodies" because "the qualities of bodies, which are accidental forms, can be perceived by the five senses."[36] It also helps to explain, as I have shown elsewhere, why all the ancient Greek philosophers, from the ancient physicists to Plotinus, were sense realists. They started their philosophical reasoning from principles they abstracted from their sensory apprehension of the physical universe.[37]

The philosopher's realist grasp of first principles further helps to explain why Socrates was put to death with the help of ancient poets and sophists (because the rise of philosophy, with its appeal to sensory evidence, helped to undermine the control exercised by the Greek poets over Greek education and weaken the growing educational power of the sophists) and why Aristotle was driven out of Athens (because this same sort of appeal made by Aristotle helped to undermine the influence of Greek religion, which the poets largely controlled).[38]

Because Pope Leo recognized this essential quality of ancient Greek philosophical realism, which he understood the Medieval Scholastics had continued, he was hopeful that, by reviving Scholasticism, he could breathe new life into philosophy and theology. Leo approvingly noted how God, in His goodness, allowed "pagan sages

36. Gilson, *Christian Philosophy: An Introduction,* p. 16.

37. See my *Wisdom's Odyssey.*

38. For a more detailed defense of these claims, see my *Wisdom's Odyssey,* pp. 1–40, and "Poetic Revenge and Modern Totalitarianism," in *From Twilight to Dawn: The Cultural Vision of Jacques Maritain,* ed. Peter A. Redpath (Notre Dame, Ind.: University of Notre Dame Press/AMA, 1990), pp. 227–40. Regarding the influence of Aristotle on Greek religion, see Etienne Gilson, *God and Philosophy* (New Haven and London: Yale University Press, 1970), pp. 32–37.

with nothing but natural reason to guide them" to discover certain truths that God later proposed to Christians for belief.[39] Leo thought that philosophizing within faith, by reinforcing our sense realism, strengthens our ability to exercise natural reason, thereby improving our philosophizing.

In place of principles extracted from sensible being, modern "philosophy" adopts the posture of the ancient poets and sophists. In Plato's *Gorgias,* Gorgias responds to Socrates' critique of his supposed "art" by asserting that his profession gives him great comfort precisely because "without learning any other arts but this one" he is able "to prove in no way inferior to the specialists."[40] Just like ancient Gorgias, Descartes persuaded himself that he had found *The Method* for doing science buried in his soul. In so doing, he substituted authority, his own act of self-persuasion, for the being of sensible things as the starting point for natural reasoning.[41]

Just as for Protagoras "man" was the measure of all things, for Descartes and his modern and contemporary descendants, "Enlightened man," the person of "pure reason" becomes the measure of truth.[42] As Pope Leo said, "A multiform system of this kind, which depends on the authority and choice of any professor, has a foundation open to change, and consequently gives us a philosophy not firm, and stable, and robust like that of old, but tottering and

39. Pope Leo XIII, *Aeterni Patris,* in Etienne Gilson, *The Church Speaks to the Modern World* (Garden City, N.Y.: Doubleday, 1954), p. 34.

40. Plato, *Gorgias,* trans. W. D. Woodhead, in *The Collected Dialogues of Plato,* ed. Edith Hamilton and Huntington Cairns, Bollingen Series 71 (New York: Bollingen Foundation/Pantheon, 1966), 459B–D.

41. For a more detailed critique of Descartes as a rhetorician, see my *Cartesian Nightmare,* especially pp. 19–132.

42. For a more detailed critique of modern and contemporary "philosophy" as neo-Protagorean sophistry, see my *Cartesian Nightmare* and *Masquerade of the Dream Walkers.*

feeble."[43] Indeed, as Aristotle quipped, thinkers like Protagoras "say nothing, while they appear to say something remarkable, when they say 'man is the measure of all things.'"[44]

Leo traced this anti-realist, and anti-historical, way of philosophizing back to "struggling innovators of the sixteenth century" who pleased "to philosophize without any respect to faith, the power of inventing in accordance with his own pleasure and bent."[45] While he does not mention the names of these "struggling innovators," the description he gives of them fits Renaissance humanists, who, by trade, were rhetoricians, not philosophers.[46] Whatever the case, the chief purpose of Leo's encyclical was to end the divorce between Catholic theology and classical philosophical realism in order to help restore the whole order of higher education. Hence, he said:

In short, all studies ought to find hope of advancement and promise of assistance in this restoration of philosophic discipline which we have proposed. The arts were wont to draw from philosophy, as from a wise mistress, sound judgment and right method, and from it also, their spirit, as from a common fount of life. When philosophy stood stainless in honor and wise in judgment, then, as facts and constant experience showed, the liberal arts flourished as never before or since; but, neglected, and almost blotted out, they lay prone, since philosophy began to lean on error and to join hands with folly. Nor will the physical sciences themselves, which are now in such great repute, and by the renown of so many inventions draw such universal admiration to themselves, suffer detriment, but find very great assistance in the restoration of the ancient philosophy. For, the investigation of facts and the contemplation of nature is not alone sufficient for their profitable exercise and advance; but, when facts have been established, it is necessary to rise

43. Ibid., p. 46.
44. Aristotle, *Metaphysics,* trans. W. D. Ross, in *The Basic Works of Aristotle,* ed. Richard McKeon (New York: Random House, 1968), Bk. 10, 1, 1053a32–1053b3.
45. Ibid.
46. Paul Oskar Kristeller, *Renaissance Thought: The Classic, Scholastic and Humanist Strains* (New York: Harper & Row, 1961), pp. 11, 100–101, 109.

and apply ourselves to the study of the nature of corporeal things, to inquire into the laws which govern them and the principles whence their order and varied unity and mutual attraction in diversity arise. To such investigations, it is wonderful what force and light and aid the Scholastic philosophy, if judiciously taught would bring.[47]

Clearly, by putting "natural reason" at the service of Christian faith, Pope Leo had in mind reason as a faculty of the human soul possessed by an organic person. He did not have in mind the disembodied pure reason of Descartes, the time-bound poetic *Dasein* of Martin Heidegger, or any of the other mythological musings, or excited imaginative projections, that moderns often use to masquerade as the ground of our being in order to subordinate speculative reason to the wandering poetic imagination or the modern will to power.

If a Christian philosopher is a person who puts natural reason in the service of Christian faith, not a non-believer with an interest in Christian philosophy as an external guiding star, natural reason so utilized must be of the sort envisioned by Pope Leo. Envisioning use of any other sort of natural reason involves employment of natural reasoning without sense realism. And the attempt to use natural reasoning without sense realism is to engage in fantasy, not philosophy.

Since all human knowledge essentially depends upon external sensation as the starting point for all natural knowing, including natural reasoning, Gilson repeatedly indicates that sense experience is the first principle of all philosophical reasoning for the ancient Greeks and for all time.[48] This, in turn, means that philosophy is essentially a habitual, abstractive activity. For philosophy is essen-

47. Ibid., p. 49.
48. See Gilson's *Methodical Realism* and *Thomist Realism and the Critique of Knowledge.*

tially the act of a habit. And this habit involves abstracting principles from sense images that we habitually use to measure the behavior of substances. This activity, not logical coherence of ideas, formally distinguishes philosophy from other human activities.

Because modern philosophers have lost their sense realism, they
have lost their comprehension of philosophy as an essentially abstractive activity, and have become reduced to the condition of what
I call transcendental sophists, or as Maritain called them, of ideoso-
phers and neo-Protagoreans.[49] They have no real ground upon
which to base intellectual distinctions. As a result, they resemble a
dog chasing its own tail. Using poetic musings and esoteric jargon
to give their empty ideas the veneer of substance and air of authority
not justified by their vacuous content, many modern and contemporary philosophers engage in one long circular argument to find
the ground of real being within consciousness. They have the habitual tendency to confound philosophy with logical systems and logical systems with metaphysics. As I have shown elsewhere, their activity is mostly, if not entirely, secularized Augustinian theology,
which they inherited through Descartes from Renaissance rhetoricians.[50] Through historical and philosophical ignorance, we have
been duped into mistaking this secularized theological sophistry for
philosophy, which contemporary thinkers often call "philosophy of
subjectivity." Modern thinkers have a hard enough time carrying off
this masquerade when only dealing with natural reason and naturally grounded arts and sciences. When they have to try to explain
their occupation as Christian philosophers, their flights of fancy
border on the mystical.

Since, strictly speaking, modern philosophy is sophistry mas-

49. Maritain, *The Peasant of the Garonne*, pp. 84–126.
50. For a detailed defense of these specific claims, see my *Masquerade of the Dream Walkers, Wisdom's Odyssey*, and *Cartesian Nightmare*.

querading as the genuine article, in no way can I conceive of Christian theology putting modern philosophy to use in the service of the faith. This is especially so because modern philosophy, in particular since the Enlightenment, presumes as starting points of enlightened or philosophical reasoning that (1) we do not extract philosophical principles from sense reality, (2) no hierarchy can exist on the level of spirit, (3) no real mysteries exist (in modernity mysteries largely, if not entirely, become imaginative projections or past and future dream states), (4) efficient causality has no place in the physical universe, and (5) tradition is, at best, an occasional cause of transcendence. Like Rousseau's *Emile*, Enlightenment thought generally contends that human beings must emerge entirely out of themselves.[51] As Kant tells us:

*Enlightenment is man's emergence from his self-incurred immaturity. Immaturity* is the inability to use one's own understanding without the guidance of another. This immaturity is *self-incurred* if its cause is not lack of understanding, but lack of resolution and courage to use it without the guidance of another. The motto of enlightenment is therefore: *Sapere aude!* Have courage to use your own understanding![52]

By this, Kant means that tradition cannot bind succeeding generations to unalterable doctrines. Indeed, he thinks that to do so "would be a crime against humanity." As he says:

But should not a society of clergymen, for example an ecclesiastical synod or a venerable presbytery (as the Dutch call it), be entitled to commit itself by oath to a certain unalterable set of doctrines, in order to secure for all time a constant guardianship over each of its members, and through them over the

51. For a more extensive critique of Rousseau and Kant on the matter of enlightenment as self-emergence, see my *Masquerade of the Dream Walkers*, pp. 67–136.

52. Immanuel Kant, "An Answer to the Question 'What is Enlightenment?'" in *Kant: Political Writings*, ed. Hans Reiss and trans. H. B. Nisbet (Cambridge: Cambridge University Press, 1992), p. 54.

people? I reply that this is quite impossible. A contract of this kind, concluded with a view of preventing all further enlightenment of mankind for ever, is absolutely null and void, even if it is ratified by Imperial Diets and the most solemn peace treaties. One age cannot enter into an alliance on oath to put the next age in a position where it is impossible for it to extend and correct its knowledge, particularly on such important matters, or to make any progress whatsoever in enlightenment. This would be a crime against human nature, whose original destiny lies precisely in such progress. Later generations are thus perfectly entitled to dismiss these agreements as unauthorized and criminal.[53]

Shame that Moses, not to mention many of the American founders, did not realize that they were engaged in crimes against humanity!

Because modern and contemporary philosophy generally deny the ability of philosophical reason to come into contact with the being of physical things, generally undermine any distinction between the natural and supernatural orders, generally deny and tend to be hostile to the notions of mystery, of spiritual hierarchies, and of binding a community of believers by religious tradition, modern and contemporary philosophy generally undercut the foundations of the Christian faith.[54] For these reasons, I contend that these modes of reasoning are totally inadequate tools to use in doing Christian theology. Indeed, attempts to apply them as handmaidens to Catholic theology are largely responsible for the current, generally pathetic condition of Catholic colleges and universities. Clearly, Pope Leo did not have this type of philosophical malpractice in mind as the model of Christian philosophizing.

At the same time, I have a problem with the notion of Christian philosophy as articulated by thinkers like Gilson and Maritain. Generally, I think they mistakenly articulate this notion from a his-

53. Ibid., p. 55.
54. For a more detailed critique of modern and contemporary philosophy, see my *Masquerade of the Dream Walkers.*

torical, consumer standpoint, not from a metaphysical, Christian-producer standpoint. If we consider Christian philosophy from the standpoint of its being, I do not think Gilson and Maritain's analysis is correct.

Like every other human act, Christian philosophy is consequent upon Christian being. Act is consequent upon being. And we act according to the way we exist. Consequent upon the human way we exist, we exercise specific human operations, one of which is philosophy, and Christian philosophy. Regarding philosophical acts, Gilson rightly says that sensation of external being is always philosophy's first principle. He also says that the whole person knows and senses, not the intellect or the senses. As he puts it, we sense with our intellect and intellectualize with our senses.[55] St. Thomas, in turn, tells us that the faith we receive through grace is a revelation and a theological virtue.[56] We receive this grace into our wills and intellects. And we sense with our intellects.

This means that, as Christians, we sense with faith and revelation. As Christians, we can never divorce the first principle of our philosophizing from our faith or revelation. Faith and revelation are imbedded in our sensation, and our sensation is the starting point of our philosophizing. As believing Christians, we cannot abstract from grace's influence on the sense act. And the sense act is the first principle of all philosophical reasoning. This presents a problem that contemporary Thomists have not adequately recognized, much less addressed.

As Maurer observes, "We may do mathematics, but the total action involves not only doing math but acting with our whole selves, including our Faith. Everything we do, we should do for the glory

55. See Gilson's *Methodical Realism* and *Thomist Realism and the Critique of Knowledge.*
56. St. Thomas Aquinas, *Summa Theologiae,* II–II, q. 4, a. 1 and a. 5.

of God and for our salvation."[57] Maurer, however, immediately cautions:

> But this does not mean that when we are doing math we should bring our Faith into the mathematical demonstrations. When a Christian does math he should do it just as non-Christians do it, using the method of mathematics. Of course, if God had revealed some math in Scripture, this would be a guide for the Christian mathematician and enable him or her to do math better. Unfortunately for the mathematician, there seems to be no help in revelation. There can't be a Christian mathematics. Regarding philosophical matters, Scripture is an indispensable aid to the Christian, but for the Christian philosopher revelation should not feature as a premise in his conclusions. Otherwise he is not doing philosophy but theology. In short, Christians have to respect the autonomy of the sciences and their methods. Thomism as a philosophy is "strictly rational."[58]

Maurer's advice is sober and helps to clarify the point at issue. If God had revealed some mathematics in Scripture, the Christian mathematician could use this and do math better. To my knowledge, and despite the musings of thinkers like Newton, Maurer is right. God has made no such revelation in Scripture.[59] God, however, has made scriptural revelation about creation. As physicist Stanley L. Jaki has meticulously documented, because some cultures and civilizations cannot dynamically imagine the physical universe as non-cyclical and non-deterministic, they cannot progress as far in physics as can people capable of imagining the universe as created.[60]

Maurer rightly cautions that "we should not bring our Faith into

---

57. Letter from Armand A. Maurer to Peter A. Redpath dated 1 December 1999.
58. Ibid.
59. Regarding Newton's view of the relation of faith and revelation to physics, see my *Masquerade of the Dream Walkers*, pp. 9–32.
60. See Redpath, *Masquerade of the Dream Walkers*, p. 241; see also Stanley L. Jaki, *Science and Creation: From Eternal Cycles to an Oscillating Universe* (Edinburgh: Scottish Academic Press, 1986).

our mathematical demonstrations" and "for the Christian philosopher revelation should not feature as a premise in his conclusions."[61] Should the case be the same for the Christian physicist?
Apparently not, if God has revealed some things in Scripture to us
about the nature of the physical universe.

As I see it, however, the main point at issue has nothing to do
with *bringing our faith into our demonstrations,* in physics, mathematics, or metaphysics. In a believing Christian, faith already exists
as a necessary condition for forming premises and conclusions of
demonstration. The theological virtue of faith is an effect of grace
present in the first principles and methods of Christian philosophical reasoning. The sense act is the first principle of philosophical
reasoning. The human intellect is present in the sense act, in the abstractive intellect working on imagination's phantasms to extract
from sense images the intelligible content of simple apprehension
and judgment. The grace of faith is present in the agent intellect,
which is present in the imagination and the senses as the act of abstraction of first principles takes place. Since grace perfects nature,
it elevates the ability of this abstraction to take place. It helps us abstract better and, therefore, reason better philosophically. Moreover,
we take the methods of the sciences from the way the soul's powers
and habits operate in relation to their proper objects.[62] If we divide
the sciences on the basis of the aims, methods, and principles we
use in conjunction with our intellect, and the grace of faith is present in all of these, then, since faith is a theological virtue, Christian
philosophy would appear to be a special way of theologizing.

---

61. Letter from Armand A. Maurer to Peter A. Redpath dated 1 December 1999.

62. St. Thomas Aquinas, *Commentary on the de Trinitate of Boethius, Questions V
and VI, and St. Thomas Aquinas: The Division and Methods of the Sciences,* trans. with
an introduction and notes by Armand A. Maurer, 3d rev. ed., q. 6, articles 1–4
(Toronto: Pontifical Institute of Mediaeval Studies, 1963).

Granted, Christian philosophers should not use revelation, in the sense of premises expressing Christian mysteries, to justify their conclusions. Not all revelations are scripturally derived mysteries, however. And, crucially, some scriptural premises are knowable to the unaided natural intellect. The grace of faith is a revelation. And the premise that God created and sustains the physical universe in existence is a revelation *and* naturally knowable to the human intellect. Because this is a revelation to some people, does this mean we cannot use it as a philosophical premise to justify a philosophical conclusion?

When I talk about philosophizing within faith, I am not talking about mixing premises of philosophy and premises related to Christian mysteries taken from Scripture. In its most precise sense, philosophy is an abstractive intellectual activity, an act of a habitual way of abstracting. More than anything else, this complete act, not simply the premises philosophers use, distinguishes philosophers from other kinds of thinkers. The fact that I use mathematical premises does not primarily make me a mathematician. And the fact that I use philosophical premises does not mean I am necessarily a philosopher. To be a philosopher I must discover these premises through my own abstracting ability, through my own power, and then be in the habit of reasoning logically from premises to conclusions, according to these principles I have derived from observing the behavior of things in the physical world, or of things causally connected to such things. If I add some supernatural aid to my abstractive ability, and use this aid as a guide and measure of truth throughout my process of reasoning from premises to conclusions, then, strictly speaking, I am engaged in an ancillary activity of philosophizing within faith. To me, since faith is a theological virtue, such reasoning is a theological act. Those who think of philosophical activity principally in terms of premises and conclusions think of philosophy from the consumer's, historian's, or logician's perspective—as a system. Thinking about Christian philosophy primarily in this way will never help us understand its precise nature, any more than it will help us understand the nature of philosophy in general. In this systematic sense, Thomism as a philosophy is "strictly rational." As the act of a *habitus,* however, Thomism as a Christian philosophy, is "more than strictly rational."

While considering Christian philosophy from a chiefly historical perspective can dull our understanding of its precise nature, ancillary historical analysis can throw some light on the problem. Ancient philosophy started as a movement away from the superstition of Greek poetry, that sought, among other things, to liberate natural reason from intrusion of any higher lights. In Book 10 of the *Republic,* Plato speaks of numerous examples of an ancient feud between philosophers and poets.[63] This feud existed because ancient poets claimed that inspiration from the gods, not natural ability and naturally acquired habits, caused human virtue or skill. Widespread acceptance of the poetic view of learning gave the ancient poets special authority among the ancient Greeks. Growth of philosophy challenged the ancient poets' monopoly on education. Philosophy arose among the ancient Greeks as a conscious attempt to remove the gods and inspiration as sources of human learning. For this reason, in Plato's dialogues, Socrates constantly ironically attacks poetic claims to knowledge by inspiration.[64]

The ancient Greeks, in short, intentionally thought philosophy to be measurable by principles (ones) derived by unaided natural reason from sense experience of the behavior of physical beings or

63. Plato, *Republic,* Bk. 10, 607B.
64. Redpath, *Wisdom's Odyssey,* pp. 1–29, and Plato, *Apology,* 18B, and 21A–23E, *Ion,* 536A–D, *Meno,* 99D–100A, and *Phaedo,* 65B.

from things causally connected to such beings (a many). As I have said elsewhere, as envisioned by the ancient Greeks,

Philosophy is the highest form of unaided natural reasoning. It is the highest form of secular or pagan intellectual activity. From its own perspective, as an intellectual habit in a secular or pagan soul, philosophy cannot reasonably be expected to recognize any science higher than itself. In a Christian, philosophy can never exist as the highest human science. It must always exist in an ancillary position. This creates a problem. How can the habit of philosophical activity exist as an ancillary science and still remain philosophy? The only way it can do so is as the material object of a higher science, a science of revelation.[65]

In saying this, I do not deny that philosophy can exist apart from the influence of supernatural faith and theology. It can, in the soul of a non-believer or pagan. Nor do I deny that something akin to the habit the ancient Greeks called philosophy, that is open to, and ordered to, direction by a higher science, can exist in the Christian soul as a habit distinct from the supernaturally infused virtue of faith. It can. But since it operates in an ancillary position to the infused theological virtue of faith in its aims, method, and principles, the result is not univocally the same essence as Greek philosophy.

For the ancient Greeks, in the pagan soul, in its absolute or relative state, philosophy is a habit and activity totally unaided by any higher lights. In the Christian soul, philosophy must, as Gilson maintains, be open to Christian revelation's influence and theology's guidance, and supernatural faith must actually be present in the act of philosophizing. The person, not the faculty, is the knower. In a Christian philosopher, faith acts as a first principle of knowing present in the act of sensing and reasoning that intensifies a person's ability to discover, reason, and comprehend. Hence, in the Chris-

65. Ibid., p. 44.

tian philosopher, theology contains by way of eminence the natural habit of reasoning that the ancient Greeks called "philosophy."[66] As Gilson recognized, those who study the works of philosophers, or engage natural reasoning through first principles under the influence of faith within their faculties, do not mix water and wine. They change water into wine.[67]

To support my claims in the above paragraph, let us consider Gerald B. Phelan's succinct and lucid presentation of the Christian philosopher's procedure, a procedure I suspect many contemporary Thomists would accept. Phelan says:

Confronting the universe as it presents itself before him the philosopher asks questions—every question he can think of—and seeks to find answers that he can understand without relying upon the authority of anybody's word. . . . If the philosopher is also a man who has received the gift of faith he is aware that God would never teach what is false. Consequently, should his reflections lead him towards conclusions at variance with revealed truth, he realizes that he is on the wrong track and he will retrace his steps and subject his philosophical thinking to rigorous criticism until he finds the flaw in his thought.[68]

My question is: how is this possible? Gilson says that the *person* philosophizes, not a faculty or pure reason. If, as Phelan states, a philosopher "seeks to find answers that he can understand without relying upon the authority of anybody's word," are we to believe that the Christian philosopher can put a hold on supernaturally infused faith while philosophizing, as if all this involves is an act of intellectual abstraction through which we hold in abeyance the Holy Spirit's influx? If a person can so act, is that person actually a

---

66. See Gilson, *The Philosopher and Theology,* p. 100.

67. Ibid.

68. Gerald B. Phelan, "Philosophy and Theology—A Contrast," in *G. B. Phelan: Selected Papers,* ed. Arthur G. Kirn (Toronto: Pontifical Institute of Mediaeval Studies, 1967), pp. 171–73.

believer? If the person is a believer, then, according to Phelan's criteria, can that person's philosophy be anything other than pretension?

A person can be a believer and still argue impartially using as measures principles abstracted from an observation of the behavior of things. Indeed, faith improves our ability to abstract such principles. A philosophically trained believer will not include in philosophical argumentation premises related to scripturally revealed mysteries because these transcend the philosopher's natural ability to abstract from sensible images. Christians hold that grace perfects, but does not destroy, nature. But no Christian can do what Phelan apparently contends and Mortimer J. Adler asserts: "if he has faith, he must hold it in abeyance in order to proceed as a philosopher."[69] How? Would not such an ability to hold supernatural faith in abeyance require supernatural and miraculous power? Christians do not consider faith an obstacle to objectivity. It does not prevent us from accurately expressing philosophical principles. If what we believe is true, when we shine the light of faith's principles upon philosophical principles, we comprehend these principles more, not less, intensely. Christian philosophy is more than natural reasoning: natural reasoning under the influence of supernatural power. Hence, even if we could do it, why would any Christian want to suspend faith? Better to be inspired than to be a second-rate thinker.

To maintain that this sort of reasoning is identical with the natural philosophical mode of ancient Greek reasoning is misleading: somewhat like a professional athlete on steroids maintaining that his activity is completely natural, or merely *open* to artificial stimulants. When we use the term "philosophy" to refer to Christian philosophy and totally natural philosophical reasoning, we do so in a

69. Mortimer J. Adler, *Truth in Religion: The Plurality of Religions and the Unity of Truth* (New York, Macmillan, 1990), p. 45.

way similar to our application of the term "sighted" to a human being and a dog: analogously.

As a Christian philosopher, I think I do something more than
philosophical. Since measures must be homogeneous in nature with
the things measured, no purely philosophical or historical means exist to measure the truth claims of faith's influence on philosophical
acts. Such truth conditions transcend the ability of ordinary philosophical and historical experience. To attempt to measure them by
purely philosophical or historical means would be philosophically
unreasonable, as philosophically unreasonable as a philosopher's
claim that such transcendent truth conditions cannot possibly exist
because philosophy is the highest mode of knowing. While, for a
Christian, philosophical and historical experience belie such claims,
I think that, for the non-believer, such claims are, at best, hypotheti-
cal, not real, possibilities. As an excellent Christian philosopher and
Christian historian, Gilson could easily see Christian philosophy in
philosophy's history. Not so for a secular philosopher or historian or
a mediocre Christian scholar. If the history of philosophy teaches us
anything, it teaches us the limited range of philosophical and historical reason, even when working under faith's influence.

Only people with experience of an act are good judges of it. Just
as people with no experience at being just or courageous cannot re-
liably recognize such behavior, and are not good judges of it, so
people who do not try to philosophize under faith's influence are
not competent judges of its reality. We prove supernatural influences by apprehending or performing supernatural acts. Such acts,
however, need not be miraculous acts. They simply need to be ab-
normally improving and beyond ordinary natural ability. If saintly
people exist, and if the Church is God's main earthly reporter, then,
by constantly looking to saintly scholars and the Church to guide
us in our reasoning (like a myopic person who recognizes that his

or her vision is improved by putting on a pair of glasses), we avoid making a lot of stupid mistakes.

This does not mean that I think some grace of my own enables me to reason better than other thinkers or even better than myself without this grace. I am far from claiming that any direct infusion of grace improves my reasoning ability. I am more like a parasite, vicariously living off the grace-filled acts of others. My proof of grace's influence is the improvement I experience when I stand on the shoulders of faith-filled giants. They elevate me by their stature. I have direct experience that, with their help, philosophically, I imagine things more richly, understand things better, reason better, and am better at protecting myself from making philosophical errors, than I would be on my own or with the aid of secular intellects alone. I do not claim that this improvement makes me work better philosophically than a non-believer with a lot of natural ability and secular training. I simply know how my practice helps me, and, given my natural penchant to be dull-witted and make stupid mistakes, I shudder at working in any other way.

Still, as a Christian Scholastic, philosophizing within theology, my concern is not chiefly to defend or elucidate faith's scripturally revealed mysteries (*revelatum*). I am interested in seeking and defending truth as apprehensible by natural human reason through principles that I can naturally abstract from the behavior of sensible beings. These principles, in turn, not my faith, objectively measure for others (historical and philosophical observers) whether my philosophizing is any good. I consciously seek to defend or elucidate what the Church teaches insofar as this coincides with the truth I discover through principles I abstract from the being of things accessible to my natural reason and sense faculties strengthened by faith. As a Christian philosopher, my area of concern is *revelabilia*, not *revelatum*.

As a Christian philosopher, I know the answers to many of the major metaphysical and moral questions that puzzled the ancient Greeks. This poses another problem for me about thinkers who claim that the Christian philosopher seeks "to find answers that he can understand without relying upon the authority of anybody's word." I already know the answers to many of these questions before I start reasoning philosophically about them. As a Christian, the whole of my natural reasoning is in an ancillary position to the metaphysical principles I know by faith. How, then, can I actually find the answers to these without relying on anybody's word? How can I use the same abstractive method that other philosophers use when the way I abstract my principles essentially differs from the way they abstract theirs and I have God's Word that my metaphysical and moral principles are true?

Moreover, all philosophical principles are metaphysical principles or analogous transpositions of metaphysical principles to respective subject matters. Moral principles are not metaphysical principles, and physical principles are not moral ones. Nonetheless, these principles cannot nullify each other. The ancillary relation that the act of a philosophical habit always has within the Christian soul is an essential part of its being, not an accidental condition of its relative state. Christian philosophy considered in its absolute or pure state is philosophizing ordered to, and imbedded with, faith's grace. This is what gives it its Christian being and makes it Christian philosophical practice. Philosophy does not exist as the act of a habit in the Christian soul like mathematics exists within military science. Military science does not give the mathematician answers or hints to the questions that the mathematician seeks to answer. Nor does military science enter into the mathematical habit, infuse it with intelligible light, and intensify its activity's precision. Supernatural faith does all these things within the philosophical habit of the Christian philosopher.

As a result, as Pope Leo tells us, Christians who philosophize in this way engage in "the best way of philosophizing." This is the way I try to philosophize. How well I succeed at the practice I do not know. I do know that the attempt makes me more active, imaginative, inquiring, and original than I could be left to my own resources. For example, doing philosophy in this way has led me to interpret philosophy's history in a radically different way than most of my contemporaries. It has also led me to interpret the nature of Christian philosophy differently than do most of my contemporaries.[70]

Armand Maurer rightly cautions that "we who stand on the shoulders of giants are not giants ourselves."[71] I concur. This is especially true in my case. Still, even Lilliputians come in different sizes. I would rather be a philosophical Lilliputian standing on the shoulders of faith-filled, realist Lilliputians in touch with the being of things than a modern or postmodern giant walking in circles trying to drag Socratic reason out of the head of Protagoras. Whether I have chosen the better path is up to future Christian and non-Christian philosophers to answer.

70. See my *Masquerade of the Dream Walkers, Wisdom's Odyssey,* and *Cartesian Nightmare.*
71. Letter from Armand A. Maurer to Peter Redpath dated 1 December 1999.

*Mary Elizabeth Ingham, C.S.J.*

# 6. THE LOVE OF WISDOM AND
# THE DESIRE FOR GOD

ॐ

The question of the relationship of faith to the intellectual life is an intricate one. How one approaches it depends to a great extent upon a prior question, that is, the possibility that human reason is equipped with a capacity to understand reality. This possibility suggests multiple manners of approaching all that is. One of these manners involves taking seriously both personal experience of the transcendent and the data contained in revelation. Both refer to the realm of faith. In the case of the first, that of personal experience, it is often difficult to demonstrate or explain satisfactorily the content of what is experienced. Nonetheless, one does not doubt the fact of the experience, nor does one deem it a weakness not to be able to offer an exhaustive explanation. In the second, more traditional understanding of faith, the authority of Scripture is taken to record both the individual human experience of the writers and the inspiration of the Holy Spirit in revealing the divine intention operative in the history of salvation. In both cases, however, the requirements of coherence and consistency are used to validate the rational quality of the experiences, the way they are seen to make sense, either to oneself or to another.

I take it to be true that human reason is able to approach and make sense of what exists. Some of this sense-making results in deep understanding and exhaustive demonstration; some of it results in awareness of (apprehension) the existence of something, but not such profound understanding (comprehension) of its nature. Both are related to a deep sense of wonder before reality that completely transcends the capacity of human reason. My own growth in this sense of wonder has been fed by the insights of the medievals who understood both the distinction and the complementarity of the realms of faith and reason.

My first exposure to medieval thought was Dom Jean Leclerq's *The Love of Learning and the Desire for God*.[1] In this work, the Benedictine presented the principal insight of monastic scholarship: that the intellectual ascent to truth and, ultimately, to wisdom is central to the spiritual journey toward union with God. This insight has guided my work both as educator and as scholar for over twenty-five years. It informed my interest in medieval thinkers as religious who, like myself, sought to integrate their spiritual lives with their intellectual interests and pursuits.

More recently, I have to come to appreciate the work of Pierre Hadot, who currently calls our attention to the original vocation of the philosopher: not scholar but sage.[2] Hadot seeks to recapture the earliest understanding of the study of philosophy as an entry into a way of life richly satisfying and personally rewarding. Our challenge today, he asserts, is to rediscover the unity beneath two apparently different visions of philosophy. On the one hand, the discipline has scientific standards and exists as one scientific discourse among

1. Dom Jean Leclerq, *The Love of Learning and the Desire for God* (New York: Fordham University Press, 1961).

2. Pierre Hadot, *Qu'est-ce que la philosophie antique?* (Paris: Editions Gallimard, 1995).

many. It is a specialization, just as medicine and law are areas for concentrated study and research. Philosophy today can and does compete at the highest levels of research and speculation. Professional philosophical societies host conferences all over the world. On the other hand, philosophy continues to attract the non-specialist, who sees in it a way of spiritual enlightenment. In reading philosophical texts not as articles for publication but as records of the meditative journal of great minds, we discover the common human aspiration to understand the world and our place in it. Philosophy must be lived in order to be authentic.

Together, the scientific and existential dimensions of the love of wisdom reveal the deepest richness of human rationality. We are both theoretical and practical beings, and we seek to express our grasp of truth in the way we live our lives. As we enter the third millennium, with the imminent collapse of the modern Enlightenment project with its emphasis upon scientific objectivity and individual autonomy, we may have a remarkable opportunity to uncover the truth beneath both philosophical dimensions. This truth involves the spiritual nature of intellection.

To understand the spirituality inherent in the intellect is to grasp how the philosophical activities of investigation, critique, and speculation take place within the context of a much broader and foundational human aspiration that is religious in nature. Conversely, to understand the intelligence inherent in the human spirit and the desire for self-transcendence and communion is to recognize that the fullest experience of happiness requires the discovery of meaning, not merely in one's own life, but at a foundational level. In my reflections here I consider the mutual relationship of the love of wisdom called philosophy and the desire for God. I intend to proceed from within each of the two perspectives that make up this relationship. It is in their fragmentation or opposition to one another that the most important human vocation is frustrated. In other words, our coming to know God is itself accomplished in the search for wisdom.

## I. THE INTELLECTUAL AS SPIRITUAL

Pierre Hadot's work on ancient philosophy points to the original aspirations of philosophers: to provide rational salvation in a world of suffering and death. This salvation involved embracing a higher perspective, a philosophical way of life, whether Stoic, Epicurean, or Platonic. This original vocation is in part lost to us today as we witness the increased specialization and fragmentation within the academy. In philosophy itself, logical analysis figures as the central activity. Questions of more ultimate import have been increasingly located within the domain of the religious or spiritual, completely divorced from the intellectual and rational. Indeed, it is a common assumption of our university students today that believers generally do not need to think and thinkers do not need to believe.

When I say that ancient philosophers saw themselves as offering a type of spiritual salvation, I do not mean to suggest that they disregard soundness of argument or logical rigor. Rather, these techniques were understood within a much broader context framed by the ultimate questions of meaning, especially the broad issue of determinism versus human free choice. One obvious example of the balance between techniques and ultimate concerns can be found within Stoicism. The propositional logic of the Stoic thinkers and the advances they made on Aristotelian logic helped them deal specifically with issues of fate and free will. Stoics were able to make peace with the cosmic order of nature by means of careful study of the meaning of terms and the relationship of propositions to their referents. For them, the method of logical analysis played a central role within a much larger intellectual-spiritual journey to escape the caprice of fate. Reflection upon language and its relationship to reality was the ladder for transcendence to the realm beyond space and time, a ladder visually depicted on the tattered garment of Lady Philosophy in Boethius' classic *The Consolation of Philosophy,* Book I, I. The purpose of philosophy is to enable transcendence from the unpredictable world of human suffering to the world of changeless perfection.

A concrete example of the way in which philosophical questions are re-framed as questions of faith can be seen in the way human free will in light of fate or destiny appears to the believer. The perspective of belief transposes this question beyond the Stoic's "accepting what one cannot change." The question now touches the believer's relationship to God. For, if an impersonal divinity or divine plan governs all reality, then the only relationship would be conformity to the higher law. Additionally, if God were a personal being who only required unquestioning submission, then why would a believer want to cultivate any spiritual relationship inspired by love? Fear would be foundational to the spiritual life.

Let us consider how one's faith in a personal God informs both the purpose and the method of intellectual speculation. Take the question of free will. In the tradition of Christian reflection upon the exact nature of human freedom in light of divine omniscience, several assumptions frame the investigation. First, it is assumed that God is a personal being who loves us and wills our good. This insight is contained in revelation. Second, the existence of some human free choice is affirmed at the outset. While this too is contained in Scripture, it is also the result of logical argument (the critique of physicalism about the mind), and it recognizes the way societies are organized. As Aristotle states clearly in the *Nicomachean Ethics* Book II, 1, were human persons not in control of their actions, then neither praise nor blame would be appropriate.

No one would be punished for actions over which they had no control. Thus, for the philosopher, the affirmation of free will is a more rational position than its denial.

The interesting aspect of the fate/free will question for the believer, however, goes beyond that of finding a solution. True intellectual success here would involve finding a solution that, in fact, supports and reconciles the data of revelation about God's love, the predictability of the natural order, and the desire of human aspiration about the possibility of having some control over our own choices. Augustine's solution in the *City of God* uses logic to correct the way in which the problem results from a misunderstanding of the term *fate*.[3] Boethius offers the imagery of the higher divine perspective (the man in the tower) to reconcile temporal and eternal points of view.[4] This shift in perspective offers a solution based upon the way the situation would appear to someone inside of time and to another outside of time. Finally, the solutions of Aquinas and Ockham[5] depend upon the way in which God's knowledge of the future is understood to be necessary. In all four cases, the possibility for human free choice is defended in light of divine knowledge and, more importantly, divine goodness. These are clear examples of how intellectual reflection and analysis aids the spiritual journey in coming to a better understanding of concrete, human experience.

But the contemporary situation admits of another difficulty. The modern penchant to specialize narrows philosophy and separates it

---

3. *City of God*, Book V (New York: Penguin Classics 1980 ed.), pp. 188–96.

4. *Consolation of Philosophy*, Book IV (Chicago: Regnery Gateway, 1981), p. 84.

5. Aquinas, *Summa Theologiae*, Ia, q. 14, a. 13, trans. by the Dominican Fathers (New York: Image Books, 1969), pp. 42–46. Ockham, *Predestination, God's Foreknowledge and Future Contingents*, trans. Marilyn McCord Adams and Norman Kretzmann (Indianapolis: Hackett, 1983).

from the larger human questions about the meaning of life and the purpose of suffering. In such a separation, the domain of philosophy is re-defined to fit a curriculum where transcendence no longer has a place. Thus do we find excluded what can no longer fit into neat categories. As a result, one must justify on logical terms the broader context within which the philosophical method was meant to function. One is forced to demonstrate the larger by means of the smaller. Demonstrating why such questions are important or philosophically significant resembles the task of the liberated prisoner in Plato's *Allegory of the Cave.* How can one demonstrate to those chained in the cavern that an outside world does, indeed, exist?

Here we discover the greatest challenge to the philosopher who is a believer and who does not wish to separate her spirituality from her intellect. The challenge involves expanding the limited realm of philosophical inquiry beyond the empirical. The project requires a shift of perspective in order to see the activity of intellection as more than mere data gathering and analysis. Both ancient and medieval thinkers understood philosophy to promote not a theory or way of knowing, but a lived wisdom, a way of living according to reason.[6] Such a life involved a practical discernment of the value of things, where one could judge either according to the world (the visible or apparent) or according to the world to come (the spiritual or real). This discernment was key to the moral order and, ultimately, to happiness.

Centered around such an existential question (that of a happy life), medieval thinkers saw themselves involved in a reflection that transcended religious tradition and united all rational inquiry in a common human search. The philosophers and theologians of the

---

6. Leclerq, *The Love of Learning and the Desire for God,* p. 101.

twelfth and thirteenth centuries encountered something of a multi-cultural world. Although each culture was faithful to its own religious tradition, all realized the value of the intellectual contribution of the other as an expression of a much deeper intellectual spirituality. At that moment in history, Islamic, Jewish and Christian intellectuals formed a community of scholars around the Philosopher, Aristotle, himself seen by all three traditions as a "pagan." Thinkers within the Arab tradition happily integrated what they thought was an "Aristotelian theology" into their philosophical understanding. This theology was not Aristotelian, but Platonic and Neoplatonic. Thomas Aquinas was pleased to find the truth in all his sources and wrote with great respect of Rabbi Moses (Maimonides) and the Commentator Averroes (Ibn Rushd). Even Peter Abelard, famed logician of the twelfth century, wrote his *Dialogue between a Philosopher, a Christian and a Jew* to exemplify the points of contact between the major religious traditions of Judaism and Christianity, and the spiritual-philosophical tradition of Stoicism. The three partners in his discussion focus on natural law, human happiness and the greatest good. Each example (how Arabs read Aristotle, how Aquinas read Maimonides, and how Abelard read the relationship of various traditions) illustrates the way in which one might consider the intellectual ascent as a manifestation of a deeper spiritual journey that belongs to human rationality. Abelard provides a convergence of perspectives made possible by a deeper intellectual commitment to ultimate reality shared by philosophers, Christian and Jews.

My interest in ancient and medieval thinkers is fueled by a deep commitment to the harmony between the spiritual and intellectual. In these earlier voices there is no attempt to fragment aspects of human rationality into the opposed categories of *faith* and *reason*. Such a separation misrepresents how the human mind understands reality. There is not a category of propositions which we take on faith that constitute a parallel track to those propositions whose truth is known to us. Rather, as Augustine suggests in his *Confessions,* belief is itself a prelude to any intellectual endeavor. For what, if anything, do we hold to be true that has not been told to us by another?[7] Debaters take premises to be true at the outset. Many contemporary philosophers take it to be true that there is no transcendent dimension. Reflection upon what is given deepens human understanding. This means that rational reflection deepens faith. The relationship between faith and reason is better understood as an ascending spiral rather than parallel lines. At the outset, some information is given on the authority of another.

Consider, for example, the proposition "God is Love." Here, understanding functions at a superficial level of *the meaning of terms.* Once the terms of a proposition are understood, then the mind assents to the truth of the proposition as certain or based upon belief. But this assent is not the end; it too points beyond itself to further understanding and deeper assent. If, indeed, God is love, then we have reason to expect certain behaviors of God rather than others. We check our experience to see if we can produce verifiable evidence in favor of the divine essence as love. The process of such reflection leads naturally to deeper and deeper understanding of the nature of God and of the divine relationship to us and to the world. Thus, as Bonaventure would say, does apprehension of truth give way to its comprehension, by means of rational reflection. Comprehension is itself foundational for a different sort of faith-stance, one that resembles confidence or trust in another. Here is the *engagement* of existentialism. At this point, the person is ready for a commitment based not upon certainty but upon the confidence of

7. *Confessions,* Book VI, 5 (New York: Penguin Classics 1988), p. 117.

friendship. This commitment involves more than mere intellectual assent to a proposition about the divine essence (love), but also involves an existential acknowledgment that expresses itself in trust. Here I not only think that God is love, but my actions are informed by my confidence that, in everything I do, the divine loving presence accompanies and sustains me. This awareness expresses itself in an attitude of presence to the world that reflects a deeper understanding and can itself be the object of reflection and self-awareness. I understand my assent/engagement as the fruit of a journey that began on the basis of faith, yet grew and deepened because of the skills of reflection and awareness.

Such an understanding sees the relationship of faith and the intellectual life as organic in nature. It is a dynamic manifestation of reason that develops through moments of questioning, certainty, risk, trust, and conviction. It does not isolate the operations of the intellect from other human experiences, especially emotional experiences. It is unifying and integrating because reason seeks the whole. One impoverishes both faith and reason, I believe, to set them either in opposition to one another or in a linear relationship where one must claim superiority. The result would be to view faith either as the fairy tale of the poor (Ibn Rushd), the opiate of the people (Marx), or as belonging to a domain so vastly superior to reason that we cannot even understand what it is we believe (Tertullian, Meister Eckhart).

The dynamic relationship between the intellectual and spiritual suggests that all areas of human life belong to the domain of the rational. Human emotions, for example, are potentially rational insofar as they lie within self-awareness and can be integrated into the *engagement* referred to earlier. All that is human belongs (at least potentially) to the rational whole. This insight opens contemporary philosophy to include the emotional both as reflective of the human experience and as potentially rational, insofar as my emotions register my interaction with the world around me and are part of my own self-reflection. In addition, the insight challenges us to view the aesthetic/poetic as more-than-merely-subjective response to what is pleasing. Here again, medieval thinkers hold a wealth of resources yet to be reclaimed by contemporary scholars. Spiritual writers like Hildegard of Bingen, Bonaventure, and Duns Scotus link the spiritual to the aesthetic. The discovery of beauty requires a spiritual intellection, a higher sense that is prelude to the beatific vision.

Our era witnesses the return of spiritual awareness in popular circles. After four centuries of rationalist, modern philosophy, the domain of the transcendent has been rediscovered. This new spirituality, if it is to offer the integration so deeply needed today, must not neglect the intellectual/rational dimension so vital to true human fulfillment.

## II. THE SPIRITUAL AS INTELLECTUAL

At the end of the eighth book of the *Confessions,* Augustine refers to an experience that he considered to be the existential culmination of his years of intellectual search. Shortly before his death, Thomas Aquinas is reputed to have abandoned his project of the *Summa Theologiae* on the grounds that it was "all straw." In 1932, Edith Stein put aside her scholarly career to enter the Carmelite monastery of Cologne. In all three cases, and in many more, both well known and anonymous, the journey of intellectual questioning and development led more deeply into an arena of faith-experience. This movement of deeper penetration into the spiritual guided the intellectual until, at a precise moment, the domain of the transcendent so completely overshadowed the capacities of intellectual analysis and explanation that the individual could not speak of the experience in any way that would do it justice. Silence was the only appropriate response.

The domain of the spiritual, within which faith is a central element, expresses itself intellectually in the major questions asked, the over-arching themes that recur, and the manner by which the goal of the human journey is conceived. The remarkable story of Augustine illustrates this most clearly. It is also here that my Catholic Christian identity plays the most significant role. The rational optimism of the Catholic intellectual tradition has always informed and guided my work. This rational optimism refers to the conviction that questions do have answers. The optimism points to the way in which every question expects and anticipates a certain sort of answer. The only acceptable answer is the one that satisfies *this particular question* and not another, similar one. Questions, then, are self-transcending activities; they point beyond themselves to a greater reality whose contours are suspected and anticipated but not fully grasped. As such, the so-called *ultimate* questions (the meaning of life, the nature of evil, the nature of God, the possibility of immortality) are human intellectual questions that point to the existence of answers we may not yet fully grasp.

This optimism refers as well to the natural human capacity to know and love God. We can never know God completely, that is, in terms of God's own self-knowledge. But we can know those truths of God that come as the result of reflection upon our experiences, especially those experiences where we are conscious that we are not alone. Scripture offers evidence of encounters with the divine in which we may indeed see our own life parallels—Jacob's wrestling with the angel, Joseph's reconciliation with his brothers, Mary's encounter with Jesus at the empty tomb. The history of Christianity thrives on these and other stories of individuals who had common and extraordinary experiences, and who interpreted them as encounters with God. We have our saints and our martyrs.

The necessity of multiple witnesses points as well to the value found in many perspectives of human experiences of the divine. In a manner similar to the multiplicity of intellectual approaches, the spiritual too can accommodate a variety of cultural vantage points. Here I do not merely point to the many members of the Judeo-Christian tradition who have gone before us, but indeed to all human persons. Christianity may make a privileged claim about the basic message that Jesus is Lord, but this message can be seen to ground all other spiritual and religious experiences. In other words, if "God loved the world so much that He sent his only Son" (Jn 3:16) then the nature of God is love and generosity. This love and generosity have been given specific expression in the person of Jesus Christ, but this is not to say that other religious or spiritual experiences outside of Christianity are false. One can argue for the value of all religious traditions and still claim that there is a specificity to the Christian revelation.

The centrality of the Incarnation is a singular aspect of the project of John Duns Scotus, both as philosopher and as theologian. In his discussion of the difference between philosophy and theology, Scotus considers the role of *formal object* or manner of consideration in any activity of human reflection. For the philosopher, the ultimate reality, the ground of being, is understood as *ens infinitum* or infinite being. This term stands at the limit of human reflection unaided by any revelation. For the believer, God's self-revelation to Moses in Exodus 3:14 stands in remarkable complementarity to the fruit of philosophical investigation. When God chooses the term "I am Who am" as the most appropriate mode for self-revelation, the believer is provided a referent for a philosophical concept. This referent is *ultimate being,* at once personal and capable of self-manifestation. In addition, this ultimate personal reality longs for friendship and relationship with humanity. All the attributes philosophers logically hold to belong to such an ultimate being (necessity, unity, perfection) continue to belong to such a personal being. The believer does not dismiss the value of philosophical conclusions, but he recognizes as well the particular and specific contribution of revelation.[8]

Today, such an insight about complementary perspectives is timely. It points to the value of affirming all cultures in their particular manifestation of the spirituality of the intellect. Multiple perspectives are necessary because, first, the individual human mind is limited and, second, the reality that we would understand far surpasses our ability to do so fully.[9] Thus, scholarship is not an individual endeavor of discovery, but a conversation with earlier generations and with other cultures. The purpose of the conversation is not the acquisition or possession of quantities of information, but the transformation of the knower. This transformation is an intellectual-spiritual dynamic of growth into a dimension that is *personalized,* a reality filled with other persons.

Here we see clearly the contribution of the Judeo-Christian tradition. The central insight of the tradition affirms that the transcen-

8. *Treatise on God as First Principle,* trans. Allan B. Wolter (Quincy, Ill.: Franciscan Press, 1966).

9. Aquinas makes this point very clearly in his *Commentary on Aristotle's Metaphysics II,* lectio 1, nn. 276–288. See, for example: "In spite of the fact that what one human being is able to contribute to the understanding of the truth, by means of his own study and talent, is something small by comparison to the whole consideration of the truth, nevertheless, what comes together from all the collected partial views becomes something big. . . . While each of the predecessors has discovered something of the truth, the product of all these discoveries brought together into one leads posterity to a great knowledge of the truth." Rowan translation (Chicago: Regnery 1961), pp. 116–19.

dent is a personal being. The record of divine initiative contained in Scripture grounds the natural human intuition about being with a divine guarantee. One could reflect upon the ontological categories independently of revelation, but the fact that revelation offers its own secondary support of this intellectual activity transforms the meditation from mere introspection to an activity of transcendence, an activity that is itself a bridge to an encounter with a personal God. In this way, the spiritual integrates the intellectual within a much larger human activity. Thus does faith enlighten the intellect.

In addition to the centrality of divine initiative, the recognition of a triune deity further specifies the nature of this God with whom we are in contact. Thus does relationship become necessary not only for human survival but, as Aristotle states, for living well. Relationship mirrors divine life. Self-gift, the love of friendship, generosity are not simply luxuries. They constitute the human spiritual journey and, in relationship to the divine, are its fullest expression.

Finally, the important insight of divine initiative transforms the human journey from attainment to response. Our fullest experience of happiness is to be found, neither in making ourselves worthy of the divine, nor in self-perfection. The key to the spiritual journey is openness to receive the gift of life, of love, of divine generosity.

Within the larger view of Christianity, aspects of the human person are significant because they mirror the divine: relationship is central, generosity is the model for love, delight is the fullest human experience of satisfaction. For the medieval discussion of happiness, the experience of *frui Deo* or delight in God was central to sanctity. When we lose sight of these key insights centered in revelation, we fall prey to the temptations of the modern world: autonomy replaces relationship as the moral goal, acquisition is the model for perfection, and self-divinization is principle and measure for human fulfillment.

So, in light of all this, can a Christian be a philosopher? I take the term *philosopher* in a primary sense, as one who loves and seeks wisdom. As a philosopher, the Christian seeks a particular and specific wisdom, identical with the God revealed in Jesus Christ. For Justin Martyr in his *Second Apology*,[10] this wisdom was the fullness of divinity sought by Socrates and Plato. For Clement of Alexandria, the earliest yearnings of lovers of wisdom were only to be realized in Christianity as true philosophy.[11] For Paul, it was the recognition that the "unknown God" of the Athenians was indeed the God revealed to Abram, Isaac, and Jacob. For Thomas Aquinas, it was the connection between that which "all call God" in the *Five Ways* and the One Who Is. Finally, for Duns Scotus, it was the realization that the goal of metaphysical speculation, *ens infinitum*, was the starting point for theological reflection. Theology begins precisely where philosophy leaves off. Faith specifies what reason encounters.

Theology, however, as an activity of human reflection, does not exhaust the reality under consideration. Moses Maimonides and, to a lesser extent, Thomas Aquinas point clearly to the limits of language and predication when it comes to explaining the divine. For Rabbi Moses, language must stop as soon as the existence of the divinity has been affirmed, because this being has "nothing in common with the beings he has brought into existence, nothing in common with them in any respect."[12] Thomas is willing to allow

10. St. Justin Martyr, *Second Apology*, Fathers of the Church, vol. 6 (Washington, D.C.: Catholic University of America Press, 1948), pp. 129–30.

11. *Stromata*, Book VI, 7 in *Greek and Roman Philosophy after Aristotle*, ed. Jason L. Saunders (New York: Free Press, 1966), pp. 319–22. In this work, Clement uses Aristotle to place faith at an intermediate level between initial knowledge and deeper understanding. Faith is that voluntary assent necessary for any scientific inquiry, in the manner of accepting the truth of first principles.

12. *Guide for the Perplexed*, I, 58, in *Philosophy in the Middle Ages*, ed. A. Hyman and J. J. Walsh (Indianapolis: Hackett, 1984), pp. 381–84.

language a larger role, all the while agreeing that no human word is sufficient to represent God to the human mind. All names referring to God "signify the divine substance, but in an imperfect manner."[13]

For Maimonides, the Divine Being lies so far beyond the limits of human understanding that no exercise of rational reflection suffices to bring us to union, not even the activity of negation. For Aquinas, human understanding in its fallen state is so dependent upon creatures that anything we can assert about God must be done on the basis of our understanding of the world around us. Our awareness of the limitation of human cognition supports and informs our affirmations about the divine.

This does not imply that at a certain point the believer ceases to think. Rather, faith focuses on the content of the intellectual journey, on the First Mover, First Efficient, Necessary Being, Infinite, One. In the pattern of friendship, there is not only the affirmation of the existence of the other, but the mutual self-revelation that enables a deeper, interpersonal encounter, as in Martin Buber's *I-Thou* relationship. At this point a threshold has been crossed. Something has been revealed that is new. This new revelation must now become the focus for understanding and reflection. What had previously been the *intellectual*-spiritual now is transformed into the *spiritual*-intellectual. The dynamic remains; the emphasis has shifted.

In Scotus's work *De Primo Principio,* he claims that the notion of *ens infinitum* is an empty concept to the philosopher, an abstract category that is the culmination of the journey of intellectual reflection upon being *(ens)* as the natural object of the human mind. There is no contradiction in bringing together being *(ens)* and infi-

---

13. *Summa Theologiae,* Ia, q. 13, a. 2.

nite *(infinitum)* as a mode of intensity. The mind detects no dissonance between these two terms; they are therefore logically possible.

But the move from the logically possible to the actual requires an
experience. This experience must come from divine initiative for
self-revelation, for how can one be known in the absence of self-
disclosure? Scripture records events of encounter with the divine.
These events serve as models in our effort to understand our own
inner experience. In the most silent moments within our hearts we
recognize that we are not alone. Thus do both philosophy and revelation support a deeper comprehension of an intensely personal experience, one that exceeds the mind's own ability to explain.

### III. REFLECTIONS

In light of these comments, I would describe the relationship between faith and research in my own life to be one of mutuality of
influence. I accept the harmony between the spiritual and intellectual journeys. My areas of research interest are strongly informed by
my own spiritual concerns: the primacy of interpersonal over individual, the possibility of beauty as a moral category, the experience
of delight and creativity as revealing the divine presence within. In
all these aspects, medieval thinkers offer the most promising resource. All of them, Christian, Islamic, Jewish, take it to be true
that there is a larger spiritual dimension and that this dimension is
rational and personal. They hold themselves to the requirements of
logic and reasonableness. They fall neither to the extreme of fideism
nor to immanentism.

Specifically, the Christian thinkers seek to identify what precisely
distinguishes their religious perspective from others. In doing so,
they identify what all share. For Thomas Aquinas it was the rationality of doctrine that enabled him to use the work of Moses Maimonides, Averroes and even Aristotle himself. In his use of such

sources, both religious and non-religious, Thomas affirms the grounding of the spiritual in the rational. In his discussion of perfect happiness *(beatitudo)* he shows how the highest rational experience is indeed the ultimate spiritual experience and grounded in Scripture of the Beatitudes. Early in his commentary on the *Physics,* Thomas notes the need to study natural science, since it is easier to make mistakes about God when one is mistaken about the natural order.

For Duns Scotus it was precisely the distinctive character of Christianity that guided his use of other thinkers. This led him both to affirm the natural, metaphysical order of all being and to point to those particular aspects of revelation needed to confirm what we suspect but cannot prove. Among these are truths about God's free choice to create our world, to enter into contact with Moses and Abram, and finally, to become incarnate. These truths are coherent. They seem also too good to be true.

The ascent to and experience of the divine within the self brings together both spiritual and intellectual journeys. For the Christian, the insight that God dwells within opens the philosophical command to "Know Thyself" as no mere self-absorption. Self-knowledge is the key to awareness of God's existence, the first step in the journey of transcendence. And, as with Augustine, the discovery of the divine presence within the human heart requires a conversion of attitude and life, a re-ordering of values in light of the ultimate value. For Scotus, the realization that the Incarnation lies at the heart of the divine relationship with the world (and not, as Anselm said, in view of an act of ultimate reparation) cannot leave us unchanged. If this world possesses such value that God desired from the beginning to take flesh with us, then we cannot treat creation as a means to our ends. The value of this created order, the value of each person as *imago dei,* the value of community as mirror of divinity, the value of human action as an incarnation of value in imitation of divine creativity: these insights emerge as the fruit of reflection and revelation.

But the project has its limits, as Aquinas, Maimonides, and Bonaventure would be quick to point out. Language is not enough. Human reason cannot come to the end of an analysis of Mystery. The silence of Bonaventure on the seventh day of the *Itinerarium Mentis ad Deum,* the silence of Aquinas at the end of his life, the continual appeal of Rabbi Moses that we do better to negate, rather than affirm, truths about God—these are the silences of those who have met the Holy and whose intellectual careers have been transformed by the encounter. Here is a final silence that can speak but refuses to dare reduce so great a mystery to the poverty of human language. Here is a silence that affirms both the grandeur of the Other and the limits of the self.

*Mary F. Rousseau*

# 7. FAITH FINDING UNDERSTANDING

❧

My faith and my intellectual life began to come together shortly after my conversion to Catholicism, though I didn't know it at the time. For what was to be my intellectual, specifically philosophical, life began the day I entered my Catholic high school. The Leonine Revival was at its high point in North America. Seminaries and houses of religious formation based their teaching of the faith on the philosophy of St. Thomas Aquinas. That philosophy, thus, was part and parcel of the lives of the nuns and priests who were my teachers. *Mutatis mutandis,* it was the usual content of the catechesis of children, of Sunday sermons, of advice in confession, of marriage preparation, and of the instruction of converts. It was reinforced by Catholic books, newspapers, and magazines. It was to become the focus of my entire intellectual life.

In fact, it had already been implicit in my preparation for Baptism, just prior to my beginning high school. That preparation was a fifteen-month series of weekly catechical sessions with an Oblate of Mary Immaculate. He, too, had been formed by the philosophy of Thomas Aquinas. The instruction he gave was unashamed apologetics, following the Baltimore Catechism. Its implicit Thomism, I am convinced, is one reason that the gift of faith entered my conviction with ease. For Thomism is first and foremost a philosophy of common sense, showing the truth and goodness of the daily lives of ordinary people.

The *Summa Theologiae* is, indeed, a philosophical counterpart to Aaron Copland's "Fanfare for the Common Man." Its originating data, the stuff of its philosophical reflection, is not the esoteric result of science or mathematics or semiotics, but the ordinary daily perceptions of the world of ordinary people. It does not originate in the private intuitions of an individual, nor in an analytic deconstruction of texts. It does not require us to deny the truth of our ordinary experience of the world in favor of a contrived empiricism. Nor does it require that we somehow justify the use of our minds prior to, and thus without, our using them. The originating data of Thomistic philosophy—*pace* a common misunderstanding—do not come from the decrees of a pejoratively authoritarian Church. They are, instead, the ordinary, straightforward perceptions of our common daily world, most fundamentally the sheer facts of the multiplicity and mutability of the things we see and hear and feel.

Thomistic method, moreover, is not complex or highly specialized. It is the logic discovered and transmitted by Aristotle, which has persisted to this day because it conforms to the natural tendencies and capabilities of the human mind. As the late Professor Julius Weinberg put it to me in conversation some years ago, "I like to read the Scholastics because they always try to make sense. They don't always succeed, but they try. That is more than can be said of some of our more recent philosophers."

Not for me, then, as an adolescent convert to Catholicism, the doubts and difficulties about Catholic faith that seemed to torment some others. It all seemed true at first hearing, and does to this day. Nor did I suffer the notorious anguish of "Catholic guilt" imposed by harsh and judgmental priests. Catholic life was, from the start, all about love—God's love for us, and our love for God and each other. Thus, I also made an easy entry into the sacramental life of the Church—daily Mass, weekly confession, and regular spiritual reading. Given what I had come to believe, it seemed the obvious thing to do, and does to this day.

What thus began in my baptismal instruction, without my explicit realization at the time, was a love affair with logic applied to everyday life. My desire to become a Catholic arose while I was living in an abusive foster home, having lost my parents traumatically and then being separated by 1000 miles from the rest of my family. The abuse was verbal—explicit, frequent, and sustained, and it produced in me an inordinate need to seek elsewhere for some basic rational order in my daily life. That need eventually developed into a more explicit desire to know what is and is not real, especially as regards human love and human relationships. That drive, in its turn, was later transformed into an enthusiasm for metaphysics, not as an abstract mind-game, but as an ever-deeper entry into the mystery of Being.

A Freudian might say that I was seeking an unhealthy escape from my painful daily reality. But what I consciously experienced was an intellectual comfort that continues to this day. In high school, my teachers, all products, as I said, of an implicitly Thomistic religious and priestly formation, showed me a real and obvious love, simply by treating me as they did everyone else, with basic human decency and respect. They had no knowledge of my home life. But they made me feel loved when no one else was doing so. They knew that God is Love, and their love made that God credible to me. I admired my teachers and became attached to them. Again, a Freudian might say that I was unconsciously seeking my missing mother and father, to fill in these gaps of my adolescent psychological life. But what I consciously experienced was the simple reality of human love. Love of God and love of neighbor—that is how those teachers *actually lived.* Given what they knew and believed, it was the only thing to do. They certainly saved my sanity and my faith, and quite possibly my life as well.

They also set me on the intellectual path that I was to follow through all my adult life. Without thinking that they were doing anything special, they gave us, their students, an excellent intellectual formation. In a parish high school that was quite ordinary for its time, we received four years of Latin, four of English, and two of French. We had three years of mathematics and one of chemistry; three years of history and one of sociology; and, of course, four years of religious instruction. The languages stood me in good stead in my subsequent graduate studies in philosophy. But I, all unknowing, also met some of the content of Thomistic philosophy in my sophomore sociology and senior religion courses. Sociology was not what currently passes under the name—an uncritical, value-free cataloging of various social arrangements. It was, rather, Thomistic social ethics, taught from papal encyclicals. We actually read *Rerum novarum, Quadragesimo anno,* and *Casti connubii.*

Of course our understanding of these documents was sophomoric. But we received the lasting impression that they were true and good and important for our lives. Hence, recent discussions in these areas have not come as news to me. I have known for fifty years the arguments that workers have rights: a right to work, a right to part ownership in the enterprise that employs them, a right to a family wage, and a right to organize and strike so as to secure these other rights. I subsequently learned that these teachings are all rooted in St. Thomas' "Treatise on Justice" in the *Summa.* Nor did *Humanae vitae* take me by surprise in 1967. I had known the teaching against contraception for twenty years. More recently, I have seen it argued more cogently, in *Love and Responsibility.* Its author, who now sits on the throne of Peter, was at the time of its writing one of the Thomist philosophers at the Catholic University of Lublin.

Our senior Religion class was also implicitly Thomistic. Its focus was moral decision making, not mere "values clarification," but a model which I was later to recognize in St. Thomas' "Treatise on Law" and "Treatise on Prudence" in the *Summa*. Our priest didn't tell us his source. He simply said, "Here's how to make your moral decisions," and gave us the model. We then made applications and practiced with examples. We considered object, end, circumstances, and consequences of concrete moral acts and evaluated them by applying the secondary and primary precepts of the Natural Law. We were expected to apply this model in our lives and to structure the confession of our sins accordingly.

This model of moral decision making, St. Thomas' prudential judgment, has stood me in good stead ever since. It all made sense to me. It seemed right and true and good. Its entry into my mind was also made easy because it was modeled in the justice, the prudence, and the chastity of my teachers. I later gained a more explicit and more refined understanding of it, thanks to my college and graduate school studies of St. Thomas. But I have never had to replace it by something better.

Needless to say, I haven't always abided by that model. But I have always known how to decide moral matters. Time and again I have been able to approach our current moral problems—such complexities as artificial reproduction, nuclear defenses, a global capitalist economy, variations on the traditional family—with confidence that there are reasonable and true answers to them. We need not despair in advance of knowing how to live in this age of technology. On the one hand, we are not reduced to a "cookie-cutter" morality that mindlessly applies abstract medieval principles to the concrete realities of our postmodern lives. But neither are we condemned to flounder in endless, unresolvable considerations of the circumstances of unique moral events that have no intrinsic moral value and no transcendent norms.

Thus I had handed to me on a platter what I have seen many colleagues struggle for. The prudential judgment of St. Thomas does not yield mathematical certitude. But it gives a reasonable assurance of moral truth that enables us to act, confident enough in the rightness of our judgments as to make a life of human virtue possible. Moral judgments are not expressions of volatile feelings or subjective opinions, nor mere variations in the uses of language. They truthfully state that things are the way they are—human nature, human destiny, and human actions as the path to that destiny. They are founded on ontological truth, a truth that is quite accessible to the minds of all who sincerely seek it.

When I took this religious and intellectual background to Creighton University, every student—whether in business, pharmacy, journalism, nursing, pre-law or pre-medicine, or the liberal arts—was required to take a sequence of five courses in the philosophy of St. Thomas Aquinas. The late, great Father Henri Renard, S.J., was there then, and in his prime. Father Renard was one of the early heroes in the struggle to bring genuine existential Thomism to this country, by way of the Gregorian University in Rome.

I was privileged to have him as a professsor in only one course. But all sections of all five of the courses required in the core curriculum were taught out of his textbooks: *The Philosophy of Being, The Philosophy of Man, The Philosophy of God, The Philosophy of Morality,* and *The Philosophy of Conduct.* These pioneering books had their weaknesses, as did their teachers. But such a sequence of five coherent courses, almost unheard of today, had the advantage of taking us deeply enough into a single philosopher's system to see it *as* a system. Moreover, we learned one possible philosophical method as a mode of thought, which made other philosophers accessible as well. My subsequent experience, many times over, has been that Thomists are more open to the thought of other philosophers than other philosophers are to Thomism. Thanks to Father Renard and his books, I became instantly and permanently enamored of metaphysics, which answered to my drive to make sense out of daily life.

The one course I had from him was on the "Treatise on Grace" in the *Summa*. That treatise had been influential at the Council of Trent, whence came, eventually, the catechism that had drawn me into the Catholic Church. And so, in this intelligent theology of the spiritual life, one that was not embarrassed to use philosophy as its handmaiden, the reciprocal influence of my faith and my intellectual life reached a new depth. My academic life continued to grow out of my living the sacramental life of the Church. As I had no practical life-goals in mind (the possibility of college teaching hadn't occurred to me, nor had it been suggested), I became a double major in my first two loves, Latin and philosophy. I graduated, and kept my day job as a waitress.

Soon after, an unexpected opportunity to teach philosophy arose when the only philosophy teacher at a local women's college became ill in the middle of a semester. I was pressed into service to finish her logic course. My first day in the classroom convinced me of a vocation to teach philosophy, and so I did, for three more years. Then I married a Thomist metaphysician and began doctoral studies at Marquette University while also teaching at local colleges. My husband, who has always found the motivation for his intellectual life in his faith and the sacramental life of the Church, had done his doctoral studies at Fordham University. Among his professors were Dr. Elizabeth Salmon and Dr. Anton Pegis, as well as Dr.

Emmanuel Chapman and Dr. Dietrich von Hildebrand. When I enrolled at Marquette University, it was also a center of the Leonine Revival. My professors were such notable Thomists as Drs. Beatrice Zedler, James Robb, Charles O'Neill, Marc Griesbach, and the Jesuit Fathers Gerard Smith, Thomas Davitt, and Francis Wade. I also knew and associated with Drs. Donald Gallagher, James F. Anderson, and John Riedl. Indeed, beyond the philosophy department, the entire atmosphere of the university at that time was the intellectual life as inspired by Catholic faith.

Early in my graduate studies, the wounds of my earlier psychological abuse found a healing that made my adult intellectual life possible. Its instrument was, once again, the sacraments of the Church, notably Jesuit spiritual direction in the context of confession, given by a theologian with a strong Thomistic background. This confessor quickly identified in me a deep and pervasive self-seeking that threatened, first of all, to be a major barrier to increasingly intimate relationships with both my husband and with God. The abuse I had suffered as a child and adolescent (as does any abuse) had left me with inordinate needs for success and approval, thus causing a near constant self-absorption and efforts to use other people as means to meeting those needs. He encouraged me to make these wounds matter for confession and spiritual direction— not necessarily as voluntary sins, but as psychological disorders that were genuine barriers to more loving, trusting relationships with God, my husband, and other people. These emotional bonds would also have seriously distorted my intellectual life, or, more likely, made it impossible. For any intellectual life requires a certain measure of objectivity and self-forgetfulness.

Over a period of several years, with the help of guided readings, this Jesuit brought me to a psychological healing and liberation that astonishes me to this day. We read three books by Josef Goldbrunner, the Dominican (thus Thomist) theologian and Jungian analyst: *Cure of Mind, Cure of Soul; Holiness is Wholeness;* and *Individuation*. Goldbrunner's pages on *persona* construction and the dissolution of a *persona* struck me as my exact psychological biography, written by someone who had never met me. But then, Goldbrunner had learned that two kinds of people are especially susceptible to *persona* construction: religious believers and professional people. And I was aiming to be both.

Faith thus became a deeper *fons et origo* of my professional philosophical life. For through this healing, my intellectual life not only became possible, but found its permanent specific focus in Thomistic personalism. As we progressed, my confessor and I looked at my motivation for teaching, and my reasons for finding it so gratifying. Without denying the conscious motivation of my faith and love of God, we found it mixed with less healthy, less genuine elements, such as the need for a sense that I could do *something* right, and to some degree a flight from reality into abstractions. But as I took some small steps towards seeking "not so much to be loved as to love," in the words of the prayer attributed to St. Francis of Asissi, my philosophical focus on Thomistic personalism was sharpened.

I asked myself, for the first time, not "What can I do successfully?" but "What do my students need from me?" I was encouraged to stay with Thomistic metaphysics, since my talents and training therein met a genuine need of my students. I soon saw, however, that they did not need what I most enjoyed at the time: abstract and abstruse arguments for the existence of God, the freedom of the will, the immortality of the soul, and the truth of the existential judgment. These would come back into the picture later, in more existential fashion. But my undergraduate students, for the most part, were not going to be professional philosophers, or even philosophy majors. All of them, however, were going to be someone's friends, and most of them someone's spouses and parents. What my students needed more immediately was something that was nowhere offered in their entire curriculum: careful reasoned reflection on the daily realities of ordinary life, such as friendship, love, sex, marriage, and family life.

But could such topics be done philosophically? Were they appropriate for "serious" philosophy? Were usable teaching materials available? Would they be seen, by those on whom my professional security and progress depended, as girlish fluff? (What eventually came to be true didn't occur to me at that time. Thanks to recent massive cultural shifts such topics as love and sex and marriage are widely regarded, even by professional philosophers, as beyond the pale of any intellectually serious consideration. Recently a colleague, reading a dissertation on the Thomistic notion of creation, referred to a section comparing that doctrine to neo-Platonic emanationism as "religious pieties" not worthy of inclusion in a dissertation. And this respected colleague is more of a metaphysician than many in our profession). To my shame, I had not yet discovered Plato's *Lysis,* Aristotle's treatise on friendship in the *Ethics,* or Marx's *Holy Family.* Indeed, as recently as six years ago Michael Pakaluk gave us a still badly needed anthology of writings on friendship throughout the history of western philosophy, *Other Selves.*

But in this practical dilemma, I was once again saved by three books recommended by my confessor: Jean Mouroux's *The Meaning of Man;* Robert Johann's *The Meaning of Love;* and Abel Jeannière's *The Anthropology of Sex.* Mouroux's book is a Thomistic theology of the human person. But Thomistic theology, done correctly, presupposes Thomistic philosophy, in this case, a metaphysics of the human person. Mouroux makes his philosophy explicit, in a separate section of each chapter, so that the Thomistic synthesis of faith and philosophy is immediately evident. One whose interest is merely philosophical finds in Mouroux's pages an obvious and integral philosophical personalism. Its central point is the overcoming of ontological solitude through a communion with other persons in love.

Johann's book is entirely philosophical, an explicit metaphysics of love according to the questions on love in the *Summa*. His main point, a continuing key point for my purposes, is that every human person suffers from an ontological loneliness, thanks to his individuality, that can only be healed by communion with others. Such communion comes about in only one way: through *amor amicitiae* (literally, *loving love*). One who exercises such love takes the well-being of another as his own end or good, willing it to the other for the other's sake. He thereby comes to possess that other's good without losing his own, thus expanding his own existence beyond his original ontological limits. His loneliness is thus healed, to the extent of his loving in each situation. Moreover, thanks to the unity of the many beings of our world, each act of love of any single entity has the potential to be a communion with all of reality, God included.

Jeannière's book comes out of the French existentialist school, with a strong dose of Heidegger, taking sexual intimacy as a healing of our ontological loneliness. Here, the healing comes about through our appropriating, by personal choice, the nature that is ours by birth: a human nature both desirous and capable of such an intimacy. One common mode of this appropriation is sexual union motivated by love rather than self-seeking. This book, then, is quite consonant with Mouroux on human fulfillment and Johann on the healing of ontological loneliness. But Jeannière gives these a focus on the sexual that has important implications for marriage and family life.

The central notion grounding these three studies is St. Thomas' *amor amicitiae* (whose English equivalent I still seek; the modifier is an intensifying formation from the same root as the noun). This primary, genuine, most perfect form of love consists in wishing to someone his own well-being for his own sake. We thus make him, not ourselves, the ultimate end/final cause of our actions toward him. Once we thus identify his good as our good, too, then thanks to the realism of willing, it becomes ours. That single good held in common binds us in a real, existential unity that enhances our own individual reality. To apply this analysis to Aristotle's homely example, a mother staying up to care for a sick child *for the child's sake* really possesses his restored health as her good, too. It is a common good that binds the two in a true, existential unity.

This *amor amicitiae* of *S. Th.* I–II, 26–28 is fundamentally similar to Aristotle's friendship of the third kind, in which the one who makes himself the friend of another becomes his own best friend in the process. Such love is both ecstatic and unitive, unitive by reason of being ecstatic. It is not masochistic, for with it we welcome the reciprocity of the one we love. We also cherish our own self-development, so as to have something to give to the one we love. But despite its being self-fulfilling, it is not self-serving. For once we seek it for our own sake, it ceases to be *amor amicitiae*. It becomes, instead, *amor concupiscentiae,* a desirous love. We then wish a friend his well-being for our own sake. We make his good a means and our own good the end/final cause of our benevolence. We then have what is rightly called an ulterior motive, and fail to generate a common good which could bind us into a real union with our friend. For in desirous loving, the good I wish to my friend is separate from, and, indeed, subordinate to, the good I wish for myself. He has his well-being, and I have only my own.

In a wonderfully clear and concise analysis, Aquinas elaborates the metaphysics of all of this. His analysis forecloses all the problems resultant to the modern egoism/altruism distinction by undercutting its false start. The opposites in human loving are not love of self and love of another, with all the resultant problems of balancing these two. Modern thought requires us to mitigate the war of all against all with a certain minimal concern for others so as to ensure their minimal concern for ourselves. Otherwise universal egoism would destroy us all. But too much altruism is unhealthy and self-destructive. Self-preservation mandates self-concern. Self-sacrifice, especially the final one, giving up one's life for another, makes no sense. So altruism and egoism have to be balanced by contracts, tacit or explicit, in which every *quid* is balanced by an equal *quo*. And the contracts have to be constantly renegotiated.

For Thomists, love of self and love of others coincide, for self-fulfillment comes through, not in spite of, self-sacrifice. The ultimate sacrifice of oneself is one's ultimate fulfillment. Paradoxically, altruistic love fulfills the one who gives it, while egoistic self-seeking is self-defeating. The resonance of *amor amicitiae* with the biblical "Love thy neighbor as thyself," and with "He who loses his life will find it, but he who seeks to keep his life will lose it," is obvious. Here again, faith finds understanding in Thomistic personalism.

When I came to Marquette in 1957, as a part-time graduate student, the required undergraduate courses in the core curriculum numbered five, and they had a strong Thomistic content, just as at Creighton in my undergraduate days there. For Marquette, too, was one of the centers of Thomism at the high point of the Leonine Revival. The graduate program, while it provided a broader philosophical education, also had a strong Thomistic focus. Four historical courses were, and continue to be, required: Plato, Aristotle, Aquinas, and Kant. I had several more specialized courses in Aquinas, as well as courses in Medieval Islamic philosophy; Locke,

Hume, and Berkeley; Locke's philosophy of law; natural law jurisprudence; contemporary analytic philosophy; contemporary psychological theory; metaphysics of knowledge; and medical ethics.

There are obvious gaps in this record—logic, for example, and aesthetics, as well as contemporary continental philosophy, American philosophy, and political theory. But overall the offerings of my *alma mater* were, and continue to be, broader than those of many other departments. The quality of my courses was high, thanks to the excellence of the professors. They enabled me to publish several of my course papers in the standard journals. My M.A. thesis was easily developed into a published book in the prestigious *Medieval Philosophical Texts in Translation* series of the Marquette University Press, and the book *(The Apple, or Aristotle's Death)* was favorably reviewed in two prominent journals.

I brought this background and focus on Thomistic personalism to the faculty of my *alma mater* in 1978. By then Thomism had undergone its surprising and dramatic decline in this country. Required courses in Thomism had all but disappeared from core curricula everywhere, including Marquette. Thomists had become a minority of the faculty. Their number was still smaller when I recently retired—myself and one junior professor, and a few others who could, if pressed into service, teach such courses, but whose focus in research and teaching lay elsewhere.

Required undergraduate courses in philosophy now number four, but none are primarily Thomistic, and there is practically no continuity from one course to the next. Printed departmental policies require a substantive Christian philosophical component in philosophy of human nature and a substantive presentation of natural law in theory of ethics. But these policies are regularly ignored. Since our hirings for some twenty years have been overwhelmingly non-Thomist, even when these Thomistic components are taught, they are taught by professors who have no background or special interest in them.

To date, this departure from an earlier Thomistic focus has not been a notable improvement to our program, at least in meeting the existential needs of the great majority of our undergraduate students. To take just one example, our typical theory of ethics course now consists of hurried, superficial, and uncritical comparisons and contrasts of four ethical theories: utilitarianism, deontology, virtue ethics, and natural law. Students regularly come out of such courses with vague and confusing impressions, and no sense of systematic philosophizing. To do philosophy at all requires a certain clarity, complexity, and depth that cannot be achieved by, say, a four-week reading of selected texts of such great minds as Kant, Hume, Aristotle, or Aquinas. Our undergraduate students, as Father Francis Wade used to remind us, are "only four short years away from grade school." By and large, then, such survey courses not only fail as introductions to philosophy; they also fail to give our students any clear, coherent, or relevant guidance for their lives.

I do not, of course, mean to equate Thomism with the intellectual life, or with Catholic intellectual life, or even with philosophy. I mean only to report the context of my own intellectual life as it has been influenced by my faith. As my venture in trying to meet the existential needs of my students has turned out, my three early sources—Mouroux, Johann, and Jeannière—continue to be my basic sources for research and public speaking. Their fundamental ideas have enabled me to write and publish a metaphysics of community, which has been favorably reviewed, *Community: The Tie That Binds*. My conclusion therein is that community constituted by *amor amicitiae* is the human existential good, which directly translates into our moral good. Thus community becomes a moral norm, and the foundation is laid for a communitarian ethics such as that called for by Alasdair MacIntyre. I am confident now that I can write a sequel to my *Community: The Tie That Binds* that will outline a basic theory of communitarian ethics. The decision-making model will be the Thomistic prudential judgment, in which object, end, circumstances, and consequences of each voluntary act are brought under a norm that determines their moral goodness or evil. That norm will be community as constituted by *amor amicitiae* and as violated by *amor concupiscientiae*.

A few short months after my joining the faculty at Marquette, Thomistic personalism ascended the throne of Peter in the person of the Cardinal Archbishop of Cracow, Karol Wojtyła. I was slow to notice Pope John Paul II as a philosopher. In fact, I was advised in 1980 by a noted colleague, who knew his work much better than I did, that he wasn't much of a philosopher. I was told, bluntly, that he wouldn't have been noticed as such except for his election to the papacy. He was one of the lesser lights of the Lublin School of Thomism, not worth my serious attention. But one fine day I picked up his 1958 *Love and Responsibility*, just translated into English in 1980, as a small curiosity to occupy my mind during a coffee break. With that, my intellectual life once again received a major stimulus from my faith. I spent the rest of that day and the next in a careful, extensively annotated reading of the book. For in it I had found a truly creative development of Thomistic personalism, a sexual ethics in which the communion of persons constituted by self-giving love is a moral norm for all of sexual behavior.

Indeed, this sexual ethics offered a more general moral norm that its author has made the theme of nearly all his writings and public addresses in the twenty years of his papacy. With an obvious assist from Kant, Karol Wojtyła/Pope John Paul II has touched on every moral problem of our day, making a coherent and plausible assessment of each one by bringing all of human behavior under the personalistic norm: Persons are always to be loved, never used. This Thomistic distinction between the two kinds of love, *amor amiciti- ae* and *amor concupiscientiae*, has now been brought to bear on con- temporary moral questions related to sex and marriage and family, but also to economic behavior, the punishment of criminals, mod- ern warfare, biomedical behavior, education, entertainment, inter- national relations, global finances, and every other theater of hu- man behavior.

Since that providential coffee break, the philosophy of Pope John Paul II, who is now widely recognized as one of the major philoso- phers of our time, has been the focal point of my own Thomistic personalism. As his pre-papal philosophical writings have become available in the two languages that I began to learn in high school, I have discovered a new role model for my own integration of faith and philosophy. His life has been just such a growing integration since his underground studies during World War II. It was in that vein that he wrote his early poetry and plays, such as *The Jeweler's Shop,* that dramatize faith understood as the ongoing basis of our lives. For every day of every human life, no matter how ordinary and hidden, is a drama that each of us must play out for himself. Each choice is a challenge to our freedom, a challenge to either con- struct or destroy a communion of persons, depending on our choice to either love or use each other. The drama lies in the responsibili- ty—for with freedom, our actions become so deeply and truly our own that we, and we alone, are responsible for them. We and we alone are responsible for what we make of ourselves. The primary object, or receiver, of each moral act is its subject, the very person who performs it.

This drama of *amor amicitiae* (called, in various papal writings, "self-gift," "self-giving love," "love" *tout court,* and—most recently —"fairest love") as against its opposite, *amor concupiscientiae* ("self-seeking," "desire," and/or "use") is not just the common theme of all of this pope's writings and speeches. It is the guiding principle of the final document of Vatican II, of which the then Cardinal Archbishop of Cracow was a principal author: *Gaudium et spes (The Church in the Modern World)*. This principle undergirded Wojtyła's support for *Humanae vitae* when that document was being prepared for Pope Paul VI's signature. And the catechism of Vatican II, the *Catechism of the Catholic Church*, would fall apart if the passages dependent on that theme were somehow excised. If and when my communitarian ethical theory comes to life, it will be less creative than I used to think. For the writings of Pope John Paul II will be a major source of its Thomistic personalism.

Thus what began as an attempt to meet the genuine needs of my students for reasoned reflection on friendship, love, sex, and marriage has turned out to be just what I needed as well. My childhood desire to make sense of the world, especially of human relationships, has been fulfilled beyond anything I could have imagined when the quest began. My focus in retirement remains fixed on the metaphysics, the anthropology, and, finally, the ethics of community. For to a great extent, faith has found understanding in philosophy, in the personalism of St. Thomas Aquinas.

There are hazards in attempting such an integration. An obvious one, of course, is in bringing my own psychological needs into my professional life. There was the very real danger that instead of solving my personal problems, I would merely impose them on my students, leaving their last state worse than their first. I leave it to others to judge my success or failure on that important score. My conscious way of guarding against such an evil has been to teach and write in a mode of philosophical argument that is as logically rigorous as it can be and that is verified in ordinary experience, and to use only those sources that do the same.

My chosen mode of argument has been that of Aristotle and St. Thomas and their disciples. In that mode, philosophy begins with some fact or other of common, ordinary human experience. The explanation of the fact is then sought, through the syllogistic logic set forth in Aristotle's *Organon*. The final results, which yield purportedly true conclusions about the world of common, ordinary human experience, are then taken back to that world for their ultimate "reality check." In Wojtyła's pithy statement, "Philosophy begins in experience and is verified in experience."

Much intellectual elaboration of the truth of things, though, comes in between that beginning and that verification. Errors happen, obvious errors, in our very first perceptions of the world. We make mistakes in logic. And our verification process is not infallible. Ordinary experience is a problematic source of data. But a paralyzing skeptical objection to this starting point is self-refuting. The mere fact that we know we make mistakes is a sure sign that we are not mistaken all the time. If we were, we wouldn't know the difference, and then could never even wonder how to avoid or overcome our errors.

Nor need we be deterred by opinions (and that is all they can be) that such topics as friendship and love, sexual desire and sexual actions, marriage and family are not appropriate, or even possible, topics for philosophical reflection. Such an objection rules out, as beyond the range of reasoned understanding, these basic and important areas of every person's life. The burden of proof rests with those who would make philosophy purely abstract, or purely empirical in an especially crude materialistic fashion, or secular. Despite the contempt with which recent intellectual fads label reflections on such basic realities as love, sex, and family as pietistic, they can be examined as rigorously as any other facts of our lives.

However, a synthesis of faith and intellection, specifically philosophy, must guard the integrity of each. Otherwise we fall into one of two opposite disasters, one religious, the other intellectual. Fideism, in which faith is supposedly kept pure from any so-called intellectual contamination, is actually a corruption of one's faith. For we are intelligent beings, and faith itself tells us that this God-given gift is meant to be put to the service of God and men. Such use of philosophy in the context of faith is not, however, an attempt to prove the truths of faith by way of a demonstration that would compel assent to them. Contrary to the proverb, seeing is not believing, and believing is, precisely, not seeing. The truths of faith are those that transcend our intellectual capacities. They come to us only by God's direct revelation in Scripture, and our assent to them is by choice rather than by proof. And no matter how much these accepted revelations are elaborated and clarified and systematized by theologians, our assent to them always remains an act of choice.

A crucial intellectual act must intervene right here, however, for without it faith would not be faith but superstition. That act is a judgment that it is good to choose to assent to that which we do not, and cannot, prove to be true. That judgment requires some sort of adequate intellectual warrant. For example, the breakdown of philosophy in demonstrating some sort of embodied life after death makes our belief in the resurrection of our bodies *prima facie* plausible. Thus our assent to the doctrine has no proof, but is a reasonable choice nonetheless. Those, on the other hand, who would make philosophy a way to prove the truth of the content of religious belief would destroy faith by obliterating its transcendent content. Those who would rule such assents by choice, and thus religious belief, out of human life place a gratuitous restriction on the uses of reason. They make philosophy perforce secular and atheistic. And in so doing, they corrupt the intellectual life. That life, including philosophy, can then only be an academic game with no ex-

istential import. Most importantly, however, these two views—
fideism and secularism—are simply false.

As St. Thomas shows, faith and reason are intimate bedfellows
joined in an embrace which enhances rather than blurs their distinct identities. He makes their union intelligible by assigning a
clear and explicit, carefully nuanced, primacy to reason over faith.
The foundation of that primacy is the definition of faith as an assent to supra-rational truth by choice rather than by proof. The
choice is free, not compelled by intellectual insight into the truth of
faith, but drawn nonetheless to the goodness of giving such assent.
Faith is thus one of the voluntary actions that are the subject-matter
of the entire Second Part of the *Summa,* the treatise on morals. All
such acts, done knowingly and freely, are either right or wrong
morally, and we bear responsibility for them (hence Wojtyła's title
*Love and Responsibility*).

The immediate and always binding guide for such actions is
each person's sincere conscience. Conscience is a reasoning process
in which we apply some general principle of morality, or precept of
law, to a concrete, particular action. Thus the assent that is faith,
the choice to believe what we do not see, comes out of a prior judgment of conscience that it is good to so choose. The late, great Father Gerard Smith, S.J., made this point at a funeral Mass for one
of his Jesuit confreres. The congregation began to sing, "He who
believes in me will never die," and, "If you eat My body and drink
My blood you will have life eternal." Father Smith whispered to
me, in full view of the casket of one who had done those things,
"By God, if you can believe that, you can believe anything." His
point, of course, was the *prima facie* implausibility of the most important truths of our faith. And yet, he believed them, and so did I,
and each of us knew full well that the other did so. And we had
good philosophical reasons for doing so.

Conscience, of course, as a human reasoning process, can go astray and make an honest mistake. But its agent must then follow it nonetheless, for he has nothing else to go on. He then chooses something that is objectively wrong, wrong in itself, but appears right to him. He is absolved of any moral responsibility for his wrong action because he has no such responsibility for the act of conscience that guides it. St. Thomas' choice of an example to illustrate this argument could hardly be more stark: a conscientious refusal of the true faith itself. If, he says, someone were to sincerely think that belief in Christ is wrong, then, for him it would be wrong to believe, and he must not do so. We might think, for example, of someone born and raised in a Muslim culture, having heard from his earliest days, "Cursed be he who says God is three," and then encountering Christian missionaries.

There could hardly be a stronger affirmation of the priority of reason over faith. And this priority is what allows Catholic intellectuals, indeed, compels us, to integrate our faith into our intellectual lives. Our intellection lacks some of its crucial content if we don't, and our faith lacks its ongoing intellectual foundation, thus disintegrating into fideism. But once conscientiously chosen, faith then becomes normative over reason, even over philosophy. Catholic faith commits our minds to the truth of the Bible, as interpreted by the Church. The content of this revelation, God's very revelation of Himself, is infallibly true, as is the guidance of the Church, while reason is not. Reason can go wrong in philosophy, in many ways. For a believer, faith is a corrective to such errant reason. When his philosophizing leads to conclusions that contradict the truth of faith, he has a wake-up call to re-examine his philosophizing. He will find an error in it somewhere. That is not the end of his philosophical work, though, but only its beginning. He cannot simply substitute a teaching of the Church for an error in his philosophical system. The error has to be corrected by the hard work of philosophy, as he re-examines his originating data, his argumentative elaboration of that data, and his verification of it in reality. But at least he has the advantage of knowing when and where to start. And the possibility of needing to do such a re-examination is a constant of his philosophical life. Once he closes it off, he is no longer a philosopher, a seeker of wisdom.

Thus, faith and philosophy, when correctly integrated, have a reciprocal influence. Philosophy, though, as the guide to a conscientious choice to believe, has the final priority over faith. A believer whose sincere conscience should ever come to judge that faith is wrong must give up his faith at once. Otherwise he is a fanatic. But one whose ongoing conscience calls for faith must constantly heed that call. When he does, his faith then—but only then—becomes normative over his subsequent uses of his mind. What keeps this intertwining from being a vicious circle is that the binding force of conscience is rooted not in its correctness, but in its subjective sincerity. One who seeks truth, including moral truth, specifically the moral truth that it is good to believe, must do so for the sake of truth itself. If he holds to his belief for any other reason than its being true, he is either a hypocrite or a fanatic, not a sincere believer. His reason for clinging to faith is self-serving—social acceptance, perhaps, or fear of family rejection.

The test of sincerity is the willingness to die for the truth rather than deny it—as did St. John Fisher, for example, and St. Thomas More. One who lacks such openness to martyrdom for the truth must ask himself why he adheres to that to which he clings. His answer will be something other than, "because it is true." But one who adheres to truth for truth's sake, and thus sees that giving up life rather than giving up truth makes sense, sees the truth of truth itself. That is, he sees truth as a reality, not a mere abstraction or construct of his mind. When abstractions and constructs become inconvenient, we simply change them in favor of other abstractions and constructs. Moreover, a sincere adherent of truth for the sake of truth sees the truth as a reality that is transcendent to him, able to make demands on him, including the final demand of his life. Once again, if he sees himself as independent of, or superior to, truth, he is not sincere in his adherence to it. He is a self-serving manipulator of the truth.

To carry this logic of sincerity one last step, we must ask what is this real transcendent entity known as truth, to which a sincere person of conscience subordinates his life choices, and even his life itself? The answer lies in metaphysics, specifically in the philosophy of God, where it is argued, first, that there is a First Cause of Being, and then that this Cause has certain attributes. He is Supremely Real, Personal, Transcendent to us, Creator Who is Truth. In short, the sincere adherence to truth—a necessity for both faith and philosophy as well as their integration—implies that Truth exists, as real, and as transcendent to us. From there, philosophy integrated into faith can take us to a further understanding that the vision of Truth is the last end and ultimate fulfillment of our lives. Fidelity to a vocation as a Catholic intellectual can lead us finally to that vision of which Gregory the Great asked, "What do they not see, who see Him who sees all things?"

*Jude P. Dougherty*

# 8. CHRISTIAN PHILOSOPHY:
# SOCIOLOGICAL CATEGORY
# OR OXYMORON?

꙳

The theses to be entertained here can be set forth simply. I will advance several. To address the question "Is there Christian philosophy?" it is necessary, first, to acknowledge that there is no such thing as "Christianity." As a sociological category "Christianity" may have some content. People the world over profess to be Christian. But, when we look to the content of belief we find so little in common between professed Christians that the designation becomes almost meaningless. Professed Christians subscribe to a multiplicity of faiths with varying degrees of sophistication; they adhere to tenets many of which are contradictory, many irrational, many unexamined. Orthodox Christianity is difficult to define even within the Roman Catholic community, where a premium is placed on universality, unity, and the apostolic mandate. That is my first observation: the lack of unity in Christianity that might give meaning to the term "Christian philosophy."

The second is that, logically and chronologically, philosophy is

Portions of this article originally appeared in *The Monist* 75 (1992), pp. 283–90.

prior to Christianity. The type of philosophy one espouses, implicitly or explicitly, either opens one to faith or closes it as an intellectual option. Furthermore, the type of philosophy one espouses determines the kind of Christianity one embraces. Classical Greek and Roman intelligence gave rise to, and forever will lead to, the institution shaped by the Fathers and Doctors of the early and medieval Church. If one starts with modern philosophical nominalism or epistemology, one will not end up in the belief system which shaped Aquinas and to which the Parisian master contributed. The differences between Plato and Aristotle, for example, or between realism and nominalism, are carried through history as Christians attempt to understand their faith. Ancient skepticisms and Pyrrhonism have their modern counterparts which make belief for their adherents as impossible today as those outlooks made it impossible in antiquity.

The third thesis, which is likely to meet with no dissent from the orthodox, but will nevertheless be challenged within the group that may be called "sociologically described Christians," is that Christianity is based on divinely revealed truths inaccessible to human reason. Such truths consist of propositions such as "Christ is God," "Christ redeemed mankind by his sacrificial act on the cross," "Eternal beatitude consists in union with God in a life hereafter," "God has revealed himself as triune, Father, Son and Holy Spirit." All will admit that Christ taught truths accessible to human reason, but not all will subscribe to the literal truth of assertions which go beyond those provided by reason itself. In sum, if one distinguishes between types of Christianity, one soon realizes that for the orthodox there may be one type of relation between faith and philosophy and for the non-orthodox another. If, in the spirit of the *Redaktionesgeschichte* movement, the whole of Christianity can be reduced to metaphor or to moral teaching, there is no problem concerning the relation of philosophy to revelation. Supposed revelation is nothing but a poetic manner of stating truths accessible to purely human intelligence. Averroes took this approach when he identified three modes or levels of teaching, each proportioned to or determined by the audience sought.

Distinguishing between religion, theology, and philosophy, Averroes held that these are but three modes of discourse corresponding to the three classes of men. Religion is truth made accessible to the common man who must be induced to live virtuously by eloquent preaching, that is, by appeals made to the imagination rather than to the intellect. Theology is the attempted rational justification of common belief, but it is only philosophy which provides the nucleus of truth contained in the fancies of the men of faith. The three approaches to the same truth ultimately agree with one another. The beliefs of the common people and the teachings of the theologians are simply philosophical truths adapted to inferior minds.

Yet Averroes did not consider religion to be merely a rough approximation to philosophic truth. It was for him much more. It had a definite social function which could not be fulfilled by anything else, not even by philosophy. The *Koran* he believed to be a miraculous book and one "divinely inspired," because he found it more effective than philosophy in raising people to the level of morality. Thus Moses, Jesus, and Mohammed can be considered true prophets and messengers of God to mankind, but their religions were only popular approaches to the truth found in its purity in philosophy.

This position was to be partially reiterated in Hegel's all-embracing system in which Christian faith was treated as a moment in the unfolding of Absolute Spirit. For Hegel, religious language expresses in a symbolic manner the universality of truth which philosophy alone brings to rational explicitness.

It is appropriate to recall that Marx as a believing Jew learned from a Protestant biblical exegete how to interpret Isaiah in a purely secular fashion. Engels, too, lost his Pietist faith under tutelage by similarly disposed biblical scholars. If the so-called "sacred Scriptures" are but poetic ways of teaching certain truths about human nature, morality, and the social order, then philosophy is the proper science of those things, although other modes of discourse may have indispensable educative roles to play.

For the orthodox believer, such as Augustine, philosophy retains its proper methodology, yielding important truths about nature and human nature, but it begs to be completed by divine revelation. Augustine can assert that he believes in order to understand, that is, *fully* understand. For Augustine, the understanding provided by faith is greater than that available to natural reason; a contemplative union with God in whom all is manifested is seen as the goal of human life. Aquinas is well known for his doctrine that the natural prepares the way for the supernatural, that the two complement each other, revelation adding to the store of natural truths about God and man. These two intellectual giants used the categories inherited from Greece and Rome to understand the faith they received from Jerusalem, and they developed theologies which remain alive today.

St. Thomas, in constructing his theology, employed the philosophy of Aristotle to such an extent that not only his strictly philosophical works but his theological treatises are studied for the philosophy they contain. Most who use Aquinas recognize the distinction and keep the two modes of discourse separate.

This distinction is universally recognized in the ordering of higher studies within the Catholic educational complex. One will never find a department of philosophy and religion in a Catholic institution, although the two disciplines have been and continue to be placed under one organizational schema in state and many private institutions. The name, "American Catholic Philosophical Association" is a name that has through the years given pause to many a novice, but each generation of scholars seems to find through experience that it is a sociological category and not the designation of a particular *ism,* membership in the organization consisting mostly of Catholics or of those who teach in Catholic-sponsored institutions.

I implied earlier that there is a major difference between Protestant and Catholic attitudes toward philosophy. Of course, it is no more possible to define "Protestantism" than it is to define "Christianity." If we distinguish between "high" and "low" churches, or between "evangelical" and other denominations, and concentrate on those that have clearly separated themselves from Catholicism, we find little resort to philosophy *per se.* Yet in many quarters a previous suspicion of philosophy has been replaced by its cultivation. Fundamentalist seminaries, in the latter half of the twentiethcentury, added philosophers to their staffs and even created departments of philosophy where none existed a generation ago.

Protestant attitudes toward philosophy are in part determined by the biblical theology embraced by the reformers. Luther's doctrine of the "fall" certainly colored his attitude toward speculative philosophy. Accepting the biblical account of the Fall of Adam, he was convinced that intellect was so darkened as a result of the Fall that it could not unaided conclude to the existence of God. Consequently, Luther had little regard for philosophy. Sworn enemy of Scholasticism, he once remarked that God had sent Aristotle as a punishment for the sins of mankind. Calvin, too, was suspicious of the intellect's ability to achieve unaided a knowledge of God, although he was convinced that at least God's existence was ascertainable apart from revelation.

Kant with his *Critique of Pure Reason* became for many the Aquinas of Protestantism. His boast that he had destroyed reason to make way for faith was compatible with a fundamentalism that emphasized the gratuitous character of faith. Whereas Catholic apologetics insists on a rational preamble, that is, upon the reasonableness of belief, the tradition represented by Luther, Calvin, and later by Kierkegaard called for a leap into the dark.

The Enlightenment reaction to both the fideism of mainstream Protestantism and a weakened Scholastic legacy established a rationalism that still holds sway. For nineteenth- and twentieth-century English-speaking philosophers such as John Stuart Mill and John Dewey, the problem is one of justifying the moral legacy of Christianity by providing a proper rationale for many of the values formally justified on a religious basis.

History suggests that the problem of Christian philosophy is largely a problem of the relation of faith and reason. It is a problem for the Christian who wishes to keep distinct the sources of his knowledge, that is, what he has learned, from revelation and its development in sacred theology, on the one hand, and the natural sources of his knowledge, on the other. It is an issue for the nonbeliever, who tends to regard the philosopher who is open to the testimony of faith as a "theologian in disguise," distrusting a tainted witness. There is no doubt, as Etienne Gilson has shown, that Western philosophy has been influenced by religion and that the believer often has distinctive interests in the practice of philosophy. Clearly, philosophy employed in the analysis and development of doctrine is theology. No one questions the use of philosophy by the theologian who is disposed to use it. The fundamental question is, can philosophy remain unalloyed in the presence of biblical revelation? And need it do so? The answer to the second question, as I have suggested above, depends on the type of Christianity embraced.

The answer to the first is, philosophy must remain unalloyed if it is to be true philosophy. It must justify to its hearer every conclusion it reaches by the evidence it produces and the inferences it makes. This explains a peculiar affinity to classical philosophy on the part of the believer, who finds in Greek and Roman thought the rational preamble without which he would find it difficult to believe.

Contributions to philosophy by Christians can hardly be denied, even when that philosophy is developed within a theological context. The Christian is not compelled to defend, even against the most strident agnostic, the work of Augustine, Anselm, Albert, Aquinas, Scotus, Suarez, Maritain, or Lonergan. Aquinas' commentaries on Aristotle, even today, in spite of centuries of similar work, remain a valuable guide to the work of the Stagirite. The plurality of philosophical approaches among believers is noticeable. There is no one philosophy among those whose faith may be in substantial agreement. The term "scholastic philosophy," for example, embraces a heterogenous collection of systems from Albert and Aquinas, through Bonaventure and Scotus, to Ockham and Suarez. There is no single method, no single doctrine; one may say, paraphrasing Gilson, "only intellect in the service of Christ." Philosophy is obviously employed by those who seek to understand the "mysteries" of their faith and to probe the implications of what they take to be revealed truth. Most who profess the Catholic faith guard the integrity of their philosophy because it alone provides a common language, a common set of distinctions, which enable the believer to enter into dialogue with those who do not share his faith. Sidney Hook could challenge the believer with the assertion, "We have as much evidence for the existence of God as we have for the existence of leprechauns and fairies." Ernest Nagel could proclaim reason "sovereign" against those who invoked Scripture. John Dewey could explain to the believer, in the fashion of a Schleiermacher or a Ritschl, the true secular meaning of the doctrines to which the believer subscribes. But with each, the believer, philosophically equipped, remains in a position to argue the evidence pro and con.

In the last analysis the battleground is metaphysics. Without the principles of intelligibility, causality, substance, finality, and potency and act, intellect is left, so to speak, dead in the water. There can be no movement from contingent being to self-existent being, the cause of the existence of things. Without an acknowledgment that intellect can achieve a notion of "being," there can be no inference to Being Itself. Without intellect as a collaborator supporting the proposition that God exists, and that things insofar as we can know them are as revelation presents them, those propositions which reason does not teach will necessarily have to be accepted on blind faith.

The Catholic mind cherishes philosophy as the rational preamble to its faith, but the philosophy cherished is of a select strain. It is largely the philosophy of Aristotle and Stoics as developed and commented upon through the ages; it is not the empiricism of Hume, or the critical philosophy of Kant, or the materialism of Marx. It is a philosophy confident of the intelligibility of nature, of the power of intellect to ferret out the secrets of nature, and of the intellect's ability to render at least partially intelligible that which is not self-intelligible. To ask about Christian philosophy inevitably forces one to raise the question, "What think you of the Greeks and their detractors?"

The position defended here is not unlike that taken a generation ago by Jacques Maritain, one of several twentieth-century giants who debated the issue. In his *An Essay on Christian Philosophy,* Maritain distinguishes between philosophy considered in the abstract and philosophy considered in its concrete state of existence.[1] Philosophy as abstracted from its concrete conditions of existence is a purely natural and rational discipline: it cannot be "Christian." But

1. Trans. E. H. Flannery (New York: Philosophical Library, 1955). Two major

as found in those who philosophize, it will be characterized one way or another. The Christian is apt to be influenced by his faith even as he philosophizes. On that point one may question Maritain. If the influence is regarded as subliminal, so to speak, there is no way to ascertain whether it is operative or not. If the guidance is open, as in the case of the biblical account of God revealing Himself to Moses as "Yahweh," interpreted as "He who is," we can acknowledge with Gilson, "Any Christian convert who was at all familiar with Greek philosophy was then bound to realize the metaphysical import of the new belief."[2] "I am who am," restated in metaphysical terms, becomes "self-existent being," or "I am he whose essence it is to exist." And from the biblical account of creation, it is easy to add, "the cause of the existence of things." Thus revelation has suggested to the philosopher a key distinction, namely, that between essence and existence, between *what is* and the act *whereby it is.* This distinction is either philosophically defensible or it is not. Similar distinctions from the natural sciences, particularly from quantum mechanics, are absorbed by philosophy and defended philosophically without troubling effect. The distinction, for example, between iconic and mathematical models of natural structures is not one to be ignored and can readily be incorporated into philosophy without leading one to doubt the difference between physics and epistemology.

Etienne Gilson took a position somewhat different from Maritain, but one which I believe is compatible. Gilson, invoking the

---

explorations of the Maritain and Gilson positions should be mentioned: Joseph Owens, *Towards A Christian Philosophy* (Washington, D.C.: The Catholic University of America Press, 1990); and John Wippel, "Thomas Aquinas and the Problem of Christian Philosophy," in his *Metaphysical Themes in Thomas Aquinas* (Washington, D.C.: The Catholic University of America Press, 1984).

2. E. Gilson, "God and Christian Philosophy," in *A Gilson Reader,* ed. A. Pegis (New York: Image Books, 1957), p. 193.

fact may lead us back to a renewed appreciation of something recognized by Gilson.

The nineteenth century produced an abundance of philosophers who took as one of their principal tasks the criticism of Christianity on presumably philosophical grounds. Karl Löwith notes: "Philosophical criticism of the Christian religion began in the 19th century with Hegel and reached its climax with Nietzsche. It is a Protestant movement, and therefore specifically German; this holds true of both the criticism and the religion at which it was directed. Our critical philosophers were all educated Protestants, and their criticism of Christianity presupposes its Protestant manifestation."[7]

## I I

It is evident that the cultural and social setting do indeed matter. In recent years I have had the occasion to prepare lectures on three late-nineteenth-century philosophers—Miguel de Unamuno, George Santayana, and Edith Stein. Unamuno and Santayana were born a year apart in Spain. Both were, in their early years, the beneficiaries of a Catholic education. Edith Stein by contrast was reared in Breslau, Germany, within a traditional Jewish family. All three abandoned the religious faith inherited from their families, in each case as a result of their University educations. All were reading more or less the same books. Only one escaped the influence of those books because of a perceived logical deficiency.

Unamuno was to become a distinguished rector of the ancient University of Salamanca, and at his death he was famous the world over as a philosopher, poet, dramatist, novelist, and essayist. Born in 1864 in the Basque coastal city of Bilbao, at age sixteen he left his

7. Karl Löwith, *From Hegel to Nietzsche: The Revolution in Nineteenth Century Thought,* trans. David E. Green (New York: Columbia University Press, 1991), pp. 327–28.

native city for Madrid. One of his biographers notes that shortly after he arrived in Madrid, the formerly pious youth stopped going to Mass. What he took up is not fully disclosed, but he began reading German philosophy: Schopenhauer, Kant, Nietzsche, and Hegel. He learned English in order to read Herbert Spencer, the prophet of evolutionary process, who was the intellectual fad in those years.

Unamuno eventually married his childhood sweetheart and the couple had eight children. When he was in his early thirties, they lost their third child. The experience was shattering. It brought Unamuno to his knees and briefly, at least, to contemplation and prayer, although he never returned to the practice of his faith. Though Unamuno was culturally and emotionally a Mediterranean Catholic, he failed to develop a Catholic mind to go with it. Years later, as an influential academic and politician, he was trusted neither by the Catholics nor by his secular colleagues. His literary legacy remains ambiguous, a kind of reverent humanism without adequate foundation.

Unamuno was fifteen years of age when Leo XIII promulgated his famous encyclical *Aeterni Patris* (1879), which recommended to the Catholic world the study of St. Thomas. Leo XIII recommended Aquinas both as a philosopher and as a theologian, for he was aware that the critical philosophy of the Continent, not to mention the empiricism of Scotland and England and the various materialisms which commanded the allegiance of intellectuals throughout the West, provided no foundation for the Catholic faith. To one of the Catholic faith, belief makes sense not only for the understanding it provides, but because it forms a continuum, adding to what one knows to be the case from experience and reason. Leo XIII recognized that some philosophies open one to the faith, just as some philosophies close it as an option. Unamuno was born too early to profit from the Thomistic revival.

Picture now a young woman schooled in the German philosophy of the same period, newly a student of Husserl, discovering Catholicism. Edith Stein was born twelve years after Leo XIII urged the study of Thomas. She was eventually to experience the fruit of a renewed interest in Aquinas. Edith's path to St. Thomas was complex. It began with philosophical study which eventually led, through her acquaintance with Max Scheler, to an appreciation of Catholicism. That is the same Max Scheler on whom Karol Wojtyła was to write a doctoral dissertation.

Reared in a conservative Jewish home, Edith Stein, not unlike Unamuno, abandoned her faith as an adolescent. Between the ages of thirteen and twenty-one she considered herself an atheist. Intellectually precocious from childhood, as a University student she found herself dissatisfied with the dominant German philosophy of her time, the same philosophy which separated Unamuno from his religious heritage. By accident she discovered the two volumes of Husserl's *Logical Investigations.*

Husserl's philosophical realism came as an antidote to both Kant and Hegel, insofar as he affirmed the existence of objective truth and the existence of a knowable world apart from the mind. As we have already noted, a philosophical realism enables one to embrace the Christian faith as a compelling objective account and not as a mere subjective conceptual schema, because that faith is measured against external standards. Husserl himself, partially trained in Vienna, was indebted to two Austrians, Franz Brentano and Bernard Bolzano, both trained as priests, both steeped in the Scholastic philosophy of the Thomistic revival.

At age twenty-one Edith left Breslau for Göttingen, where she hoped to study with Husserl, whom she had already come to regard as the leading philosopher of her day. It was in Göttingen that she met Max Scheler, a Jew, as well as an on-again, off-again Catholic.

Scheler opened her eyes to the fact that one could be a philosopher of rank and a believing Christian. It was be ten years before she entered the Church, but under Scheler's influence she discovered what she called "the phenomenon of Catholicism." Husserl taught her the method of phenomenology, a method she used to look closely, in a detached way, at the world and into herself.

Long before her baptism she began to study St. Thomas. Later, on the advice of the Jesuit philosopher-theologian Erich Przywara, she began the translation of St. Thomas' *Questiones Disputate de Veritate*. It was that translation which brought her into intimate contact with the mind of St. Thomas, but to say that she admired his style would be to leave a false impression. The Scholastic practice of stating a thesis, listing the objections to the thesis, defending the thesis, and then answering the objections to the thesis would, in her judgment, discourage the modern reader. Thus she dispensed with the objections and their answers and got to the meat of Thomas's own systematic thought on the topic.

To each question she appended an analysis showing the contemporary bearing of the discussion, with particular emphasis on the metaphysical and epistemological issues involved. She was writing for a literate audience, not for scholars. Martin Grabmann provided an introduction. Father Przywara was to say of her work that it was St. Thomas and nothing but St. Thomas throughout, but he is brought face to face with Husserl, Scheler, and Heidegger. The translation gained for her a reputation as a student of St. Thomas, and she received numerous invitations to lecture on his thought.

But it wasn't Thomas alone who prepared her for her reception of the Catholic faith. Husserl and Thomas both opened the way. Husserl's realism opened her to theism; it was from Thomas that she acquired a Christian outlook; but it was Teresa of Avila who led her to the final step. Visiting the home of Hedwig Conrad-Martius in the Summer of 1921, she read *The Life of St. Teresa of Avila,* an autobiography. Upon finishing the work in the early hours of the morning, she put the book down proclaiming to herself, "This is Truth." Thomas' *De Veritate* was about "truth" in the abstract; Teresa gave her truth concretely.

The same morning she set out to buy a catechism and missal. Frau Conrad-Martius relates[8] that she had the impression that Edith attended Mass daily from the night of her encounter with St. Teresa. Edith studied both the catechism and the missal and one morning after Mass, she followed the priest into the sacristy and asked to be baptized. Surprised at the abruptness of her request, he informed her that she would have to take instructions. Her response was quiz me, which he did. Needless to say, she had prepared herself well. She was received into the Church on January 1, 1922. As de Fabregues puts it in his little biography, "Edith found her source in the intellect and came home to her Creator: the love dwelling in her soul responded to the searchings of her mind."[9] Without Husserl and Thomas, Edith might not have been positioned to appreciate Teresa. Clearly, in her case, faith came as a gift perfecting nature.

Permit me now a third exhibit, and then I will draw some conclusions. My third protagonist is George Santayana. Born in Madrid in 1863, Santayana spent the first nine years of his life in Spain. By his own account, as an adolescent he oscillated between solipsism and the Catholic faith. Although Santayana was to become as a result of his philosophical studies a materialist and therefore a non-believer, he never lost an affection for his Mediterranean upbringing. Throughout his life he could recall with fondness his early

8. Cf. Hilda Graef, *The Scholar and the Cross: The Life and Work of Edith Stein* (Westminster, Md.: Newman Press, 1955), p. 32.
9. *Edith Stein* (Staten Island, N.Y.: Alba House, 1965), p. 53.

experiences of religious pageantry, of the many feasts, such as Corpus Christi, celebrated in his boyhood Avila. Strangely in later life, he claimed never to have practiced his faith. His estrangement seems to have occurred during his college years when he began the study of philosophy, particularly the work of Spencer, Hume, Mill, Schopenhauer, and Nietzsche. While he was enrolled at the Boston Latin School he continued to attend Mass, but at Harvard College his faith in the literal truth of Christianity began to fade. After studying with William James and Josiah Royce he subsequently spent two years in Germany and then returned to Harvard for graduate study, eventually joining its faculty.

Santayana's years at Harvard spanned a watershed period, with an inherited idealism sometimes called "the classical period of American philosophy" on the one side, and various realisms and materialisms which were to replace it on the other. Idealism of the Germanic variety was at that time thought to be an adequate prop or metaphysical underpinning for a religious outlook. But confidence in Hegel was soon to erode as achievement in the sciences seemed to entail philosophical empiricism, and the critical movement in biblical studies cast doubt on the supernatural sources of the sacred Scriptures. The new realism and the critical realism which soon replaced idealism were materialisms of one sort or another. Santayana's reflections on religion were always the reflections of a materialist, but he was appreciative of Catholicism in the same way that he was appreciative of other coherent systems of belief which produce effects in the practical order. In *Persons and Places* he tells us, "I had never practiced my religion, or thought of it as a means of getting to heaven or avoiding hell, things that never caused me the least flutter. All that happened was that I became accustomed to a different *Weltanschauung,* to another system having the same rational function as religion: that of keeping me attentive to the lessons of life."[10] Elsewhere, he said, "I have found in different times and places, the liberal, the Catholic and the German air quite possible to breathe."[11] George Herbert Palmer once said of Santayana, "He had Hume in his bones."

One could multiply these intellectual biographies a hundredfold and touch only the surface of an intellectually turbulent period. Löwith, recognizing the power of Hegel, credits him with an absolute destruction of Christian philosophy and of the Christian religion.[12] Löwith similarly charges David Frederick Strauss with the reduction of Christianity to myth, and Ludwig Feuerbach with the reduction of Christianity to a humanistic anthropology.[13] Influenced by all three, Marx demanded the abolition of the social circumstances which prompt men to turn to religion.

Is it then surprising that in the midst of these nineteenth-century currents Leo XIII felt obliged to encourage a return to the philosophy of St. Thomas and to the classical sources upon which he drew. In Aquinas, as with Aristotle, one finds a philosophy at once compatible with common sense, modern science and the Catholic faith. But Leo, in *Aeterni Patris,* is remarkable for several other insights. He saw that wherever philosophy is regarded as a science, there is necessarily a respect for the past: there is the acknowledgment of a wisdom to be mastered, augmented, and conveyed to a new generation. Leo noted that it was under the influence of the sixteenth-century reformers that men began to philosophize in complete disregard for the faith, with the result that instead of coordinated and focused enquiry there came to be a spectrum of di-

10. *Persons and Places* (Cambridge: M.I.T. Press, 1986), p. 419.
11. *Soliloquies in England and Later Soliloques* (New York: Charles Scribners and Sons, 1937), p. 189.
12. Löwith, *From Hegel to Nietzsche,* cf. chap 1, pp. 31ff.
13. Ibid., pp. 71–82.

verse and incompatible systems. A passion for novelty, Leo thought, produced a proliferation of philosophical opinions which resulted in intellectual hesitation and doubt and finally disbelief. Catholics were not exempt from the *Zeitgeist*. Many failed to appreciate the value of their inheritance and chose instead to repudiate and to build anew. In retrospect we can say that, as discordant as things may have been in the nineteenth century, they are even worse today. In the last part of the twentieth century we have witnessed whole schools of philosophy isolate themselves from each other, failing to communicate even with respect to fundamentals. We have seen persons trained in the same philosophical techniques become so specialized that their individual work has no bearing on the work of others or relation to any common effort.

While there may be no Catholic philosophy *per se,* there is a Catholic intellectual tradition, which takes philosophy to be a science indispensable to theology, one that engenders a respect for the past and an openness to serious enquiry wherever it is conducted. This is manifested in its appreciation of classical philosophical texts and the tradition of commenting on them, a tradition begun with the Fathers and one carried through the Middle Ages into our own time. We draw upon Thomas as he drew upon the best of his predecessors. And in doing so we acquire a sure guide as we attempt to understand nature—our own nature and things divine.

*James V. Schall, S.J.*

# 9. FROM CURIOSITY TO PRIDE: ON THE EXPERIENCE OF OUR OWN EXISTENCE

ॐ

*The metaphysical proofs of God are so remote from the reasoning of men, and so complicated, that they make little impression; and if they should be of service to some, it would be only during the moment that they see such demonstration; but an hour afterwards they fear they have been mistaken. Quod curiositate cognoverunt superbia amiserunt. This is the result of the knowledge of God obtained without Jesus Christ; it is communion without a mediator with the God whom they have known without a mediator. Whereas those who have known God by a mediator know their own wretchedness.*

—*Pascal*[1]

*The ground of existence is an experienced reality of a transcendent nature towards which one lives in tension. . . . There is that openness of the soul in existence which is an orienting-center in the life of man. . . . We all experience our own existence as not existing out of itself but as coming from somewhere even if we don't know from where.*

—*Eric Voegelin*[2]

---

1. Blaise Pascal, *Pensées,* trans. W. F. Trotter (New York: Modern Library, 1941), p. 127.

2. *Conversations with Eric Voegelin,* ed. R. Eric O'Connor (Montreal: Thomas More Institute Papers/76, 1980), pp. 8–9.

I

In a famous passage at the beginning of his *Metaphysics,* Aristotle observed that "all men by nature desire to know. An indication of this is the delight we take in our senses; for even apart from their usefulness they are loved for themselves" (980a23–24). This rather laconic passage in one of the greatest of all books is, nonetheless, on examination, charged with surprise. It is not just that we know but that we "desire" to know. We know that we know; we know that we desire to know; we know that desiring to know is not knowing. And the proof of this "desire" is nothing less than the "delight" we take in our very knowing. The correspondence between knowing something and the delight in knowing something intimates an unanticipated relationship, something that perhaps need not exist but, when it does exist, indicates some kind of plan or order that is already present in us without our causing it. We simply notice that it is there.

Furthermore, we do not just want to "know"; we want to know something. In the beginning our mind is the famous *"tabula rasa,"* that alive power with nothing in it, a blackboard with nothing written on it. Our mind seeks to be informed, to be written on, as it were. Our very act of knowing itself depends on our first knowing something that is not itself an empty "knowing" but a something out there, something capable of being known. Aristotle already distinguishes here between what is useful for us and what is somehow beyond use, something that is delightful by its own experience, something we would do even if it were not also useful. We would still want to see, he tells us elsewhere, even if we did not delight in seeing. Furthermore, he notices that what is for its own sake is more important than what is useful for something else. The things that are for their own sakes are more worthwhile, more elevated. When we know something, affirm it, we are, on reflection, surprised that things in us are working, that in their working they delight us.

Aristotle is not giving us here a "theory" of knowledge. Rather he is guiding our attention to what it is we regularly do if we would only pay attention, only reflect on our own reality and its constituent activities. From the first, our own reality, which is most immediate to us, is a reality that knows and delights in knowing. We do not begin our knowing, moreover, primarily out of need, or fear, or physical desire, as we might at first suspect. These things too can eventually be things or experiences that incite us to know, but our knowing them is not itself a fear or a desire or a need. Knowing what fear is, for instance, is not the same as being frightened at something. The former is a knowledge and we delight in knowing it. Knowing what fear or need or desire is involves knowing the fullness of what we already are. We find that we can examine ourselves while knowing. Aristotle compares the light of seeing with the light of knowing. What is not us enlightens us, yet the light is also in us.

There is more. *"Nulla est homini causa philosophandi, nisi ut beatus sit,"* as Augustine put it in *The City of God.* The very reason we philosophize, why we seek to know *what is,* to know the order of the whole in which we ourselves exist, is in order that we might be happy. Otherwise, we would not take the trouble to know. To be happy means that we are experiencing and directing our given faculties to operate on their proper objects, neither of which have we ourselves made. Aristotle told us in his *Ethics* that the reason we do all that we do is precisely in order that we might be happy; thus our lives are nothing less than an unavoidable examination of the things that might fulfill this search. "A man who is puzzled and wonders thinks himself ignorant," Aristotle realistically added. (982b37). This recalls Socrates' paradoxical wisdom, that he knows what he did not know.

To be puzzled and to wonder about things, evidently, indicate our condition, what we are to be about. On first being ourselves, we begin by not knowing, but we want to know. Our ignorance discontents us, but we are pleased that it does. "For it is owing to their wonder that men both now begin and at first began to philosophize" (982b12). The science that has no other purpose than to know is the free science, the first science, the one that exists for its own sake, only to know, and to delight in this knowing what it can know. Aristotle, in a marvelous insight, notes that it is this same wonder which first caused men to philosophize that now causes us to philosophize, to come alive, to become luminous to ourselves by knowing what is not ourselves.

The mind is a faculty of a certain kind of being. There are beings that know and know even when they also sense and feel. These beings are ourselves. "God, having made the heavens and the earth, which do not feel the happiness of their being," Pascal wrote, "He has willed to make beings who should know it, and who should compose a body of thinking members" (#482). We are capable of knowing *all that is;* we are *capax omnium.* We are designed so that what is not ourselves can, in the order of our knowing, become ourselves. We are not deprived of all things just because we are limited and finite things in our own makeup. To know is to be, and to be ourselves in a fuller manner.

Yet, when we know, we do not change what is known. What is known remains *what it is,* unless we, with the help of our knowing, act upon it to change it. But if we are capable of knowing all things, including reflectively something of ourselves, of knowing that we too exist, that we too are not nothing, nevertheless we know that we do not cause ourselves to stand outside of nothingness or cause ourselves to be what we are. That we are and what we are, both are given to us. They are the starting points of our mind's searching for *what is;* they are not the ending points of our own making. We know what we make; but we find ourselves already made, intricately made and ordered. This too puzzles us. What we are seems to bear imprints from beyond what we are, almost as if we were also somehow "words," somehow intelligible in our own uniqueness.

## II

In English, at least, the phrases "to be curious" and "to wonder" can have the same meaning, but often the former word, curiosity, has a slightly pejorative tinge. It means to be overly meddlesome or prying into things beyond proper bounds. Socrates was accused of this very vice. Perhaps, like Prometheus' stealing of fire from the gods to aid man, there is a kind of defiance or challenge to the gods contained within much of our curiosity. The latter phrase, "to wonder," has a more innocent connotation to it. It is more accepting of what we are, even in our initial not knowing. Wonder indicates an honesty, an admission that we do not know something other than the fact that it is there, without our putting it there. Wonder also suggests that the desire to find out the reasons for things is essential to what we are, or rather, it simply *is* what we are in our fullness or completion. In knowing, we remain substantially ourselves. We do not want to be some other sort of being, even when within ourselves we know about other sorts of beings.

We delight in knowing what is not ourselves, as if somehow this knowing of something not ourselves is designed to constitute our perfection, our happiness even. We notice, furthermore, that we do not know even ourselves directly. Nothing is more sobering, or more fascinating, than this realization that we know ourselves only indirectly. We know ourselves, as it were, reflexively in the very process of knowing something else. We are luminous to ourselves only when we are actually knowing what is not ourselves. We are, so to speak, given ourselves because we are given what is not ourselves. This is the grounding of both our dignity and our humility.

Things not ourselves in our knowing make us aware of ourselves, make us aware that it is an "I" that is knowing. My very self knows that I am a self, that I have a soul, that I look out on the world. And what most fascinates us in our own knowing, even of ourselves, is when it is another "I" that is being known. The whole drama of love and friendship, and yes, of hatred and enmity, begins here. Thus, we seem to disclose an order in our parts that leads everything we encounter back to our knowing faculty, to a power we have, which power, in turn, contains for us all that is not ourselves. Truth, as Plato says in *The Republic,* is "to say of *what is* that it is, and of what is not, that it is not." When we say of *what is* that it is, it is we who say it. That is, the *what is,* while remaining itself, also becomes luminous in our own *to be,* in our own reality. We wonder if somehow everything does not belong to us in some way. We wonder about this paradox wherein our seeming paucity of being is related to all actual beings.

Yet, the difficulty in knowing and knowing accurately and fully does, in fact, make us, as Pascal said, "wretched." Some of our greatest thinkers, like Descartes, because they begin with thinking and not with thinking something, are forced to examine the suspicion that we are simply deceived in all we do. But if it were true that we are deceived in our very faculties, in all we know, we wonder why then we can consider the proposition "it is true that we are deceived?" Descartes' grandiose insight carries with it an implicit contradiction. Why are we not deceived about being deceived? Is it because in fact that, about basic things, we are not deceived unless we choose to be? "There are things and I know them," is the truth Gilson taught us adamantly to affirm in the face of every sort of skeptic, including Descartes.

In what then does our wretchedness consist? Surely it does not consist in knowing the truth of our condition, in knowing what John Paul II called "the whole truth about man." Nor does our wretchedness consist in knowing and in delighting in knowing. For when we know and delight in knowing, we are least wretched and most ourselves. Again to know that we are wretched is itself, like all knowledge, a good. Aristotle said (*Politics* 1267a1–15) that the greatest of our crimes come not from hunger, but from a lack of philosophy, or perhaps from the wrong philosophy. The pagans knew of the mystery of our wretchedness. The Jews knew of the Fall. We know of original sin and are surprised that it pertains to us, even when we know that it does. Perhaps the greatest perplexity of philosophy is its inability to propose a solution to the evil that we keep encountering in our souls, generation after generation.

Pascal, aware of these issues, said that what little we could know through genuine curiosity could subsequently be lost by our pride. What did he mean here? He did not mean that we could not know some things, even the proof for God. He knew that there were proofs that, in themselves, did hold water, however difficult the holding. Pascal meant that, at some point, we could impose ourselves on the world as its cause, as the source of its order or at least its potential order. He understood that it was possible for us to want to rival God Himself and to want to set out to do so. This is what pride, *superbia,* means. It means reversing the order of our knowing by holding our artistic or creative capacities, legitimate in their own order, to be superior to our knowing capacities, which themselves, in order to flourish, require something else not themselves, that is, reality itself. Our temptation is to be like gods, not merely in establishing by ourselves the distinction of good and evil, to recall Genesis, but in formulating the distinction between *what is* and what is not. We want to say, in Plato's sense, of what is, that it is not, so that we ourselves are not dependent on *what is* in what we do.

Our ultimate wretchedness consists, then, in mis-understanding what we are, in refusing to live what we are. Hell, thus, is not directly a consequence of God's judgment or of the structures of the world, but of our own choice to define what we, and hence the world, are. The worst thing that could happen to us, Plato told us, would be freely to accept a lie in our souls, knowingly to say of what is not, that it is; and of *what is,* that it is not. But this mis-understanding of what we are, to repeat, is a chosen mis-understanding. It does not happen apart from our willing. It is not neutral or innocent. Here is the source of the real wretchedness that afflicts us: the condition of our wills. Our god, in pride, is, to recall Pascal, without a mediator. Our communion with God, we claim, bypasses revelation. We affirm our own happiness. Our own minds are our only mediators with divinity.

We exchange *what is* for what it is we choose to think. And how exhilarating it is! The first chapter of Nietzsche's *Beyond Good and Evil* is entitled "On the Prejudices of the Philosophers." In it Nietzsche wrote, excitedly, yet ironically, ". . . when a philosophy begins to believe in itself, it always creates the world in its own image; it cannot do otherwise. Philosophy is this tyrannical drive itself, the most spiritual will to power, to 'creation of the world', to *causa prima.*"[3] It is interesting to observe that this philosophy that "creates the world" begins, in Nietzsche's view, precisely when "it begins to believe in itself." It begins not in power but rather in a "spiritual will."

And this claim of self-mediation, of creating in "its own image,"

---

3. Frederick Nietzsche, *Beyond Good and Evil: Prelude to a Philosophy of the Future,* trans. R. J. Hollingdale (Harmondsworth: Penguin, 1975), #9, p. 21.

in the actual order of things, invariably leads to pride, to making ourselves to be gods, *causa prima,* to the freedom to mis-interpret everything *that is.* It must lead in this direction because we implicitly deny something necessary in ourselves and about ourselves that enables us to know, after our limited manner of knowing, the truth about the real God. This is the point at which philosophy is important. Something evidently also philosophical enables us to know what God might want us to know about His inner life were it freely to be presented to us. The communion, Pascal says, is with the God known without mediator. But who is this "God known without a mediator?" Surely it is the God of pride.

Pascal hints that it is the God without the Cross; that is to say, our theories require another kind of God than the one *that is.* "Come down from the Cross and we will believe!" were words shouted at the Crucifixion, words that, had their taunts actually been carried out, would not have resulted in belief or adoration in the shouters. These words again hint at the ultimate temptation, namely, that those who "know" God in some sense as philosophers, that is, without a mediator, refuse to accept the way God in fact deals with men when they begin to suspect, even as philosophers, what it is. The Word made flesh who dwells amongst us establishes the communion with the God *that is,* with He *Who is.* The knowledge of our wretchedness, of our inability to know what we truly want to know, is, however, precisely what enables us to know God who in fact takes on our wretchedness. The mystery of suffering, of the Cross, even in the philosophic order, is the beginning of wisdom. "Man learns by suffering," as Aeschylus wrote.

### III

If we wonder and if we are puzzled, it is because we seem to encounter an order the structure of which we do not yet understand.

We can, to be sure, impose our order on things. We can claim that our order is identical with the order of things or, more likely, establishes the only order they have. This is what ideology and pride are all about. We can impose an explanation on things that does not arise from things themselves but from ourselves. It arises from ourselves because we despair of finding reason in things or because we refuse to admit that there is an order addressed to us, an order of which we are not the cause. We see that an order we did not make may require of us, since we are part of that very order, a reordering of how we live. There exists a tension between our order and *what is*. We notice this tension when something in our own explanation does not square with what is not ourselves, with *what is*. The very fact that we must revise our theories indicates that they are subject to testing from outside ourselves. But it also suggests that we do know something. The most important thing about us is not our curiosity or our wonder, but what we conclude as a result of their presence in us.

We are, it is said, question-forming animals. Some would even suggest that this is our highest definition of ourselves—man, the animal who questions, *animal quaerens*. Linus is scrunched down in his bean-bag seat reading a book. Lucy, his usually petulant sister, is standing placidly behind him. "You don't care anything about anybody!" he admonishes her out of his book. Suddenly steamed up, he leaps out of the seat, points his finger at her, and yells, "You never show any interest in what anyone else is doing. . . . You never ask questions." In the next scene, he carries on eloquently, more soberly, "You never ask me what I'm reading, how I'm doing in school, where I got my new shoes. . . ." Looking right at Lucy, who retains her unmoved expression, Linus' rhetorical embellishment again grows, "You never ask me what I think about something, or what I believe, or what I know, or where I'm going, or where I've been, or anything!" Finally, having said his piece, Linus walks away, still muttering, "If you're going to show interest in other people, you have to ask questions." In the next to the last scene, Lucy is standing all by herself, looking rather contrite but bemused. In the final scene, Linus is back on his bean-bag seat reading. She walks up to him, bending toward him familiarly. As he turns slightly around, obviously with some consternation in his eyes, Lucy asks him, "How have you been?"[4]

If we reflect on these amusing scenes, we find all the great questions there—even, above all, the fact that there are questions, puzzles, wonderments. Questions are expected, questions about what we think, about what we are, about what we believe. Interest in people means asking them questions. Lucy's question—"How have you been?"—is, of course, in context, the most difficult question of all for us to answer, even more difficult than what one believes or knows or does. Lucy asks Linus the "being" question. It could mean "How did you come to be?" Or more probably "give me an account of your inner self, of the state of your being." One suspects that to answer Lucy's question adequately we need to be ourselves divine. This is why, after all his flourish, Linus is not prepared for it.

IV

What do we believe? What do we know? These are indeed philosophic questions, but, as Linus shows us, questions that are fundamental for everyone, even non-philosophers. St. Thomas says that one of the reasons for revelation was the general condition of men in this present life, the difficulty of knowing, the limited time we have to know, the busy-ness of life that makes knowing so distracting and difficult. Chesterton says that Christianity is "democratic"

4. Charles M. Schulz, *Dogs Don't Eat Dessert* (New York: Topper Books, 1987).

in this sense that, recognizing the rarity of good philosophers, it did not leave everyone else in the lurch when it came to ultimate things. Yet, Christianity is also directed to the philosophers, to the limitations of their knowing, to the wretchedness that envelops even the philosophers.

Faith and the intellectual life of man are often posed as if they were in conflict with each other, as if we had to choose one or the other, as if we could not be both philosophers and believers. We must, it is said, walk by faith or by reason, but not by both. Kierkegaard, in a famous phrase, itself designed to recall St. Augustine's famous phrase, when asked why he believed, responded, *"credo quia absurdam."* St. Augustine had explained, *"credo ut intelligam."* Christian thought in particular, and this is what is perhaps most unique about it, has always juxtaposed the two ideas *"fides quaerens intellectum"* and *"intellectus quaerens fidem."* They belong together. If we believe, we are still to use our minds; indeed we use them better. If we think, we wonder about what it is that we cannot seem to figure out even with the best of our own powers and efforts. Knowing also leads to wondering.

In all of this back and forth between reason and faith, we are mindful of St. Thomas's phrase that "grace builds on nature." He assures us that "nature and grace are not contradictory." The proof of his assurance is to show us one case in which they are. If things of God appear to be "absurd," or if, to use St. Ignatius' phrase, "what is black is said (by faith) to be white," we are aware that the black and the absurdity are never understood to indicate chaos or disorder or lack of intelligence. What is absurd turns out, after long examination, to lead to something that makes sense, something that we would not otherwise have known without wondering about, examining what is revealed. If grace builds on nature, nature is something that must be attended to in its own order, for its own sake. Even the philosophical denial that there is a nature, an order of secondary causes, is a philosophic statement that can and must be examined with the same reason that proposes and justifies the denial.

If we are going to have an intellectual life at all, therefore, it is necessary, to recall Linus' admonitions, to pose questions to oneself and to others, to pose and to listen to and examine the answers given to the questions. Those who merely question with no expectation of or concern for answers are not really questioning. They have already taken a view of the world that sees it as intrinsically chaotic or irrational. Revelation is not designed to destroy reason, though it may indirectly have the effect of revolutionizing reason, especially a reason proud in its own independence. The status of reason addressed by revelation is in fact to become more, not less, reasonable. No doubt, it will seem unjust to a professional philosopher to learn that his lack of belief, his serene autonomy as a philosopher, may in fact be what most prevents him from being a philosopher, assuming that a philosopher is not properly understood to be one who refuses to look at or think about something simply because it is said to be revealed. The refusal to examine revelation is part of the refusal to examine *all that is.* The philosopher remains someone willing to look at, think about *whatever is.*

## V

What role does faith have in the life of the intellect? The answer I will suggest here is that revelation will make it more intellectual. At the same time, it will make it less prone to substitute its own speculations about unanswered questions for more plausible and sensible answers to the same questions presented by revelation. Both revelation and philosophy do purport to be explanations of reality. They cannot simply ignore or deny each other's claims on the grounds that their origins are different.

What is being said here? In Lecture Nine of "University Teach-ings," in *The Idea of a University,* Newman wrote: "Christian truth is purely of revelation; that revelation we can but explain, we cannot increase, except relatively to our own apprehensions; without it we should have known nothing of its contents, with it we know just as much as its contents, and nothing more. And as it was given by a di-vine act independent of man, so it will remain in spite of man."[5] Without the contents of revelation, Newman emphasizes, we should know nothing of its particular contents by ourselves. We would be thrown back on philosophy alone for an explanation of things. Once we know something of the contents of revelation, it is possible for us to examine what they might mean and how they might relate to things about which philosophers have thought. In other words, it is possible to compare what revelation has proposed to man with the claims of other religions and philosophies about these same issues. It is possible to make a rational judgment about the plausibility and superiority of one to the other on grounds that are, properly, philo-sophic.

What is revealed is given apart from any contribution of man and will remain what it is. Does this position mean that the non-believing philosopher is, by definition, unable to deal with revela-tion? Not quite, I think. In one sense, no doubt, philosophy can so organize itself, once it knows something of what revelation says of itself—this is public knowledge, after all—to make it impossible to be a religious believer. Certain positions are deliberately or implicit-ly taken that make belief impossible. In this sense, the rejection of revelation stands on philosophic grounds whose premises can be ex-amined for their truth.

Christianity, for example, is to some degree dependent for its

5. John Henry Newman, *The Idea of a University* (Garden City, N.Y.: Doubleday, 1959), p. 229.

credibility on miracles. We are long familiar with certain notions of science that are said to make it impossible to know or accept miracles or their possibility. Since this or that scientific theory is true, it is said, miracles are not possible. One preliminary Christian response to this position would be that since miracles, on the basis of evidence, do happen, there must be something wrong with the reductionist "theory" that denies their possibility. Reductionism means, in general, that we can hold only what our methodology allows us to hold—that reality is a function of our methods, not of itself. The problem here, of course, is not with miracles but with methodology, hence with philosophy.

Christianity in general and Catholicism in particular has been a religion in which philosophy played a special role. Christianity, unlike Islam and Judaism, was not a revelation of a law but a revelation of a teaching, a truth. What mattered was not primarily the observance of the dictates of a law but what was understood about God, man, and the world. Revelation was intended for everyone, including the philosophers. Indeed, in the Christian scheme of things, the philosopher performed a particularly important role. He was not, as Newman indicated, to change what was revealed, which did not properly fall under his jurisdiction or competency except to the extent that revelation did present itself as a coherent body of knowledge or understanding that could be fruitfully examined.

The Christian creeds and explanations of Christian beliefs and practices have long been formulated in orderly and intelligible concepts, themselves analogously or directly related to the subject matter they express. They may yet be capable of more clarity or perfection but as they stand they represent a tremendous work of reason reflecting on, further explaining what was revealed. This corpus is not something the true philosopher, concerned with *all that is,* can simply ignore as if it did not exist. Any deliberate refusal to confront these articulated positions indicates a refusal of intellect to examine *all that is,* to examine its own object.

It is said since at least Henry VIII that the British Crown bears the title *Defensor Fidei.* Whether it has done a good job at this noble task leads to remarkable reflections involving the papacy and the abidingness of doctrine over the centuries. It may even lead to the conclusion that the faith has not been adequately defended by the monarchical institution. Strictly speaking, the philosopher, unlike certain kings, would not want to be called a "defender of the faith." The faithful man who is also a philosopher does not admit that the two "sides" in him, reason and revelation, are incoherent. He does not wish to be an Averroist in any form. The rejection of any "two truth" theory—wherein, within the same soul, contradictories could be true—is typically Thomist in philosophy and theology.

That is to say, philosophy and revelation, since they reside in the same being, have an intimacy and coherence within the same person that allow for a retention of their distinction of origin and purpose and their inner relationship. The philosopher does not want to, nor can he, reason from his rational analysis to the truths of the faith such that he can assure us, by reason, that revelation is thinkable. The philosopher's own *modus credendi* cannot be the approval by his own reason of the truths of revelation, as if it were his reason that makes them thinkable. Some things the philosopher still must believe, even when he understands under the impetus of revelation.

Thomas Aquinas talked of certain philosophical truths that he called the *"preambula fidei."* One of the shocks that medieval theologians, Christian, Muslim, and Jewish, got from the discovery of the Greek classics, particularly Aristotle and Plato, was that the human mind, on its own, as it were, seemed to be able to know much more about the highest things, including God, than they had ever anticipated from reading the Books of Revelation themselves. Many theologians even wondered if Plato in particular did not have some sort of private revelation that would have guided him to his great explanations of the Good and the Beautiful and the Just. They were reluctant to admit that his lofty knowledge was the product of mere reason.

Aquinas, looking at Aristotle, did not think that one needed to resort to revelation to explain the extraordinary power of the human mind as instanced in an Aristotle. Indeed, Aquinas thought rather that it was not to the glory of God to downplay the works of God, especially those lodged in man. What this means in practice is that the work of the philosopher is at its best a great work. One might even expect that the meeting of reason and revelation might require in some sense that the best in philosophy be articulated before we might appreciate fully what is revealed. It is a perfection of the natural intellect, as it were, to arrange itself before truth, before *what is,* in such a way that it can be prepared to receive revelation after the manner in which revelation can be received by philosophy. Revelation is never received by philosophy as if its conclusions must be accepted *by reason.* Rather it is received by philosophy as if its conclusions are in fact at least possible or plausible answers to questions that reason has already asked itself but could not adequately resolve by itself.

The philosopher is said to seek a knowledge of the whole within which he himself exists. His questions, ever prodding, come from within the whole. They are his questions about his existence, his purpose. Even if he understood the whole, he would be aware that he is inside this same whole and not outside it in a position to establish *what it is* in the way it is. If we speak of philosophy having limits, we do so against the background of the capacity of the mind to know, as Aristotle defined it, "all things." If philosophy is the love of wisdom, the love of truth, it does not want to deceive itself.

It does not want to will what is not to be true merely to justify its own claim to know all things. This imposition of its own will on reality as its explanation would somehow skewer the mind's own direction toward *what is.*

Pride, we intimated earlier, means that we make ourselves the cause for the existence of and distinction in things. Perhaps it can be said that pride is the vice most dangerous to the philosopher. Surely Augustine and Paul thought this to be the case. On the other hand, the things that are most close to divinity are naturally the most delicate and, for that reason, the most dangerous. At the same time, they are the most glorious. The whole enterprise of creation as it is understood from the revelational side seems to intimate to us that the most dangerous creatures, both of men and of angels, are the most spiritual and prideful ones. This is why, most often, it seems that certain erroneous moral and philosophical positions seem to be most rashly defended. For, if they are refuted or shown to be inconsistent or self-contradictory, it means that the possibility at least of the truth of revelation, over against them, is unavoidably presented for rational consideration. The struggles of the philosophers thus are not usually or simply philosophical quibbles. They are most often last ditch stands that are openly or covertly seen as the only remaining reasons why our lives as we have lived them are justified, why they ought not to be changed because of what is revealed to us.

## VI

The intellectual life, no doubt, must be taken with some pleasantness if we are ever to see its relation to revelation. Evelyn Waugh recounts the story in his, for our purposes, marvelously titled autobiography, *A Little Learning,* in which he shows what a "dangerous thing" it is. He is in his college days at Hertford where the, to Waugh, distasteful subject of school spirit comes up. Waugh was suspected of a lack of said enthusiasm there. During a Freshman rally, a young man to whom Waugh refers as a "tipsy white colonial"—which I suppose could be an American—invaded his rooms threatening him and demanding to know "what he (Waugh) did for the college?" "I drank for it," was Waugh's quick and witty reply.[6] Some questions thus have unexpected answers, answers that delight us. It is perhaps not too far-fetched to suggest that the relation of reason and revelation is like this, that our legitimate questions are given unexpected answers that delight us, or at least should delight us if we will allow them. Be that as it may, the unexpected answers bear with them a delight that often contrasts with the despair or solemnity of the question as originally and frequently asked in philosophy, itself still arriving, in spite of its multiple proposals, at no proper or feasible solution from reason alone.

If we look at revelation as philosophers, we cannot simply pretend that it does not exist, that some articulated, orderly presentation of its content is not a presence in the world for our consideration. It is present as something handed down, something that is consistent, coherent, unchangeable in its foundations, something that did not originate in philosophy and did not claim to do so. Whatever our final judgment about it may be, not to acknowledge its inner coherence and the terms of its self-understanding is to deny our philosophic vocation to consider *all that is*. While it is true, from the revelational point of view, as Newman noted, that this content and the fact of revelation's existence in the world has nothing to do with human initiative, nonetheless, it is addressed to human understanding and intellect in the sense that it can be understood and reflected on by philosophers who are not also believers in the revelation, though by the latter too.

6. Evelyn Waugh, *A Little Learning: An Autobiography* (Boston: Little, Brown, 1964), p. 164.

Just as Christians can understand something of Judaism or Islam or Hinduism, so philosophers can understand something of the teachings or understandings offered by the great religions explaining themselves. Christianity in particular has been attentively reflected on by philosophers so that it does not stand without inherited philosophic depth. Contrariwise, believers are not free simply to ignore the claims and methods of the philosophers. This is not to deny that there may, in principle, be things in philosophy or in the human explanations of the revelational traditions that are not true. The philosophers and the theologians, each taken as a group, do, on certain basic points, contradict each other.

Sorting out these contradictions is one of the essential aspects of the adventure of truth, one of the reasons why philosophy remains essential to revelation's complete mission in the world. These contradictions may well mean, indeed in some cases must mean, that certain positions are not true and must be identified as such. But the judgment that something is not true does not mean that the position at issue had no meaning, that it was not a "plausible" error, so to speak. As an exercise in thought and reflection, error is well worth knowing. Indeed, as Plato and Aquinas imply, we cannot really know the truth of things unless we can also account for the errors related to the articulated truth. The real adventure of philosophy and theology is, in part, the understanding of positions that are "almost" true or that are true but only when seen in a whole context.

The link between reason and revelation cannot be, and is not presented to be, a necessary relationship such that human reason can "prove" the truths of revelation. For human reason to be able to do this "proving" would imply that this reason is, in fact, a divine reason. Nevertheless, human reason is a reason and as such capable of responding to the divine reason if in fact it is presented to it in some fashion. And while belief in the truths of revelation requires grace, what is revealed does not demand the denial of intellect, but fosters it. Since it is a fact of divine revelation that it need not have happened, human reason can find no "necessary" reason why it must have happened. This is why Aquinas will call many of his reasons for believing to be, on the philosophical side, "suasive," and not "necessary."

From the side of reason, however, itself looking for answers to its own legitimately formulated questions, revelation appears as but another possibility, or at least as another plausible answer to a perplexity that has remained unresolved by the philosophers. But it is a "possibility." In this lies the peculiar disturbance that all proper revelation gives to closed philosophic systems unwilling even to consider its possibility. And this refusal is what turns good philosophy into bad philosophy, into the embrace of contradictions it will not admit. The "bad conscience" of modern philosophy in particular consists in its unwillingness to admit that revelation appears as a response to its own best efforts. Nietzsche had it right: "Every profound thinker is more afraid of being understood than of being misunderstood. The latter may perhaps wound his vanity; but the former will wound his heart, his sympathy, which says always: 'alas, why do you want to have as hard a time of it as I have?'"[7] The "wounded heart" and the "hard time" are perhaps signs of the despair of the philosopher, the "profound thinker," who has not discovered the truth and yet knows, again in his heart, that his path has been of his own making.

The philosopher who rejects the "reason" contained within revelation, moreover, can always find some kind of alternate reason to justify his rejection. His dismissal of revelation will necessarily result in a counterproposal or thesis to answer the original question.

7. Nietzsche, *Beyond Good and Evil*, #290, p. 197.

This philosophical alternative itself will be in some degree untrue and hence will have consequences within the order of reason itself—and ultimately within the world, when its prescriptions are carried out in time and place in ways that the philosopher often did not anticipate. This is why, in modernity, there is a close correlation between the rise of ideology and the rejection of revelation or attenuation of faith. How is it that Voegelin put it?

> Great masses of Christianized men who are not strong enough for the heroic adventure of faith become susceptible to ideas that could give them a greater degree of certainty about the meaning of their existence than faith. The reality of faith as it is known in its truth by Christianity is difficult to bear, and the flight from clearly seen reality to gnostic constructs will probably always be a phenomenon of wide extent in civilizations that Christianity has permeated.[8]

Ideology bears within it not the simple unknowing of the philosopher but the deliberate refusal to accept one plausible explanation of valid human questions. Both Voegelin and Nietzsche seem to think that Christian or former Christian thinkers are most susceptible to deviant or gnostic philosophic alternatives.

The reason for this susceptibility may very well be, as Strauss maintained, that the elevated expectations of faith remain in the culture even when faith itself becomes weaker.[9] Hence, philosophy strives desperately to discover alternatives to the rejected or forgotten answers given by revelation to the legitimate questions of philosophy. Thus, while revelation directs itself to reason, it does not command it without grace and consent. Revelation does leave the lingering sense that things do in fact fit together somehow, because

---

8. Eric Voegelin, *Science, Politics and Gnosticism* (Chicago: Regnery/Gateway, 1968), p. 109.

9. See Leo Strauss, *Thoughts on Machiavelli* (Glencoe, Ill.: The Free Press, 1958), p. 176.

philosophy is at its best when prodded by revelation. It is, as it were, better than itself. But it does not and cannot, even under the prodding of revelation, forget its own humble origins in its Socratic not knowing, in its Thomist negative theology by which, as Josef Pieper said, we know the perfections of God only by denying the limits of the perfections that we do know.[10] The experience of our own existence causes us to wonder both about why we are and why anything at all is. Our curiosity can lead us to pride, in which we close ourselves in ourselves. We cannot remain closed within ourselves without justifying ourselves, justifying ourselves to the world, to the whole, to reason. Reason can examine what revelation says of itself, what it says about God, about eternal life, about resurrection, about virtue, about evil. It can also see that its own ponderings lead it to a wondering about things that it does not seem able to know or conclude. It can recognize that revelation's statements about itself are at least plausible answers to questions that arose independently of revelation.

Here lies the narrow gap, here is found the flickering light that philosophy can see and be assured that revelation is not totally implausible. The "heroic adventure of faith," as Voegelin called it, may be less tortuous than he postulated, however difficult it remains. "The flight from clearly seen reality," after all, is the very opposite of the trends and instincts both of Incarnation and of the philosophy of *what is* that it accepts from the philosophers and on which it bases itself. Revelation, in the end, is as much an affirmation of and concern for *what is* in all its human and material reality as it is a response to philosophy's own unanswered questions, questions that always arise from man's experience of existence in the world and from his unavoidable wonderments about its cause.

10. See Josef Pieper, *A Guide to Thomas Aquinas* (San Francisco: Ignatius Press, 1986), pp. 147–60.

*Alice Ramos*

# 10. FROM LITERATURE TO PHILOSOPHY: FAITH'S IMPACT ON MY WORK

乄

## I. INTRODUCTION: FAITH AND CULTURE

In an article which I wrote several years ago, titled "The Enlightened Mentality and Academic Freedom," I argued that the issue of academic freedom among contemporary theologians is not a new phenomenon.[1] In order to substantiate this claim, I referred to Kant's essay "What Is Enlightenment?" where Kant distinguishes between the public and private uses of reason and gives as an example the clergyman-scholar. In the private use of his reason, the clergyman must teach what the church teaches, that is, what he has committed himself by oath to the church to teach; but in his public use of reason as a scholar speaking to a cosmopolitan community, his scholarly findings may put him at odds with the church. In the name of enlightenment and of "mature" reason, Kant's clergyman-scholar will have no qualms in publishing research that is not in keeping with the truths and doctrines of his church; he will think, on the contrary, that his research serves to enlighten the masses.

---

1. See Alice Ramos, "The Enlightened Mentality and Academic Freedom," in *The Common Things: Essays on Thomism and Education,* ed. Daniel McInerny (Washington, D.C.: AMA/The Catholic University of America Press, 2000), pp. 35–47.

Now while it is possible to consider some present-day Catholic theologians as the contemporary counterparts of Kant's clergyman-scholar, I wish also to call attention to some Catholic politicians and how they too have fallen prey to the enlightenment mentality. It is not unusual to hear a Catholic politician distinguish between what he or she as a "private" person holds to be true, and what he or she as a "public" figure will allow. While the politician who is a Catholic may claim that he does not hold to abortion as a private citizen, nonetheless, as a public figure he may not consider it his right to "impose his moral convictions," and therefore will allow for legislation which upholds the right of women to choose for themselves. If one's faith has no bearing on one's work, as in the case of the Catholic politician, or if one's faith is to be called into question due to one's "scientific" findings, as in the case of Kant's clergyman-scholar, then is there any real connection between one's faith and one's work? I submit that faith, like knowledge, has to inform our life, our work, and where this is not the case, we begin to act somewhat like schizophrenics, having a divided life, compartmentalizing sectors of our life, so that we lack what might be called unity of life.[2]

If I speak of an informing, as it were, of our faith in our work, as form would inform matter, it is because I realize that when faith is relegated simply to the fulfillment of a Sunday obligation, and when in a sense our work week is alienated from that Sunday obligation, we probably have begun to alienate ourselves from our faith.

2. The notion of unity of life is used by Alasdair MacIntyre in *After Virtue* (Notre Dame: University of Notre Dame Press, 1984), in which he speaks of the human life not as a series of discontinuous episodes, but rather as a whole, a narrative, which aspires to truth (see chapter 15). See also on the notion of unity of life, St. Josemaría Escrivá de Balaguer, "Passionately Loving the World," homily given at the University of Navarre in 1967, published in *Conversations with Msgr. Escrivá de Balaguer* (New York: Scepter, 1968).

This is certainly not to say that in our work we become spokespersons for the Catholic Church, that the solutions which we propose in our work are "the Catholic solutions." Along these lines, it is interesting to note that the Catholic Church's social doctrine itself is not dictating solutions, but on the contrary providing guidelines and direction, so that then ordinary Christian citizens, informed by those guidelines, will responsibly use their freedom to create a more just society, wherever they may find themselves.[3] It is this response to Church teaching and to faith which, I think, Pope John Paul II has in mind when he speaks of how faith must penetrate culture: "A faith which does not make itself culture is not a faith fully received, not totally thought out, not faithfully lived."[4]

## II. HOW FAITH BECAME INTEGRAL
## TO MY WORK

The penetration of faith in culture, in work, seems of paramount importance to me, not because I have always lived it, but precisely because at one point in my life I did dissociate my faith from my work and then found myself, to a great extent, in an epistemological crisis. The dissociation had resulted not from a break from my faith, for I still continued to practice my faith, but rather in part from the influence of the liberal environment of a secular graduate school which did not foster the relationship between faith and culture, but was either indifferent or perhaps even hostile to it.

In the 1970s while I was studying French literature at New York University, I became more interested in methodology than in the literature itself; the professors who seemed most interesting to me at the time were all approaching literary texts from either a struc-

---

3. See Pope John Paul II, *On Social Concern* (Boston: St. Paul Editions, 1987).
4. Address to the Pontifical Council for Culture, Rome, June 6, 1987.

turalist, a psychoanalytical, or a phenomenological perspective. It
was to the latter that I was devoting most of my time, reading in
particular Sartre, Merleau-Ponty, and Heidegger. Although I had
attended a Catholic college and had taken at least twelve credits of
philosophy courses, I was nonetheless not equipped to critically
read these philosophers, nor to make sense out of "the conflict of
interpretations," which I perceived in my graduate courses. The
phenomenological perspective seemed to me at the time the most
appropriate for the literary texts that I was interested in. I was particularly drawn then to the French "new novel," in part because of
its non-traditional conception of the novel, but also because of the
demands placed on the reader: the reader of a French "new novel"
was to be more than a passive spectator, he was required to actively
participate in the constitution or unveiling of the world present in
the novel. The reader was being called upon to uncover the world
which emerged upon a reading of the text and to reactivate, as it
were, the intentional projection of the author, which made possible
the emergence of that world. A phenomenological reading of such
texts, that is, of French "new novels," allowed me then to consider
questions regarding the intentionality of works of art, along with
the constitution of their truth and meaning.

While I was pursuing such work at the graduate level, little or no
mention was made regarding the value of literary texts, their effect
on the reader, their moral implications. Although I was aware from
my college days that the reading of certain types of texts could be
morally harmful, this was not a question which I think I ever considered in my research.[5] It was not until I finished my course work

5. How texts, whether philosophical, literary, musical, etc. can have a negative impact on a person's moral life and/or on her beliefs are perhaps not taken seriously
enough. We often think of ourselves as being sufficiently grown-up and thus almost
invulnerable to such influence. I think, however, that this is naive and that certain

and started my dissertation—a Heideggerian-phenomenological analysis of the novels of Michel Butor, a French "new novelist"—that I was confronted with a similar question. While in Paris, beginning the research for my dissertation, which meant not only reading the novels and critical writings of Butor, but also immersing myself in the ontological phenomenology of Heidegger's *Being and Time* and in his writings on language and the work of art, an artist-friend of mine questioned me as to the value and truth of Heidegger's philosophy, and as to whether or not certain philosophical views might have a negative impact on my life as a believer.[6] The truth was that such a question had not occurred to me, and I was upset by the question; I remember going to the national library that day and starting to read more of Heidegger's works, in addition to learning more about his life. I think I decided that very day that I needed to acquire more philosophical knowledge, so that I could better judge the worth of the texts that I was reading.

The question posed by my artist-friend was meant to be of help, although at the time I suppose that I could only see it as complicating my life, or as disrupting what until then had been a rather straightforward and continuous course of study: one starts graduate school, goes through a series of courses, passes qualifying examinations, and then starts the dissertation, which one hopes to finish in

---

types of reading can be harmful not only to children but also to adults, particularly to those without sufficient moral and doctrinal formation.

6. See note 5. I do not mean here to make a negative judgment regarding Heidegger's philosophy. As with any philosopher, we should be interested in knowing how his thought approaches or distances itself from the truth. St. Thomas says succinctly: "The study of philosophy is not done in order to know what men have thought, but rather to know how truth herself stands." In *De Coelo,* lect. 22; Marietti ed. 109, n. 228, quoted in M.-D. Chenu, *Toward Understanding Saint Thomas,* trans. A. M. Landry and D. Hughes (Chicago: Regnery, 1964), p. 28. See also on a very similar question Alasdair MacIntyre, *First Principles, Final Ends and Contemporary Philosophical Issues* (Milwaukee: Marquette University Press, 1990), p. 66.

view of the tenure-track position. The question threw me into a crisis, which I think can best be described by some other questions
which I probably asked myself: What's going on here? How do I
make sense out of this situation? How could I have been so stupid
as to think that I could isolate my faith from my work? The question asked by my friend led me to think that my faith was very important to me, and that I did not want to jeopardize it. It was a moment of real conversion for me, in which I saw, perhaps not so
clearly as I do now, that God was addressing me in the most normal
of a person's circumstances, that is, her work.

I was nevertheless, at the time, presented with a dilemma: Should
I continue the dissertation or should I leave a degree program that I
had worked years on to embark on philosophical studies? The
dilemma was not immediately resolved or resolvable; I was fortunate, however, to have met at the time in Paris a student at the Institute of Comparative Philosophy. Through her, I went to see the
Dean of the Institute; I had given some thought to starting courses
in philosophy there the following year, which would have meant either dropping the dissertation in French literature altogether or at
least postponing it. After hearing my story, the Dean was more than
willing to accept me there as a student. The Institute had been established after the 1968 revolution in Paris by some laymen concerned about philosophical formation: their goal was to establish a
program in philosophy which would have as a comparative framework the Aristotelian-Thomistic philosophy, and also through such
a program to foster the complementarity between faith and reason
(a singular project, indeed, within French intellectual circles). Such
a program appealed to me very much, because it seemed to me ex-
actly what I needed; besides, through methodological problems in
literature, I had realized that I was more interested in philosophy
than in literature. I next went to see Roger Verneaux, one of the

professors of the Institute and a respected philosopher in his own right; I had about a two-hour conversation with him, which only confirmed my desire to do philosophy.

However, before undertaking another program of study, since my fellowship year in Paris was drawing to a close, I knew that I had to return to New York. While still in Paris, I had been given the name of Father Vincent Miceli, to whom I wrote for advice. He responded with a long letter, which certainly sympathized with the situation, and with an invitation to visit him at Fordham University upon my return to New York. The letter also indicated that perhaps I would do well to finish my dissertation in French literature, before starting to study philosophy. This was advice which I followed, and upon the suggestion of Fr. Miceli, I audited some of the classes of Alice von Hildebrand at Hunter College, classes which I found exciting. I suppose that she became for me the model of the academic woman, of the philosopher committed to her faith.

Fr. Miceli's advice seemed to be on target, although finishing the dissertation took more time than I had anticipated, since shortly after my return to New York, I was offered a full-time college position in French. Because my only teaching experience had been as a graduate assistant at NYU, I decided to take the position, although I knew that it would delay the dissertation. During this time, I was also trying to cultivate my faith, in part through attendance at classes of philosophy and theology, through readings and meditation which would help to build the edifice of my soul. I wanted to nurture my faith and not simply rely on what I had learned in Catholic schools from grade school to college. I thought it important to have a knowledge of the Catholic faith which would be proportionate to my graduate education.

As soon as I finished my dissertation, I looked into the possibility of studying philosophy in the States; I audited some philosophy classes at Columbia University, but decided to look elsewhere for a program of study. Some friends mentioned the University of Navarre in Pamplona, Spain. At the time, I thought that I would pursue work in philosophy of language and in aesthetics, since these seemed to me the closest to my own literary and linguistic background. When I wrote to one of the professors at Navarre asking for information regarding their program in philosophy, the response was such that I had the impression that there I would be able to acquire the type of philosophical formation that I wanted: formation in the Aristotelian-Thomistic tradition, besides work in philosophy of language. In fact, while at Navarre, I once heard a Belgian professor from Louvain say that the University of Navarre was becoming in Europe what Louvain had once been: a prestigious center of learning in the Catholic tradition.

The first year that I spent at Navarre, in addition to taking graduate courses in philosophy, I spent time doing research in analytical philosophy; readings in this area seemed to me rather dry and arid. Before the end of the second semester of my first year at Navarre, the professor who was to become my dissertation advisor suggested that I read the first question of Aquinas's *Disputed Questions on Truth* and a commentary on it written by a Spanish philosopher. This reading proved an invaluable introduction to St. Thomas, and made me realize that I wanted to pursue study in Aquinas. Years later, reading Edith Stein's life, I could understand how her encounter with Aquinas's *De Veritate* would make her think that she had finally found the truth. Such was my own encounter with the *De Veritate*.[7]

In becoming more familiar with the work of Aquinas through-

7. In my intellectual and spiritual itinerary, I am indebted to friends and fellow-travelers on the road to truth. I have been able to count on them for support and correction.

out my years at Navarre, I realized that the Aristotelian-Thomistic tradition could shed light on the "conflict of interpretations" which I had experienced in my graduate studies in New York. An appeal to this tradition provides the resources for understanding the predicaments of contemporary thought. So I embarked at Navarre on a rather singular project: through a study of contemporary theories of sign and meaning and through a recovery of the tradition regarding the sign, I proposed to arrive at a formulation of a metaphysics of the sign.[8] It seemed to me that semioticians of culture such as Umberto Eco and Jacques Derrida recognized the metaphysical implications of the traditional concept of the sign, but that they preferred to opt for the "absent structure" or for a deconstruction of the sign. I tried to show how semiotics can be considered an outgrowth of Kantian philosophy: the representational transcendentality of Kant is replaced by a signifying transcendentality, which transforms everything into a sign, such that things considered as signs are no longer knowable in themselves but are rather to be constructed, constituted, by man's knowledge.[9] The crucial philosophical problem which I saw underlying contemporary semiotics was the question regarding the truth of being, the intelligibility of things.[10] Such a question could not be resolved within the

8. Alice Ramos, *Signum: De la Semiótica Universal a la Metafísica del Signo* (Pamplona: EUNSA, 1987). See Giovanni Manetti, "A Metaphysical Theory of Sign," a review article of my book, in *Semiotica* 91, nos. 3/4 *(1992)*, pp. 359–70.

9. Kant brought about the end of metaphysics, as it were, through his transcendental philosophy. And the latter has been replaced by linguistics or semiotics in the twentieth century. Such an interpretation from Kant to Peirce is given by Karl Otto Apel in *Towards a Transformation of Philosophy,* trans. Glyn Adey and David Frisby (London: Routledge & Kegan Paul, 1980).

10. According to MacIntyre in his *First Principles,* it is because we have forgotten that truth is predicable of things that attention has shifted from this truth to new theories of truth, such as the correspondence and coherence theories, and the idealization of warranted assertibility; see p.32 and pp. 61–62.

framework of contemporary theories of sign and meaning, and so I looked to Aquinas for the resources necessary to develop a metaphysics of the sign. In so doing, I found an Aquinas not only indebted to Aristotle but also heavily influenced by Augustine and the Neoplatonic tradition. A metaphysics of the sign as developed within this tradition permits an explanation of reality, of the nature of knowledge and of the expression of this knowledge, in terms of signs, such that a universal semiotics can indeed be posited, and such that the ultimate foundation for this signifying system is an Absolute Intellect, Absolute Truth. Man's role in this signifying system or universe is to perfect himself, to return himself and all else to the origin from whence they came. Through right knowing and right acting, that is, in conformity with the truth, man brings about a return to the beginning, to the origin of all truth, to Divine Intelligence.

So, interestingly enough, in my search for the metaphysical foundations of the sign, I found myself not only in the Aristotelian-Thomistic tradition, but also in an Augustinian and Neoplatonic framework, in which man is viewed as image of God, but also as having to become more like God, which he does as he returns himself to his origin, which is also his end (the *exitus-reditus* theme). In arriving at this conclusion, I was far from those existentialist and phenomenological thinkers who had served to introduce me into the world of philosophy. The famous theses of Sartre: "Existence precedes essence," and man as "a useless passion;" and of Heidegger, the world as a system of references which points to the existence of man, as a being thrown into existence, as an "undeciphered sign." These theses, along with others, could lead one to think that neither the world nor man had meaning and yet, that it was necessary to create, to construct meaning. From there then, the turn to artistic, literary activity, which creates meaning (which is the case in Sartre), or the turn to language, to signs, as instruments for comprehension, as a vehicle to create meaning, as openness toward the world, or as "the house of being" (in Heidegger's phrase). I had gone then from language and literature, from the construction of meaning, to the truth of the concept and the judgment, to the truth of reality, and finally to Divine Truth.

## III. MY TASK AS A CATHOLIC PHILOSOPHER

Once I returned to the States, after having been at the University of Navarre from 1980 to 1986, I knew that I wanted to continue work in that tradition which fostered amicable relations between faith and reason, for the truths of faith are not contrary to reason, and the truth arrived at by rightly using our reason does not contradict what God has revealed.[11] The Catholic philosopher should definitely have a certain superiority complex, since the goal of classical philosophy, which is ultimate wisdom, ultimate truth, has been revealed in the Person of Jesus Christ. True philosophy cannot but have a theological dimension.[12] Aristotle's metaphysics clearly shows how man's natural desire to know can be satisfied only by absolute truth, a truth which without divine revelation he could not attain to in its entirety.

In characterizing Christianity as true philosophy, Joseph Cardinal Ratzinger offers two reasons from Justin Martyr for the unity of philosophy and theology in early Christianity: "First, the philosopher's task is to search for God. Second, the attitude of the true philosopher is to live according to the Logos and in its company. Christian existence means life in conformity to the Logos; that is

11. St. Thomas Aquinas, *Summa contra Gentiles* I, 7, trans. by the Dominican Fathers (London: Burns, Oates, & Washbourne, Ltd., 1929).

12. MacIntyre, *First Principles,* p. 29.

why Christians are true philosophers and why Christianity is true philosophy."[13] It makes sense therefore for the Catholic philosopher to put his intelligence at the service of Christ, Who is the Truth, the Way, and the Life.

But given that we attribute the distinction between philosophy and theology to Aquinas, one might ask how true to St. Thomas one would be if one maintained the unity of philosophy and theology as it was understood in early Christianity. According to Aquinas, philosophy makes use of unaided reason in order to arrive at the ultimate explanations and causes of reality, whereas theology is faith seeking understanding of what God has revealed. Aquinas thus distinguishes the two fields; he does not, however, oppose them; the opposition between the two came much later. As Cardinal Ratzinger puts it: "With a terminology still inchoate in Saint Thomas's works, the domains of inquiry belonging to philosophy and theology were distinguished, respectively, as the natural and supernatural orders. These distinctions reached their full vigor only in the modern period, which then read them back into Saint Thomas, thus imposing on him an interpretation which severs him more radically from the preceding tradition than is warranted by the texts alone."[14] Ratzinger notes that the strict separation of faith and reason dates back to the late Middle Ages; one has only to think of Ockham, who is often labeled the initiator of the Modern Age, and would certainly not have as his project that of unifying classical philosophy and the Catholic faith; and still later in the history of philosophy one can point to Kant's Enlightenment project, which undoubtedly pits faith against reason. Certainly, St. Thomas's own intellectual endeavors could never be seen in this light. It is clear

13. "Faith, Philosophy and Theology," in *The Nature and Mission of Theology,* trans. Adrian Walker (San Francisco: Ignatius Press, 1995), pp. 14–15.
14. Ibid., pp. 16–17.

that he does not pursue wisdom without recourse to revealed wisdom. In fact, he identifies Catholic theology with absolute wisdom, for the absolute consideration of the highest cause of the universe, the knowledge of divine things, which pertains to the highest wisdom, is precisely the object of Catholic theology.[15]

Since Catholic theology does therefore provide us with wisdom regarding the origin and end of the universe, as well as with truth regarding how man should lead his life in order to attain his final end, then why not make use of divine revelation, of the certitude of faith, in our pursuit of metaphysical and moral truth?[16] Should we not make use of truth in our philosophical inquiry wherever we may find it? What we know through faith, therefore, provides us with a definite cognitive advantage, which the greatest of classical minds, Aristotle and Plato, had no access to. Since the pursuit of truth in metaphysical and moral matters is difficult indeed (this does not mean, however, that unaided reason cannot attain to truth in these matters), faith helps reason so that it not be led astray from the truth. Of course, this is not to say that the Catholic philosopher who knows the answers through faith should not use his reason to offer sound arguments. It is precisely because at times Catholic philosophers do not present solid arguments to support what they know through faith that they are unable to bring others to the truth. And in so doing, we might even say that they deprive others of those natural arguments which might lead them, with the aid of grace, to supernatural belief, for grace builds on nature.

So given what we have said, it is time now to speak of the task of

15. St. Thomas Aquinas, *Summa Theologiae* I, q. 1, a. 6, trans. by the Dominican Fathers (Chicago: Benziger Bros., 1948). See also *Summa contra Gentiles* II, 4.

16. See Alfred J. Freddoso, "Two Roles for Catholic Philosophers," in *Recovering Nature: Essays in Natural Philosophy, Ethics, and Metaphysics in Honor of Ralph McInerny,* ed. John P. O'Callaghan and Thomas S. Hibbs (Notre Dame: University of Notre Dame Press, 1999), pp. 229–53.

the Catholic philosopher. According to Aquinas, reason helps faith by demonstrating the preambles to the articles of faith, the most important of which are the existence of God and His attributes.[17] By observing the beauty and order of the universe, the human mind can come to a knowledge of its creator. But because such knowledge is difficult to arrive at, requiring much time and effort, God in His providence has revealed even the preambles, so that those who did not have the time or ability would be able to rely on the certitude of faith and have this much needed knowledge. When I teach metaphysics, I spend a great deal of time elaborating metaphysical principles within the Aristotelian-Thomistic tradition, so that I can then show the students that St. Thomas's five ways are metaphysical and not mathematical or physical demonstrations.

Secondly, as a Catholic philosopher I consider it important to have the students understand that philosophy can help theology, that is, that reason can help us to better understand the truths, the mysteries, of faith. Aquinas's own penetration into the Trinity, the Incarnation, the Sacraments is a testimony to how reason can shed light on the truths that we believe. While this does not mean that the truths of faith are proven by reason, it does, however, mean that what has been revealed is not contrary to reason and cannot be shown by reason to be untrue. Theology itself makes use of philosophy to render its teachings clearer; it does not seek to acquire from philosophy its principles, since the principles of theology are given by revelation, by God. Given the weakness of human intelligence, we are more easily led to what is above reason through what is known by natural reason.[18]

---

17. *S. Th.* I, q. 2, a. 1, ad 1. See Marie I George, "Trust Me. Why Should I? Aquinas on Faith and Reason," in *The Ever-Illuminating Wisdom of St. Thomas Aquinas* (San Francisco: Ignatius Press, 1999), pp. 31–59.

18. *S. Th.* I, q. 1, a. 5, ad 2.

Thirdly, the Catholic philosopher should be able to defend his faith, for as we said above, reason helps faith to better understand the truths revealed by God. In an age of skepticism and unbelief, it becomes imperative that the Catholic philosopher realize that the "faith does not destroy philosophy, [but rather] champions it."[19] If the Apostle exhorts us to be prepared to defend our faith, to explain the reasons for the hope that is in us (1 Peter 3:15), then the Catholic philosopher who is faithful to the Magisterium has an important role to play here. According to Cardinal Ratzinger, "Believers are enjoined to give an *apo-logia* regarding the *logos* of our hope to whoever asks for it. The *logos* must be so intimately their own that it can become *apo-logia;* through the mediation of Christians, the Word [*Wort*] becomes response [*Antwort*] to man's questions. Faith is not a pure private decision, which as such does not really concern anyone else. It will and can show its credentials. It wishes to make itself understandable to others. It lays claim to being a *logos* and, therefore, to the never-failing capacity to become apo-logy."[20] A Catholic philosopher who recognizes the great gift of his faith should wish to enter into fruitful dialogue with non-believers who are well-disposed to the truth and who are sincere in their pursuit of wisdom. If we really love our faith, love the One Who has revealed Himself to us, Wisdom itself, then we not only seek an ever greater understanding for ourselves, which allows us, as it were, a foretaste of the Beatific Vision, a glimpse of the face that we long to see, but we also wish to make others participants of that truth. As Cardinal Ratzinger puts it: ". . . there is a coherence of love and truth which has important consequences for theology and philosophy. Christian faith can say of itself, I have found love. Yet love for

---

19. Ratzinger, "Faith, Philosophy and Theology," p. 29.
20. Ibid., p. 26.

Christ and of one's neighbor for Christ's sake can enjoy stability and consistency only if its deepest motivation is love for the truth. This adds a new aspect to the missionary element: real love of neighbor also desires to give him the deepest thing man needs, namely, knowledge and truth."[21] While we may not be missionaries sent to distant lands to convert the peoples of those lands, there are non-believers and even believers ignorant of their faith, of the Catholic doctrine, in the world of academe, who through our work may be brought closer to the truth.

The truth that we want to convey requires that we engage in the best scholarship that we are capable of, learning from believing and non-believing philosophers alike, as Aquinas himself did, but also bringing to bear Catholic wisdom on different philosophical issues. If, for example, we consider issues in medical ethics: quality of life in terminally ill patients, physician-assisted suicide, would not a serious reflection on the Christian meaning of suffering, on the redemptive significance of Christ's cross, on the part of the Catholic philosopher, bring to bear a "new" and perhaps unsuspected dimension to the discussion of the issues?[22] Could such a reflection, if articulated intelligently, clearly, and humbly, perhaps not give pause to the non-believer? Consider also how papal encyclicals might be a source for philosophical reflection: Pope John Paul II's *Veritatis splendor* comes to mind and Alasdair MacIntyre's article on this encyclical. MacIntyre shows how the moral arguments presented in the encyclical challenge rival philosophical accounts, how the philosophy in *Veritatis splendor* must be understood in the light of Catholic wisdom, and how our moral life and our philosophical work could be frustrated were we not to learn from Catholic wisdom.[23]

21. Ibid., p. 27.                    22. Freddoso, "Two Roles," p. 244.

23. Alasdair MacIntyre, "How Can We Learn What *Veritatis Splendor* Has To Teach?" *The Thomist* 58, no. 2 (April 1994), pp. 171–95.

In addition, however, to solid scholarship and learning, the Catholic philosopher who wants to defend his faith must realize that reasoning alone is not sufficient. In speaking of the great theologians of the Middle Ages, Cardinal Ratzinger reminds us of what they had seen clearly: that mere learning does not suffice for theological understanding, but that it must be complemented by a life of prayer, born of love.[24] The defense of the faith by the philosopher and theologian alike, as well as by any true Christian, requires not only reasoning but also a quest for perfection, for sanctity: man's search for and encounter with Divine Wisdom in the Bread and in the Word, in the sacraments and in prayer. It is in dialogue with the Divine that the Christian's love is nurtured, and where he comes to see and to understand. In order to defend the faith, therefore, the Catholic philosopher's learning must be coupled with an experience of the Divine. It seems to me that it is in this experience that the Catholic philosopher will also find the strength to carry on his work, despite the fatigue and the varied contradictions that he may encounter. Personally, I have always been very moved to know that St. Thomas considered the crucifix the book from which he had learned the most and that toward the end of his life, everything that he had written seemed to him to be nothing ("straw") in comparison to what he had seen. I think that St. Thomas, along with other great Catholic minds, shows us that in order to put our intelligence at the service of Christ, we need the cross and humility, not, assuredly, power and aggressiveness.

And yet, in academe, as in other work-settings, what often seems to be valued is power, not truth. "The postmodern spirit, with its relativist, subjectivist, deconstructionist tendencies, seems to have

24. "On the 'Instruction concerning the Ecclesial Vocation of the Theologian,'" in *The Nature and Mission of Theology*, p. 104. See also Ratzinger's *Behold the Pierced One*, trans. Graham Harrison (San Francisco: Ignatius Press, 1986), pp. 26–27.

abandoned any traditional quest for truth and to have turned its energies instead in the direction of power."[25] There is in effect a conception of the present age as waging battle against the truth; this conception is reminiscent of the Augustinian vision of human history as a struggle between two implacably opposed spiritual forces: the City of God versus the City of the World. The first is dedicated to God and to His will and to His glory, whereas the second is dedicated to something wholly different. According to Alvin Plantinga, the Augustinian struggle is present in the areas of scholarship and science, for we are not to think that these are religiously and metaphysically neutral, since they too are deeply involved in a three-way struggle or contest, the main protagonists of which are Christian theism, perennial naturalism, and creative anti-realism.[26] As Plantinga sees it, ". . . the contemporary western intellectual world, like the world of [Augustine's] times, is a battleground or arena in which rages a battle for our souls."[27] In addition, Plantinga, following Alasdair MacIntyre, notes that there are many contemporary academics and intellectuals who think of themselves as having no commitments at all: they are committed neither to perennial naturalism nor to any form of anti-realism, and they are of course far from Christian theism.[28] But as Plantinga sees it, this lack of commitment is rooted in the thought that there is no such thing as truth as such; as he puts it: "Commitment goes with the idea that there is such a thing as truth; to be committed to something is to hold that it is true, not just in some version, but *sim-*

25. Thomas V. Morris, "A Baptist View of the Catholic University," in *The Challenge and Promise of a Catholic University,* ed. Theodore M. Hesburgh, C.S.C. (Notre Dame: University of Notre Dame Press, 1994), p. 228.

26. Alvin Plantinga, "On Christian Scholarship," in *The Challenge and Promise of a Catholic University,* pp. 268–70.

27. Ibid., p. 269.

28. Ibid., p. 277.

*pliciter* or absolutely—i.e., not merely true with respect to some other discourse or version, or with respect to what one or another group of human beings think or do."[29] If, however, as we said before, Catholic wisdom complements and perfects the truth arrived at through natural reason, then the Catholic philosopher, who is wholeheartedly in unison with that wisdom, will be committed to the truth, in such a way that he will be exercising his freedom for the truth. The Catholic philosopher who is committed in this way will not only be transforming himself through his activity, but will also be transforming the souls of those with whom he comes in contact. He will thus be carrying out the missionary element of his work: sharing with others what every man naturally desires, that is, the truth. The Catholic philosopher has thus the privilege to put his intelligence, as we have said above, at the service of Christ, the Absolute Truth, and at the service of those who, like himself, are journeying toward the truth.

In the years since my return from Spain, I have tried to foster the complementarity between faith and reason both in teaching and in my research. I have learned much not only from the Aristotelian-Thomistic tradition and the Augustinian-Neoplatonic tradition, but also from contemporary thinkers such as the Polish phenomenological and Thomistic philosopher Karol Wojtyła and the prolific and multi-faceted Alasdair MacIntyre. In Karol Wojtyła, better known as Pope John Paul II, I see a synthesis of faith and reason, similar to that of Aquinas in his *Summa contra Gentiles,* but with the use of more contemporary language, that is, with existentialist and phenomenological terminology as well as methodology. I have learned very much from his Christian anthropology, which again shows how Catholic wisdom complements and perfects what is

29. Ibid., p. 278.

known by the light of natural reason. The Holy Father's work on the Trinity as a communion of persons, on the relations existing among the divine persons, also sheds light on the human person, on the person's relationality, a much underemphasized aspect of the person because of the former stress on substance.[30]

Just as I look to Wojtyła—John Paul II—for inspiration in presenting Thomism in language and in a framework accessible to the contemporary person, I also look to MacIntyre for something similar. As the latter points out: "We inhabit a time in the history of philosophy in which Thomism can only develop adequate responses to the rejection of its central positions in what must seem initially at least to be unThomistic ways."[31] MacIntyre makes use of a Nietzschean genealogical narrative—certainly unThomistic means put to the service of Thomistic ends—in order to show that "the predicaments of contemporary philosophy, whether analytic or deconstructive, are best understood as a long-term consequence of the rejection of Aristotelian and Thomistic teleology at the threshold of the modern world."[32] In my own work on theism and morality, whether in Aquinas or in Kant, I have gained much from MacIntyre's analyses of how the rejection of the teleological view of human nature is the reason why the whole project of morality in the modern age becomes unintelligible. MacIntyre's moral enquiry shows how an Aristotelian virtue ethics, an Aristotelian moral psychology, and a Christian view of the moral law are adequately synthesized in Thomistic ethics. Following MacIntyre's moral enquiry, I have tried

30. See Alice Ramos, "Foundations for a Christian Anthropology," *Anthropotes* V, no. 2 (Dec. 1989), pp. 225–57.

31. *First Principles*, p. 2.

32. Ibid., p. 58. See Alice Ramos, "Tradition as 'Bearer of Reason' in Alasdair MacIntyre's Moral Enquiry," in *Freedom, Virtue, and the Common Good*, ed. Curtis L. Hancock and Anthony O. Simon (Notre Dame: University of Notre Dame Press, 1995), pp. 179–93.

to show how the Christian context of human nature and moral law, through secularization and through its deviation from the Thomistic, Roman Catholic tradition, ceases to be an adequate context for an objective ethics and thus paves the way for Kantian ethics and for Enlightenment morality. So in reading MacIntyre, I have come to appreciate even more the harmony that exists between faith and reason in the Thomistic tradition, between classical wisdom and Catholic wisdom.

I think that it is this harmony which I am pursuing in my present work in the transcendentals, especially in beauty: the order and beauty of the universe is but a reflection of the Creator's mind, of the Divine Logos, that Logos to which Cardinal Ratzinger refers when he says: "Christian existence means life in conformity to the Logos; that is why Christians are the true philosophers and why Christianity is the true philosophy."[33]

33. "Faith, Philosophy and Theology," p. 15.

*Ralph McInerny*

## 11. *PHILOSOPHANDUM IN FIDE*

ॐ

When I began graduate studies in philosophy it came as something of a surprise to realize that the sustained pursuit of truth was thought to put one on a collision course with Christian faith. Bumptious tracts like A. J. Ayer's *Language, Truth and Logic* might have been rhetorically more excessive than most professors would choose to be, but such books accurately expressed the outlook of many philosophers. The basic claim was that theological statements are nonsense. It wasn't that they failed to match the reality they purported to talk about; they simply had no meaning at all. They didn't even succeed in being false.

Now that is a put-down of a rather high order. My introduction to philosophy had taken place at the St. Paul Seminary, where the writings of Aristotle and St. Thomas along with a few textbooks provided the basis of instruction. There was also a prolonged concentration on the history of philosophy. I had come to the major seminary after going through the six years of the diocesan minor seminary at Nazareth Hall—broken by a stint in the Marine Corps. From the age of thirteen, my education was in the classical languages, in literature, in history, in modern languages and mathematics. It was light on science. Thanks to this education I acquired the sense that, as a Catholic, I stood in the mainstream of western civilization. However marginalized Catholics might seem to be in the United States, it was the WASPs who had marginalized themselves. Prompted by Graham Greene, one looked for and found indications of this in Henry James. Stories of converts to the faith confirmed the sense that one was already—without merit, of course —where others wished to be.

I remember the exhilaration of reading *The Seven Storey Mountain* when it appeared in 1948. Thomas Merton's account of his escape from the secular world into a Kentucky monastery was at once an indictment of the education he had received and a celebration of such teachers as Mark Van Doren. I had read Van Doren's book on liberal education in a serviceman's edition, sunning myself on the gull wing of a Corsair as I did (while in the Marine Corps at El Toro, California, in 1946). It had acquainted me with the effort at St. John's and elsewhere to restore the kind of education that still characterized most Catholic colleges. My pantheon of contemporary writers included Greene and Evelyn Waugh, Hilaire Belloc and G. K. Chesterton. Willa Cather's fascination with Catholicism in *Death Comes for the Archbishop* and *Shadows on the Rock* seemed perfectly understandable. I mourned the backsliding of F. Scott Fitzgerald but took comfort in J. F. Powers and Flannery O'Connor. When I read "After the Surprising Conversions" in Robert Lowell's first collection, *Lord Weary's Castle,* it seemed right to me that the movement should be in the direction of the Church and of the great literary, intellectual, and spiritual patrimony that had developed under her patronage.

When I began the study of philosophy, I had already read a bit of Jacques Maritain and it was the excitement of the Thomistic Revival that captured my mind and imagination. To become a Thomist was the most natural thing in the world. When I left the seminary and continued the study of philosophy at the University of

Minnesota I was accordingly surprised by the reigning notion of what was what. There were those who thought that I had been caught in a time warp and must be urged into the delights of modernity. With Wilfrid Sellars I studied Kant, Leibniz, and Descartes as well as Sellars' own theory of knowledge. I read Russell's *The Philosophy of Logical Atomism* with the exhilaration usually induced by books in brown paper covers. With Paul Holmer I studied Kierkegaard, Jaspers, and Cassirer. I had a course in metaphysics from George Congar and another in contemporary philosophy with D. B. Terrell. I had logic from May Brodbeck. All this in a year, at the end of which I received the M.A. with a joint major in classics, having written a presumptuous dissertation, *A Thomistic Evaluation of Kierkegaard.* The following September I headed for Quebec to complete my graduate work at Laval, whose *Faculté de Philosophie* was then a stronghold of Thomism of the strict observance. Charles DeKoninck, the still youthful dean, had taught some of my first professors of philosophy, and I wanted to study with him. It was the wisest choice I could have made. I learned how to read Thomas with profit and I have been engaged in doing that ever since.

I was never tempted by the view that the Thomistic Revival was a mistake and that its curricular influence on Catholic colleges was to be expunged as quickly and as thoroughly as possible, supposedly with a go-ahead from Vatican II. My teaching career began in 1954 and thus was well under way before the ecumenical council of 1962–1965 met. In 1959–60, I had a Fulbright research scholarship to Louvain and it was there that I wrote my first book, *The Logic of Analogy.* There was a great deal of enthusiasm at Louvain for Husserl and Heidegger and Merleau-Ponty, but then it is an obligation for Thomists to be interested in any and every philosopher. The assumption is that all new truths are compatible with those already acquired. To be a Thomist is not only to be defending, explaining, clarifying what has already been achieved, but also to be adding to it. Such additions are often prompted by contemporary authors.

Not that this is mindless irenicism. Just as modern philosophy began with the assumption that everything prior to it was fatally flawed, so the *raison d'être* of the Thomistic revival was the assumption that something had gone radically wrong in modern philosophy. Its fundamental flaw was the turn to the subject, calling into question the external world, and setting as the first philosophical task the establishment of the reality of that world. But the external world cannot be deduced or produced from subjectivity. The most obvious reason for this is that we only become aware of ourselves as being first aware of other things. To doubt those other things is to take away awareness of self. In short, the mark of Thomism is epistemological realism.

No wonder then that the earliest figures in the Thomistic revival spent a lot of time criticizing Descartes. And Kant. Indeed, few figures in modern philosophy's hall of fame escaped criticism from Thomists. In *Aeterni Patris,* Leo XIII had cast a cold eye on the modern world and decided that the only remedy for its ills was a return to philosophy as practiced by Thomas Aquinas. At the time this must have seemed quaint to secular thinkers. Having set aside priest and king, civilization was about to ascend to new and undreamt of heights.

It would be easy to mock that confidence in progress on the part of the thoroughly secularized mind. Alas, we know what happened. And in recent years we have come to see more and more why it happened. Leo XIII has proved to be a prophet as well as a pope. We are all post-modernists now.

Nor am I tempted to smile at all those colleagues and friends who, having been brought up Thomists, abandoned the ship at various ports of call, confident that Heidegger or Wittgenstein or Husserl or some lesser and long-forgotten light represented the wave of the future. The kind of thinking represented by Thomas Aquinas was taken to be hopelessly naive and now definitively surpassed. In 1965 I wrote a book, *Thomism in an Age of Renewal,* which retains interest as a contemporary look at the crumbling of the Thomistic establishment. I never understood why interest in Wittgenstein should lead one to abandon Thomas. The attractions of analytic philosophy are real, as are those of phenomenology. I never felt any attraction to Heidegger, that great rival of the Wizard of Oz, but doubtless there were nuggets to be panned even from that Germanic flood. But there were no rivals for the role of principal mentor.

One was told that Thomas had made use of Aristotle and so we must make use of Husserl or Wittgenstein or Hegel or fill in the blank. Such remarks came from theologians by and large and they bespoke an odd conception of philosophy as a kind of Berlitz school offering a variety of jargons in which to couch the faith. The fads came and most of them have gone, to be replaced by a new set of hot thinkers. Foucault and Derrida et al. attract those with an eye to prevailing winds, though sails are beginning to slacken and sag. The Thomist too must read them and their inevitable successors, but he or she comes to them with many hard-won truths that become regulative of assimilation. What the supposed egalitarianism of philosophical systems overlooks is that much of modern philosophy was deliberately designed to put Christianity out of business. This was less nefarious when its cards were on the table, but it was something to be extremely wary of when it offered to put Christianity on a rational basis, expunge it of all supernatural and miraculous claims until it became simply what any rational person would think about morality. It is not surprising that theologians who allied themselves with such philosophers were soon espousing patently heterodox accounts of Christian revelation. Pegging the faith to the modern mind could be a suicidal operation.

The foregoing makes it clear that for me the resolution of the question of faith and reason, of religious belief and philosophizing, is all wrapped up in the question, Why am I a Thomist?

The first thing to say about Thomism is that it is not a kind of philosophy. It will occur that, *mutatis mutandis,* most philosophers would say the same. Hegel did not think Hegelianism was just one way among others, as if Kantianism were still equally good. He thought he was surpassing Kant and linking up with the great tradition of doing philosophy. Husserl was not proposing *his* way of doing philosophy but *the* way. And so on. I make these obvious points lest one think it hubristic of the Thomist to reject the idea that his is merely one way of doing philosophy and, as it happens, the wrong way. It is one's critics who turn doing philosophy Thomistically into a *way* of doing it. The Thomist doesn't think so. One consequence of this is that he assumes that other philosophers are engaged in the same enterprise as he is. The surface facts usually militate against this assumption and it is necessary to be patient. As often as not, the Thomist will find serious difficulties in the fundamental assumptions of other philosophers.

For a long time, this was because those other philosophers had taken the modern turn and accepted some version of the view that the primary philosophical task is to get out of one's head. Now while many have gone out of their head they have not, if they begin with mind, with thinking, with the subject, ever succeeded in rejoining the external world. It is simply an historical fact that the turn toward the subject led to skepticism, deism, and ultimately atheism, which is why there was that often unstated assumption around when I began graduate work in philosophy. Philosophy and faith were taken to be at odds with one another and sooner or later faith must fall before philosophy.

Cornelio Fabro wrote a large book showing how modern atheism had been more or less entailed by the subjective turn. I think that was Leo XIII's hunch as well. When Thomas was proposed as a philosophical mentor for Catholics, was the motive simply that he had expressed the faith in his theology and his theology had made use of a kind of philosophy? That is, was there something arbitrary and ad hoc at the beginning of the Thomistic revival? Leo XIII looked around and saw that there were theories and practices abroad which were incompatible with the faith. It is not the Catholic way to dismiss reason and preach the faith with disdain or indifference to reason. Uses of reason which led to conflict with the faith must be flawed. But there is a use of reason which is compatible with the faith and, in its way, a support of it. This turned out to be the kind of philosophy that had been rejected by Descartes and which had Thomas Aquinas as its most notable representative. The conclusion was clear. Go to Thomas.

The single greatest difference between the kind of philosophy of which Thomas is the paladin and the kind that has taken its cue from Descartes is not often noticed. The assumption of philosophy since Descartes has been that you cannot claim to know anything for sure until and unless you have done philosophy. This incredible assumption has become so familiar to us that it loses its ability to surprise or elicit laughter. Students who settle into Philosophy 101 are taught to believe that, with luck, they may at the end of the course and for the first time know something. Or they may come to see that everything they now think they know is illusory. But one way or another the assumption is that philosophy starts in midair. Or with a clearing operation that sweeps the mind clean so that at last real thinking can begin.

As opposed to what? For Thomas, the starting points of philosophy, its principles, are what everyone already knows. There are truths about the practical order, there are truths about the world and ourselves that everyone already knows. Most of them are learnt on one's own, almost unawares. Others may be the occasion of our grasping them, but we do not owe such knowledge to any one else. This knowledge is compatible with a good deal of confusion and vagueness, of course, but what it does not lack is certainty. Are you alive? Of course. Do you know with clarity and distinction what life is? No. Does this discredit your claim to know? Hardly. It indicates the starting point in certainty that any inquiry into the nature of life must have. To do philosophy is to move off from and constantly to return to such principles. This is of course a species of foundationalism but one immune to the devastating criticism of what I am tempted to call Euclidean Foundationalism.

It is this sense of starting points or principles of human thinking which provides an important link between reason and faith. When God revealed himself to men, he spoke to them in a human language which had a syntax and vocabulary fashioned to deal with the things around us. God showed himself in a burning bush, in the pillar of cloud; he likened himself to a roaring lion. He described himself as angry or sad at the behavior of men. In Jesus, God comes among us as a man like us in all things but sin. He talks, he walks, he tells stories. He teaches us how to pray. Our Father. The parable of the prodigal son conveys to us God's infinite mercy. None of this would be possible if epistemological skepticism made sense. If fire and water and oil and wine and bread are not really there they cannot serve as indicators of their maker. He is not before our eyes as they are, and he can be put before the eye of faith only by relying on the validity of perception. This is why epistemology is a big deal for the Catholic Church. This is why criticisms of Descartes are so

prominent in the Thomistic revival. Not only is Descartes convey-
ing a bad philosophy, his bad philosophy is one that becomes an obstacle to the faith. It matters who you hang out with philosophically.

That sounds perhaps overly protective, as if the winds and gales
of modern philosophy beat upon the house of faith and threaten to
blow it away. There are moments when that seems the case. The
nineteenth century was surely such a moment. Carrying over from
Kant, who instructed us that there was no need to pray, that it was
silly to fashion words to tell the deity what he already knew, a series
of German philosophers undertook to tailor Christianity to their
specifications—Fichte, Schelling, Hegel, Strauss. One almost sym-
pathizes with Nietzsche, who recognized that what was going on
was the rejection of Christianity, not its philosophical redemption.
But the arrogant confidence with which all this went on is notewor-
thy. In France, the apostate Ernest Renan spoke of Christianity
with benign condescension. He said he believed in God, but alas
He doesn't exist. Christianity is lovely, it is inseparable from our art,
our music, our thought—but of course only peasants could take it
to be true. On the assumption that miracles, for example, were impossible, Scripture was subjected to a critical reading that rid it of
things offensive to reason. The movement in the Catholic Church
called Modernism, against which Pius IX, Leo XIII, and Pius X definitively, warned, was a misguided effort to accept the unaccept-
able, to take on the assumptions of the warped modern mind, to
get with it.

Unlike the Owl of Minerva, the arrow of time flies night and
day. Yesterday's modernity is, well, yesterday. There is something
quaint in the urgency with which men were urged to sign on to
some theory now long since discredited. The greatest casualty has
been reason itself. Once reason was invoked with confidence. Finally the human mind was firmly on the track toward truth. Christian-

ity as traditionally understood could not survive such progress, so it had to be either jettisoned or rewritten to rational specifications. The little work that told me most persuasively that all this was over was Jean-Paul Sartre's *Existentialism is a Humanism.*

When I began to teach, it was this book, along with Ayer's, that one wanted undergraduates to read. Both are blessedly brief and they make their points unequivocally. Ayer reads like the tail-end of the Enlightenment, but Sartre emphasized the dark side of things. Once people had thought that Christianity could be done away with, that God could be expunged from our minds, and Europe would carry on as before only ever so much more brightly. Sartre made clear that the upshot of the Enlightenment was indeed atheism, and he then proceeded to draw out the implications of that fact. It was pleasant for a Thomist to see him make his point in terms of essence and existence.

For the theist, the believer, God is a maker and man a thing made, and on this analogy, man is provided by his maker with a nature or essence which tells him what he must do in order to flourish, how he must exist. Essence precedes existence. For the atheist, there is no maker and consequently man is not made. He has no nature. There are no antecedent guidelines for how he should behave or exist. For the atheist, existence precedes essence. Anything goes. Sartre goes on to remove any exhilaration such liberation might initially cause in his reader. A world without God is a frightening place. It is, as a matter of fact, nothingness.

In the middle of the nineteenth century, Ernest Hello published a critique of Renan, *M. Renan, Allemagne et l'Athéisme au XIXe siècle.* He spells out for Renan the nihilism implicit in his atheism, a critique that is in many way an anticipation of Sartre. But Hello wrote as a Catholic, Sartre as an atheist. The complacency of Renan has given way to the humorless and depressing outlook of Sartre.

Sartre wrote his little book over half a century ago, just after World War II. We have lived into a time where it is not the Christian critic who points out the relativism of secular morality. This is insisted upon by its proponents. The good has become privatized along with religion, and public life is an effort at cohabitation by radically incompatible partners. Ingenious theories are concocted to prove that this is possible, but other voices are heard, speaking with an odd cheerfulness, that admit that it is illusory to look for rational foundations. They propose a pragmatic, hand to mouth sort of solution, but at bottom there is simply self-assertion.

Newman, in the first of the *Fifteen Sermons Preached before the University of Oxford,* spoke on "The Philosophical Temper, First Enjoined by the Gospel." It is a sermon well worth reflecting on. Perhaps at the time it sounded a bit like "me too," but it does not read so now. Its tenor is not unlike that of Etienne Gilson's Gifford Lectures, delivered in the early 1930s, *The Spirit of Medieval Philosophy.* Confronted by the claim that no philosophy had gone on during the ages of faith, Gilson gave an historian's answer, drawing attention to the achievements of the period which were undoubtedly prompted by the faith but which were nonetheless philosophical gains. The doctrine of the Trinity required a clarity not available from pagan philosophy on nature and person and this clarity was achieved. It is a philosophical achievement of great theological importance. But there it is. And Gilson went on and on with other examples. So too Newman, but with a deeper claim, namely, that the faith is a kind of guardian of reason, shoring it up in times of doubt and difficulty. That is the note on which I shall end these ruminations.

It has long been the case that there is but one sure voice speaking on behalf of reason, as principles fundamental to a well-ordered life and society have fallen one by one before the demands of an unstructured freedom. The Church, whose primary purpose is to defend the faith, comes to the defense of natural reason when it has been all but abandoned by former rationalists. Not just practical reason, but theoretical reason as well. The Church insists on the mind's capacity to know reality. I have indicated above why that capacity is essential to the task of evangelizing. In the present time, it is those who are blessed with faith who have a sustaining conviction that reason, practical and theoretical, can be used with effect. This is an antecedent certitude, it does not provide philosophical analyses and arguments. But it is the ambience within which philosophy can be confidently practiced. That was Newman's point in the sermon referred to. How silly it seems now to have thought that reason spelled the death of faith. Now it is faith that provides the only hope for reason. That is the point of John of St. Thomas's slogan, beloved of Jacques Maritain, *philosophandum in fide*. We should philosophize in the ambience of the faith.

*Patrick L. Bourgeois*

# 12. CRITICAL REASON AND THE LIFE
# OF THE CHRISTIAN

❧

In this paper I intend to reflect upon the compatibility of critical philosophy and a post-critical faith in the life of a Christian philosopher. Within the unity of a concrete life, specifically the life of a Christian philosopher, there must be an intertwining of two commitments:[1] the commitment to the rational enterprise of philosophy, and the commitment to Christ in Christian faith. Both of these commitments make demands on this level of concrete life, requiring on the one hand that one live according to the best dictates of a guiding reason and pursue the critical life of the philosopher, while at once living within an all-pervasive commitment to Christ and to God. At first these intertwining commitments do not seem to present any difficulty, but on closer examination, the tension between them for the philosopher becomes apparent. And it is this tension which must be resolved in the concrete life of the Christian philosopher if there is to be a unity and harmony in his/her life.

Let us attempt to make this tension explicit and clear. It might

---

1. Although as a Catholic I am specifically writing about philosophy and Catholic faith, the philosophical problems with which we are concerned here are proper to the faith of all Christian denominations.

be helpful first to look briefly at the nature of the philosophical commitment and what it entails, and then reflect on the faith of the Christian and of the Christian theologian. This clarification will also spell out the tension between them by highlighting an alleged conflict between reason and Christian faith before resolving the tension by recognizing a deeper unity underlying the so-called conflict.

First, then, we must understand that philosophy, according to its entire tradition, is essentially an enterprise of reason alone and as such is independent of Christian faith. In accord with its standard definition, philosophy seeks evidence along the lines of reason independent of outside authority, and hence is autonomous from the demands of Christian faith. And today, learning from modern philosophy, especially from that of Immanuel Kant, philosophy, in being critical, must see the limits of reason. Philosophy, as rational and critical reflection, must ferret out all over-claims, and indeed, admit the limits of human knowledge.

In the unity of life of the Christian philosopher committed passionately to the love and pursuit of wisdom there is the further commitment in supernatural faith that extends beyond reason. Christian belief and life and the theology to which these give rise are often in a territory that is beyond the limits of philosophy. Thus, the same person makes a commitment to a philosophical enterprise of reason alone with its limits, and a commitment to a Christian faith that extends beyond knowledge in the strict sense, challenging the limits of reason itself for its place. And both of these commitments have their roots in the concrete life of the person; both permeate the existential situation and world of the philosopher who believes. How can such a philosopher today, open to the ancient and medieval tradition, but further enlightened by the critical orientation of modern philosophy, philosophize within this context of commitments? The focus of this inquiry has now emerged as the tension and apparent conflict between the concrete Christian life and the critical attitude of philosophy on the concrete level of living both commitments. For philosophy as critical challenges the very object of Christian belief as somehow beyond the scope and focus of reason. Thus, it seems to be impossible to maintain a post-critical Christian faith or a place for the gift of Faith. And if the claim is made that such a faith is viable, the question must be faced concerning the point of contact between the object of such faith and the limits placed on human claims. Also, the question of whether critical philosophy can find a place for the possibility of faith must then be transformed into an inquiry as to whether a Christian can be a philosopher; how can he/she actually operate independently of the faith commitment without polluting that philosophical enterprise?[2]

Three points, then, must be considered. First, postmodern deconstruction has challenged the very possibility not only of Christian faith, but also of philosophy itself; in the process it has dissolved our problem by pulling the props out from both poles of our tension between critical philosophy and Christian faith. Second, once the possibility of philosophy has been reestablished, we need then to look briefly at the dimensions of philosophical activity that are possible for the philosopher who is Christian. In this section we will focus specifically on a threefold relation between faith and philosophical activity. We will attempt to arrive at a philosophical

2. This paper does not pretend to claim that Christian belief is necessarily subject to philosophical scrutiny and limits. Rather, it allows for the total independence of Christian belief from philosophy. Within Christian commitment it is possible to believe in God and in Christ and to attain a complete mystical union without the explicit aid or influence of philosophy. Admitting this fact highlights a certain limit to the very nature of the philosophical enterprise. In this context, one could learn from Kierkegaard, who asks if it is necessary to prove the existence of one's beloved.

activity that is in some sense independent of such faith. And, third, the reflection on this second point requires that we resolve the problem of the relation between philosophy as critical and a Christian faith which seems to be excluded by this philosophy.

I

The possibility of philosophy today has been seriously challenged by a widespread postmodern deconstruction.[3] This brand of postmodernism, which claims to be non-philosophy, contends that the era of philosophy is at its end, since the very quest of philosophy has reached the limit of its possibilities. Philosophy has always been a quest to make sense of reality and of our knowledge of it. Thus, to defend the very possibility of philosophy is to defend the priority of sense, logos, meaning, and truth. Postmodern deconstruction calls such an attempt on the part of philosophy "logocentrism," the attempt to make logos central. Thus, this kind of postmodernism is anti-logocentric. Yet, this anti-logocentrism is itself parasitical in that it requires the prior position of logocentrism as its own starting point and host. For it must have logocentrism to deconstruct. Since this is the case, a subtle common denominator can be found for so-called logocentrism and anti-logocentrism. This common affirmation must be further explored by reflection on an extension of what William James calls "the will to believe."[4]

William James, in his essay "The Will to Believe," distinguishes

3. Postmodern deconstruction has become such a popular fad in continental philosophy, literary criticism, theology, interpretation theory, language studies, and many other cognitive enterprises that it cannot be avoided in any intelligent discourse today on the relation between philosophy and Christian faith. For it has touched both of these enterprises, and not in a positive way.

4. This treatment of the will to believe is close to that developed by William James in "The Will to Believe," in *The Will to Believe: Human Immortality and Other Essays on Popular Philosophy* (New York: Dover, 1956), pp. 1–31.

the basis for beliefs from the truth of the beliefs, and the beliefs emerge from two genuine options. And the two instances of genuine option are the choice to believe in God or not-God and the choice to believe in a moral universe or a non-moral universe. Such options are genuine if they are significant, cannot be avoided, and at least minimally tempt our wills for belief. At this stage, this option to believe is based on the volitional and passional dimension of our personalities, and not on cognitive evidence for objective truth. The cognitive and its justification for truth come later, so that the justification is post-belief. James is trying to explain that the basis of such beliefs, since they are forced and cannot be avoided, is not the cognitive evidence which would make them true, but the lack of such evidence, the "will to believe." And, as already mentioned, James only allows for two instances of such beliefs, the religious belief in God or no God, and the belief in freedom or no freedom in a universe. It must be emphasized that for James, this does not preclude the question of truth and evidence. The belief is true or false based on evidence that supports it, while the basis of the belief is the will to believe, understood as the passional and volitional dimensions of our nature. For James, as a pragmatist, this means that the true belief is the one that makes the most sense out of the whole picture of reality, the one that is rationally satisfying. Thus, this is not an appeal to merely subjective evidence, but is a claim based on objective evidence.

While these are the only two instances of a genuine option to believe for which James explicitly allows, throughout his essay a third type of option is latent and fully operative even though he does not advert to it in his treatise. James assumes a certain option to believe in the power of reason to arrive at truth based on evidence in knowledge, in science, and in philosophy. This option to believe has come to be referred to today as logocentrism, especially by those who are opposed to it in their own anti-logocentrism. We must focus now on logocentrism and anti-logocentrism in order to understand a fundamental challenge today that cuts beneath and against philosophy itself. This reflection is required today before attempting to discuss the relation between reason and supernatural faith. If this challenge from anti-logocentrism is not met, the discussion regarding faith and reason must take an entirely different direction than that proposed in this article, since reason, truth, and the process of making sense itself will have been deposed.

Reason's ability to make sense in arriving at truth, knowledge, and philosophy springs from a "will to believe"—a certain human faith that we can arrive at logos/unconcealment/sense. In fact, the critical philosophy of modernity arose in the attempt to check and limit reason's self-assurance, especially in the context of the success of science. And once logos, truth, and values have attained some degree of sophistication (e.g., in science or in philosophy), we can be thrown back to reflect on the pre-cognitive and pre-philosophical level, discovering and accounting more explicitly for that very level within the scope of the enlightening process itself. At this point, deconstruction and its opponents are within the same commitment of belief and are on the same level of discourse, for both admit this coming to knowledge and its claims. It is the status of this logos and knowledge that deconstruction attempts to dismantle. Yet, in spite of this shared basic belief in the human ability to make sense of reality, to arrive at meaning and value, deconstructionists immediately take a negative attitude toward ever arriving at a positive outcome. Let us make this point more explicit.

The deconstructionists here undergo what might be called a quasi conversion, a complete change-over in their way of looking at the whole enterprise. This quasi conversion entails a complete about-face or transformation in attitude toward the initial faith in obtaining any sense or logos. This basic reorientation of attitude gives rise to a further interpretation according to which the logos is considered to be incapable of doing justice to the excess or fullness of sense or to the abyss from which all sense arises. In this new attitude, any arrival at logos, as in philosophy, is considered inadequate to the fullness of its source; thus logos and philosophy distort this source by what they exclude. And rather than maintain a need for constant renewal from that source for every new expression of sense, knowledge, and truth as many in the recent past have done, the deconstructionist considers any arrival at logos to be a closure from, and exclusion of, its source. It is considered to be an effect that loses the underlying richness. Thus, deconstruction does not disavow logos or cognition; it simply reinterprets their sense and value. Deconstruction as anti-logocentrism and logocentrism itself both operate in the same basic will to believe in logos, but with differing interpretations of its basic sense. Hence, while it is true that deconstruction recognizes that logos brings something to light, it interprets logos and cognition, once attained, in a negative way— i.e., as closure from the fullness and richness from which logos emerges. Thus, this deconstructive attitude interprets the attempt to reach sense or logos as a subversive closure rather than an openness and a "making sense." It gapes at this openness to the richness of the abyss, subordinates that very openness to the priority of the flux in such a way as to see only a closure that belongs to the logos precisely as coming to meaning, and thus leads to the so-called overturning of logocentrism.

Thus, deconstruction does not attempt totally to abrogate philosophy, for it allows first and foremost the move to and from logos in order for the deconstructive process subsequently to take place by opening the closure of philosophy. It understands philosophy and any logos to entail a concomitant closure. The element of truth in this deconstructive claim is the fact that every logos, expression, and cognition is limited and thus does not "say it all". Indeed, this fact has been promoted for some time now by all existential philosophy and by many other philosophical positions as their essential legacy. Limit bespeaks the need for constant openness to renewal from the fullness of existence. I believe that the requirement on the part of deconstruction of an absolute closedness of every logos constitutes an "over-belief"[5] that we need not accept. Thus, in the contrast between these two positions, the pivotal focus is between a belief in the logos as having priority, admitting at once that it has openness—closure as an aspect, i.e., an openness to and, precisely as such, a closure from, which closure demands constant attunement to the source of the logos; or a belief in the priority of the anti-logocentric, so that the closure is absolute, and must be transgressed in a deconstructive process that cuts beneath any such logos, and aims at the process alone, thus fixating upon the tension between the openness and closure.

The ultimate issue, then, is that the will to believe of deconstructionists, while seeming to affirm the logos through which one must pass to reach closure, is basically a belief in the absolute status of closure and the priority of the abyss as non-logocentrism. And the very protestations of the deconstructionists, that their opponents have not grasped their thinking, reveal an underlying prejudice, as absolute in its claim as it is illusive and unattainable: a belief in the undecidable and the inexpressible of the abyss.[6] And to this it is

5. William James, *The Varieties of Religious Experience* (New York: Collier Books, 1961), pp.397–401.

6. It might be objected that the mystics have often spoken in such a way as seemingly to support such views of deconstruction. The remarks of mystics are not, however, meant to be normative for all discourse and meaning, as is the claim of deconstruction. Also, mystical discourse can be accounted for logocentrically; deconstruction as anti-logocentric has no exclusive claim on it.

best to reply with an alternate belief, one which makes sense out of sense, while at once seeing and admitting its limit. This limit, however, while initially a certain kind of closure in the openness of logos, is likewise an openness to its source for constant renewal from that origin in an ongoing process of interpretation. Thus, its openness consists in bringing to light and, at once, openness toward renewal in its rich source, even though there is a certain element of closure as limit in coming to sense.

## II

Now that we have reestablished the possibility of philosophy against the attack of postmodern deconstruction, we can turn to our second point, the dimensions of philosophical activity possible for the philosopher who is Christian, and the possibility for the Christian to be a philosopher. How does a Christian philosopher actually operate independently of the faith commitment and without polluting the philosophical enterprise?

First, the Christian philosopher can take issues from Christian faith—for instance, the claims of Christ—and seek to understand them by means of philosophical reflection. There is a natural tendency to apply philosophy to everything in the lived experience of the philosopher. Since this reflection begins within Christian faith, however, and proceeds to understanding, this activity is not strictly philosophical. Although it is appropriate for the Christian philosopher and can certainly lead to much insight and intelligibility, it is not limited to reason, but, rather, assumes supernatural Christian faith as its source. As such, it goes beyond the limit of reason, and therefore beyond the scope of philosophy.

Second, it is possible for a Christian philosopher to reflect on input from faith, but in a strictly rational (philosophical) manner, not as a case of faith seeking understanding as in the case above, but, rather, as a case of reason seeking understanding of an issue that could have sprung from reason, but, instead, arises from faith. For instance, the faithful Christian who worships and prays might come to reflect in a distinctively philosophical way about the possibility of knowing and thinking about God, and about the limits of such knowing. This is not quite the same as the theologian who uses philosophy for theological purposes (in, for instance, the manner of Thomas Aquinas).[7] For in our case the person is primarily a philosopher having (Christian) faith. Taking something from this faith to philosophy, our philosopher focuses on the question of the limit of our knowledge of God strictly as a question belonging to reason and reflects on it as a question that could have emerged initially from reason. One can, within strictly philosophical limits, ask what philosophy can say about the possibility of knowing anything about God as well as what philosophy can allow us to know concerning the possibility of faith itself. Such reflection can look at the underpinnings of that faith life in a strictly philosophical focus on the human dimension of the activity of a faith that also entails a supernatural dimension. This would be a philosophical look at the faith from the outside, so to speak, and would thus be held to the limits of philosophy. And in a postmodern age this would require the humility of reason and of understanding facing their limits. Such reflection also allows the move to the speculative level, going beyond the claims of descriptive accounts.

Third, there is the strictly philosophical reflection of the person qua philosopher, with no input from revealed faith. This is philosophy in the strict sense and within its limits. In this kind of reflection one could contend that the philosopher in philosophizing can

7. This remark is not meant to eliminate the possibility of Thomas even within his theology reflecting in a strictly philosophical manner.

bracket out any influence or input from a Christian faith commitment, while leaving faith operative in lived experience. This entails
allowing nothing from the faith commitment to enter philosophy
as content. The autonomy and independence of philosophy are
maintained and all seems well for the philosophy of the Christian.
Thus, we are now brought to the third point of our discussion, that
we resolve the problem of the relation between philosophy as critical and a Christian faith which seems to be outside of, and at odds
with, critical philosophy.

### III

We have seen how the Christian can be a philosopher, but not
how a critical philosopher can be a Christian, especially considering
the limits placed by critical reason on knowledge. But, on further
thought, philosophy precisely as critical might seem to exclude the
very possibility of this religious type of commitment and faith by
limiting knowledge and experience, since the outcome of critical
philosophy is precisely to see the role of reason in placing limits,
and to prevent human claims to knowledge from going beyond
those limits. And is not this the problem that Kant faced in his critical philosophy? Whatever can be said in this Kantian context
about the faith commitment is entirely beyond the domain of theoretical reason and its use within knowledge in the strict sense.

Thus far, our conclusion that the Christian can still operate
strictly as a philosopher within clear lines of demarcation is challenged by approaching the question of the possibility of the Christian philosopher from the point of view of critical philosophy. The
question remains (reversing the question from Part II about what
kind of philosophy is allowed within Christian commitment): Can
a person be at once a critical philosopher and a Christian? Does
critical philosophy preclude Christian commitment? Of course, for

some philosophers, the answer is simply that it is impossible to accept Christian beliefs, for they are not only beyond philosophy, but incompatible with it.

In order adequately to discuss this issue, we must now return to and expand on the general context of the will to believe in logos discussed above and find a place for different levels of faith in order to make clear the place of Christian faith in this context. At this point, an option to believe emerges in relation to the basic will to believe in the priority of logos that is strictly philosophical, and prior to Christian faith. We will turn briefly to this option.

The initial faith in logos discussed above in Part I is the structural foundation of all further levels of genuine options. This structural foundation must now be further considered. Several levels beyond logocentrism/anti-logocentrism can be distinguished; that of the rational belief of the theist or atheist, seated in the option discussed above, yet more basic than and presupposed by any further option of religion or theology, i.e., that of a specific religious faith, such as Christianity; and, finally, that of the explicit denominational faith commitment in its concrete situation and with its own tradition and theology. These latter options to believe cannot be considered to be genuine options in James' sense. Let us turn briefly to reflect further on the basis of belief in the light of our discussion above.

The second kind of option mentioned above is the will to believe in God or not-God rooted in, and continuous with, the initial belief in logos.[8] As seen above, according to William James such options, as genuine, are significant, cannot be avoided, and at least minimally tempt our will to believe. On this level of option, one engages a certain first naiveté, generally believing in a God handed

8. See footnote 5 above.

down from one's own tradition of belief. This option has what James calls a volitional, passional basis for belief,[9] rather than a cognitive basis on evidence. The cognitive dimension comes later onto the scene to justify this belief, whether it be a belief in God or a belief in no God. The justification is post-belief; it is a theoretical, philosophical justification of an already existing belief. Thus, there is not a lack of proofs. Rather, they come from a theoretical level after the initial belief, according to James. And such justification is easily forthcoming for both the theist and the atheist. And once the theist turns to the justification of this belief within logocentrism, the initial conviction, as a fundamental option based in the volitional, passional dimension of human existence, passes through the stage of critique admitting the philosophical limits of any claims to knowledge entailed by such belief. Thus, even after some justification of belief from a theoretical and speculative reflection, it is clear that critique limits what we can claim to know in a univocal sense.

9. This does not preclude the question of truth and evidence. The belief is true or false based on evidence, while the basis of the belief is the will to believe. Thus the truth is based on whether there is evidence to support it. For James, this means that the true belief is the one that makes the most sense out of the whole picture; which belief is rationally satisfying, i.e., has evidence supplied from the whole of experience. This is not an appeal to merely subjective evidence, but is a claim based on objective evidence. The theist sees, based on evidence, that theism is more rational than atheism. Or, put in more explicit terms, the theist sees which one has the best consequences in relation to the whole. Two points must be clear: first, that the denial of absolute certitude does not deny truth; and second, this does not take away from the typical proofs of God's existence as tenable and as taken, within a belief, to be definitive. For instance, once one believes, it makes sense to believe based on one of many possible proofs or arguments: e.g., based on the cosmological argument that the existence of the universe indicates that it does not make sense not to believe in God. One could argue that theism makes more sense out of the whole picture than atheism (or vice versa). At this point, I do believe that one could accept any of many different proofs for the existence of God: causality; beauty of the universe; nature of man; being itself. But, looking from James' view, one could simply say that the universe makes more sense with a God in it than without God.

Anything predicated of a God or of the Sacred must take the mode of indirect language of analogical or symbolic predication, allowing and fostering thought at the boundary of reason. And the type of analogy is complex, taking place first on the level of experience and existence, following those who are influenced by the Kantian third Critique, but also entailed in any further theoretical and speculative accounts of God in indirect language.

Since this indirect access allows a place for reflection that overcomes Kant's phenomenal/noumenal distinction, we can now return to the pre-philosophical realm of person to person, which philosophy cannot cut off or adequately explicate. This is the realm of the singular person for whom Gabriel Marcel makes a philosophical place, and of the face to face that Emmanuel Levinas emphasizes so much in his philosophy. The religious dimension of experience is tied to this context of encounter with the other person as person, because the experience of God for the Christian is the experience of God as personal. This personal dimension is one of the main emphases of Kierkegaard, especially in "purity of heart" before God in an Abrahamic faith commitment. This is the realm of conviction prior to critique, and even though it is subject to critique, it is prior to, and the place of return after, critique. Furthermore, such conviction feeds critique, for too often critique limits the scope of its own focus to some acceptable, preconceived prejudice—as, for example, Kant's pre-critical acceptance or conviction of science and its objectivity as the supposed point of departure for critique, which must be justified in this critique. Kant limited the nature and scope of experience itself too much, and thus he restricted knowledge in the strict sense too narrowly. Hence, in such a religious commitment as personal one is committed precisely to more than a philosophical account can give. One lives with an object of religious faith, as personal, beyond the realm of philosophy, but compatible with philosophy's limit. Thus, philosophy cannot ever "get at" the real "Other," as personal, of concrete Christian commitment and faith, but neither can it philosophically disallow it, except within the opposite option, which, like both positions, must admit tolerance for the other position (theist) since neither theism nor atheism has apodictic evidence, due to the nature of human knowledge.[10] The person of Christian faith, however, must accept the philosophical limit that this specifically Christian dimension will not ever fall within a strictly philosophical competence, except with a great loss of the personal, and in an analogical treatment.

As a corollary to the tension between critical philosophy and Christian faith, it is not a task of philosophy to change a person's religious faith, but rather to subject everything, even the place of such faith, to review, critique, rational clarity, and to ward off illusion. The task of the philosopher is to maintain rational integrity and intellectual honesty, and not to attempt to force philosophical consent on more than can be admitted from the rational point of view. And the philosopher must admit that to leave open the possibility for such a faith life is to admit that there is another discourse, based on the philosophically reflected indirect expressions of symbols, metaphors, narrative, or on the age-old concept of analogy, which heeds the critical warning not to claim something to be strictly empirical knowledge when it is not so. This philosophically recognized and founded mode of discourse, together with the spec-

10. This is not meant to belittle adequate philosophical proofs for the existence of God, but to review the realization that there is no apodictic evidence for the philosopher or for human cognition. Nor does this point destroy objectivity or reason. One must remember the epistemological limits admitted by Thomas in saying: "Quidquid recipitur, recipitur secundum modum recipientis" ("Whatever is received is received according to the manner of the receiver"). If something is received in the intellect, it is received in the manner of the intellect; if something is received in the sense faculty, then it is received in the manner of sense.

ulative account of the possibility of its object of belief,[11] lays open the possibility of Christian belief and life. Thus, what can be said philosophically is limited, not even addressing the issue of Christian belief precisely as Christian, but only the belief in God or the Sacred. To understand within these limits, we must strip layer after layer of these beliefs, finally arriving at that level that the philosopher can address, and admit the basis of belief and it limits.

The further levels of options than those considered above, for instance, the belief in Christ and then the commitment to a specific denomination, go far beyond the initial belief in God, and thus beyond philosophy. They have their philosophical place first in the will to believe in God that is rooted in the commitment to logos, and then in indirect expressions such as symbols, analogies, metaphors, and narratives, of our experience, as already mentioned. While this philosophical place allows the believer to integrate religious discourse into discourse in general and thus to have a place, this is the limit of philosophy vis à vis faith. And thanks to poetic language in a general sense, philosophy can continue to think beyond the limits of reason alone, a thinking that is sometimes still philosophical, although not claiming the status of strict knowledge. The tendency of the philosopher is perhaps to reduce faith at this point to this poetic or creative imaginative activity, unless the limit of philosophy in relation to Christian faith is admitted.

The philosopher who is a Christian believer must admit at some point the rational limit of philosophy and, at once, admit the factual belief of the Christian, e.g., in the resurrection of Christ as an

11. The discourse about God as such requires more than a descriptive approach to human experience and existence. Such a discourse would be speculative, and it could be philosophical or theological, depending on the perspective taken. See Patrick L. Bourgeois, *The Religious Within Experience and Existence: A Phenomenological Investigation* (Pittsburgh: Duquesne University Press, 1990).

event. It is the religious convictions on this level of fact and relevance that the philosopher qua philosopher cannot as such justify. Yet, it is precisely here that philosophy can help fathom the depth of the significance of these events believed in, and thus become a great help to Christian belief and to theology. And it is in the realm of conviction and faith that arises the possibility of a personal God to Whom one prays and before Whom one lives one's life. Yet, one has to admit that it goes beyond the scope of a philosophical reflection to deal with a specific religious response within a specific faith option. Yet there is the realm of conviction prior to philosophy that does survive even a critical philosophy, but in a post critical way.

There is thus such a thing as a post-critical faith. For a naïve faith passes through the sieve of a critique that shows the philosophical limits and place of faith and theology as seen above—and then in concrete life passes back to the level of a fundamental conviction or a post-critical second naiveté of living faith. We have found further that such faith is grounded in the experience of the will to believe that grounds faith in logos. It is from here, on the common level of the will to believe, that we can see an intertwining of faith in logos and belief in God, which latter leads to the possibility and commitment of Christian faith. This faith, as actual, entails Christian life itself. The philosophical analysis of the place of that faith thus arises out of that life, and in our analysis, is rooted in it. But for the naïve Christian, this is all supererogatory. For the philosopher, it enriches life and entails the intertwining of the various aspects of the Christian philosopher's life.

# NOTES ON CONTRIBUTORS

❧

*Patrick L. Bourgeois* is William and Audrey Hutchinson Distinguished Professor of Philosophy at Loyola University, New Orleans, where he has taught since 1968. His special areas of interest are twentieth-century continental philosophy (Ricoeur, Heidegger, Merleau-Ponty), Kierkegaard, pragmatism and phenomenology, and philosophical theology. He has written about 90 articles in addition to many book reviews in these areas, and has authored/co-authored eight books, among which are: *Philosophy at the Boundary of Reason* (SUNY Press, 2000); *The Extension of Ricoeur's Hermeneutics* (Martinus Nijhoff, 1975); *The Religious Within Experience and Existence: A Phenomenological Investigation* (Duquesne University Press, 1990); *Mead and Merleau-Ponty: A Common Vision,* with Rosenthal (SUNY Press, 1991); and *Thematic Studies in Phenomenology and Pragmatism,* with Rosenthal (Grüner, 1983). He is past President of the Gabriel Marcel Society, and is the current President of the American Catholic Philosophical Association.

*John D. Caputo* is the David R. Cook Professor of Philosophy at Villanova University, where he has taught since 1968. He specializes in continental philosophy and religion and has recently published *More Radical Hermeneutics: On Not Knowing Who We Are* (Indiana U.P., 2000); *God, the Gift and Postmodernism* (Indiana U.P., 1999); *Deconstruction in a Nutshell: A Conversation with Jacques Derrida*

(Fordham U.P., 1997); *The Prayers and Tears of Jacques Derrida: Religion without Religion* (Indiana U.P., 1997). He is also the author of *Against Ethics* (1993); *Demythologizing Heidegger* (1993); *Radical Hermeneutics* (1987); *Heidegger and Aquinas* (1982); and *The Mystical Element in Heidegger's Thought* (1978, rev. 1986). He is past President of the American Catholic Philosophical Association, a past member of the National Board of Officers of the American Philosophical Association, past Executive Co-Director of the Society for Phenomenology and Existential Philosophy, and is editor of the book series, "Perspectives in Continental Philosophy" for Fordham University Press.

*Jude P. Dougherty* is dean emeritus, School of Philosophy, The Catholic University of America, editor of the *Review of Metaphysics* and general editor of the book series Studies in Philosophy and the History of Philosophy published by The Catholic University of America Press. That same Press has published his *Western Creed, Western Identity* (2000), *The Logic of Religion* (2003), and *Jacques Maritain* (2003). He is author of numerous articles and reviews on medieval and Thomistic philosophy.

*Fr. Thomas R. Flynn* is Samuel Candler Dobbs Professor of Philosophy at Emory University. In addition to scores of essays, he is the author of *Sartre and Marxist Existentialism: The Text Case of Collective Responsibility* (Chicago), and the two-volume *Sartre, Foucault and Historical Reason,* Vol. 1, *An Existentialist Theory of History,* and Vol. 2, *A Post-Structuralist Mapping of History* (forthcoming). He has co-edited *Dialectic and Narrative* with Dalia Judowitz (SUNY) and *The Ethics of History* with David Carr and Rudolf Makkreel (forthcoming). He has been a Fellow at the National Humanities Center (North Carolina) and recently a Member of the Institute for Advanced Study (Princeton).

*Curtis Hancock* is Professor of philosophy and holds the Joseph M. Freeman Chair of Philosophy at Rockhurst University. He is co-author of *How Should I Live?* (Paragon, 1991), and co-editor of *Freedom, Virtue and the Common Good* (AMA/University of Notre Dame, 1995). He is co-author (with Brendan Sweetman) of *Truth and Religious Belief* (M. E. Sharpe, 1998). He has published articles on ancient and medieval philosophy, on Maritain, and on topics pertaining to political philosophy and ethics. He is a past President of the American Maritain Association.

*Sr. Mary Elizabeth Ingham* is Professor of philosophy and Chair of the Department of Philosophy at Loyola Marymount University. She is the author of numerous articles and reviews in medieval philosophy.

*Ralph McInerny* is the Michael P. Grace Professor of Medieval Philosophy and Director of the Jacques Maritain Center at the University of Notre Dame, where he has taught since 1955. Among his publications are *Ethica Thomistica, Art and Prudence,* and *Aquinas and Analogy.* He recently delivered the Gifford Lectures in Glasgow, published as *Characters in Search of Their Author: The Gifford Lectures 1999–2000* (University of Notre Dame Press, 2001). He is the general editor of a twenty-volume English edition of the works of Jacques Maritain. He is also author of the famous Father Dowling series of mystery novels, now made into a popular television series, as well as author of the Notre Dame mystery series.

*Fr. Richard John Neuhaus* is a priest of the Archdiocese of New York and President of the Institute on Religion and Public Life. He is the editor-in-chief of the Institute's journal, *First Things*. Fr Neuhaus is one of the world's foremost authorities on the role of religion in the contemporary world, and is author and editor of some thirty books including *The Naked Public Square: Freedom and Democracy in America; The Catholic Moment: The Paradox of the Church in the Postmodern World; The End of Democracy?*, and, most recently, *Death on a Friday Afternoon: Meditations on the Last Words of Jesus From the Cross*. Fr Neuhaus, who has held appointments in the Carter, Reagan and Bush Administrations, is a recipient of the John Paul II Award for Religious Freedom, and was listed by *U.S. News and World Report* as one of the 32 "most influential intellectuals in America."

*Alice Ramos* is Professor of Philosophy at St. John's University. She holds a Ph.D. in French Literature from New York University and a Ph.D. from the University of Navarra in Spain. She is the editor of *Beauty, Art, and the Polis* (AMA/Catholic University of America Press, 2000); a book in Spanish on contemporary semiotics and a metaphysics of the sign; and articles in Thomistic metaphysics, Kantian ethical theology, and Christian anthropology. She is currently President of the American Maritain Association and an executive council member of the American Catholic Philosophical Association.

*Peter A. Redpath* is the author/editor of eight books and numerous articles in philosophy, a distinguished alumnus of Xaverian High School, editor of Studies in the History of Western Philosophy and Deputy Executive Editor of the Value Inquiry Book Series (VIBS), Editions Rodopi, and a founder of the Gilson Society. He is Professor of Philosophy at St. John's University, Chairman of the Angelicum Academy Home School, a Director of the Great Books Academy Home School, and a Trustee of the Institute for Advanced Philosophic Research. Dr. Redpath is former Vice President of the American Maritain Association, associate editor of the journal *Contemporary Philosophy*, and graduate fellow at SUNY at Buffalo.

*Mary F. Rousseau* is Associate Professor of Philosophy, Emeritus, at Marquette University. She also taught at Duchesne, Alverno, and Mount Mary Colleges. Her specialty is Thomistic Ethics as applied to contemporary problems, with a focus on sex, marriage, and family. She is past President of the American Catholic Philosophical Association and former member of the Board of Editors of the North American Edition of *Communio International Catholic Review*. Her publications include *The Apple, or Aristotle's Death* (Marquette University Press, 1968); *Embodied in Love* (Crossroad, 1983), and *Community: The Tie That Binds* (University Press of America, 1991), as well as numerous articles and reviews in various journals. She is a member of the Advisory Board of the Institute for Ethics and Culture at the University of Notre Dame.

*Fr. James V. Schall* is Professor of political philosophy at Georgetown University. His more than a dozen books include: *What Is God Like?*, *At the Limits of Political Philosophy*, *Schall on Chesterton*, and *Does Catholicism Still Exist?*

*Brendan Sweetman* is Professor of Philosophy at Rockhurst University, and Chair of the Department of Philosophy. He is the co-author of *Truth and Religious Belief* (M.E. Sharpe, 1998), co-editor of *Contemporary Perspectives on Religious Epistemology* (Oxford U.P., 1992), and editor of *The Failure of Modernism* (AMA/Catholic University of America Press, 1999), as well as author of numerous articles and reviews, in a number of journals and collections, in the areas of philosophy of religion and contemporary European philosophy. He is President of the Gabriel Marcel Society.

# INDEX

૨♥

*Faith & The Life Of The Intellect*
was designed and composed in Adobe Garamond
by Kachergis Book Design of Pittsboro,
North Carolina. It was printed on sixty-pound
Glatfelter Writers Offset Smooth and bound
by Edwards Brothers of Lillington,
North Carolina.